M.G. Ramachandran

M.G. Ramchandran

Series Editor

M.A. Shewan

Editors

Saud Akhtar **R.K. Singh**

hbpl

Himalaya Books Pvt. Ltd.

'Ramdoot', Dr. Bhalerao Marg, Girgaon, Mumbai - 400 004
Tel : (022) 23863863, Fax : (022) 23877178
Email : himpub@vsnl.com

First Edition : 2012

Published by : **H.B.P.L.**
"Pooja Apartments", 4-B, Murari Lal Street, Ansari Road,
Darya Ganj, New Delhi-110 002
Phones : 23270392, 23278631 Reliance : 30180392 to 396
Fax : 011-23256286 Email : hphdel@vsnl.com

Sole Distributers : HIMALAYA PUBLISHING HOUSE PVT. LTD.

Branch Offices

Mumbai : "Ramdoot", Dr. Bhalerao Marg, Girgaon, Mumbai-400 004.
Phones : 23860170/23863863 Fax : 022-23877178
Email : himpub@vsnl.com
Website : www.himpub.com

Nagpur : Kundanlal Chandak Industrial Estate, Ghat Road, **Nagpur - 440 018.**
Phone: 2738731, 3296733 Telefax : 0712-2721215

Bengaluru : No. 16/1 (Old 12/1), 1st Floor, Next to Hotel Highlands, Madhava Nagar, Race Course Road, **Bengaluru - 560 001.**
Phone : 22281541, 22385461, Telefax: 080-22286611

Hyderabad : No. 3-4-184, Lingampally, Besides Raghavendra Swamy Matham, Kachiguda, **Hyderabad - 500 027.** Phone: 040-27560041, 27550139, Mobile:- 09848130433 Telefax: 040-27560041

Chennai : No. 85/50, Bazullah Road, T. Nagar, **Chennai - 600 017.**
Phone: 044-28344020, 32463737, 42124860

Pune : No. 527, "Laksha" Apartment, First Floor, Mehunpura, Shaniwarpeth, (Near Prabhat Theatre), **Pune - 411 030.**
Phone: 020-24496323/24496333/32326733

Lucknow : Jai Baba Bhawan, Near Manas Complex, Church Road, Aliganj, **Lucknow - 226 024.** Phone: 0522-2339329, 9305302158, 9415349385

Ahmedabad : No. 114, "SHAIL", 1st Floor, Opp. Madhu Sudan House, C.G.Road, Navrang Pura, **Ahmedabad – 380 009.**
Phone: 079-26560126, Mobiles: 09327324149, 09314679413

Ernakulam : No. 39/104 A, Lakshmi Apartment, Karikkamuri Cross Rd., Ernakulam, **Cochin – 682011**, Kerala. Phone: 0484-2378012, 2378016,
Mob.: 09344199799

Bhubaneswar : 5 Station Square, **Bhubaneswar (Orissa) - 751 001.**
Mobile: 9861046007, E-mail:- orissa@himpub.com

Indore : Kesardeep Avenue Extension, 73, Narayan Bagh.Flat No. 302, IIIrd Floor, Near Humpty Dumpty School, Narayan Bagh, **Indore (M.P.) 452 007**
Mobile: 09301386468

Kolkata : 108/4, Beliaghata, Main Road, Near ID Hospital, Opp. SBI Bank **Kolkata - 700 010.** Mobile: 09910440956, E-mail:- nkmitra@himpub.com

Guwahati : House No. 15, Behind Prajjyotish College, Near Sharma Printing Press, P.O. Bharalumukh, Guwahati - 781009 (Assam
Mobile: 07439040301; 07439040302

Printed by : A to Z Printers, New Delhi

Preface

Biography, is now a form of literature, very much in vogue. In fact, biography is a description or account of someone's life and the times, which is usually published in the form of a book. A biography is more than a mention of personal facts (life, education, work, relationships and death), it also portrays the subject's experience of events. Technically speaking, a work is biographical, if it covers, all of a person's life. Biography writing has a long history. A biography is real. Ancient Greeks developed the biographical tradition, which we have inherited, although until the 5th century AD, when the word 'biographia' first appeared, in Damascius' "Life of Isodorus," biographical pieces were called simply "lives". It is quite likely that the Greeks were drawing on a pre-existing eastern tradition. Certainly Herodotus' "Histories" contains more detailed biographical information on Persian kings and subjects. The earliest surviving pieces, which we would identify as biographical are Isocrates' "Life of Evagoras" and Xenophon's "Life of Agesilaos," both from the fifth century BC. "Parallel Lives" by Plutarch, a Greek writing under the Roman empire, is a series of short biographies of eminent men.

The Golden Age of English biography emerged in late eighteenth century, the century in which the terms "biography" and "autobiography" entered English lexicon. The classic works of the period were Samuel Johnson's "Critical Lives of the Poets" and James Boswell's "Massive Life of Johnson". Generally American biography followed English model. By World War I, cheap hardcover reprints had become popular. The decade of the 1920s witnessed a biographical 'boom'. Later, biographical writings, developed a lot and today biographies are written and compiled in the finest form of the genre. In India too, biography, as a form of literature has been evolved, cultivated and polished over the years. Here is an effort to promote this tradition further.

This series of biographies of great men, great women and celebrities in all walks of life is an adventurous academic endeavour, in its own right. A team of researchers and compilers has worked for a good period of time to accomplish the project. For this purpose, hundreds of books by eminent authors and editors have been consulted and referred to. We have benefited from various works, liberally, in order to illustrate and enrich this effort of ours. Present book is devoted to the great personality of M. G. Ramachandran.

Marudur Gopalamenon Ramachandran, commonly known, as MGR was a successful actor, director and greatly loved politician. MGR had over a 100 films to his credit. MGR joined Dravida Munnetra Kazhagam (DMK), founded by C. N. Annadurai; his mentor. Later, he founded his own party, All India Anna Dravida Munnetra Kazhagam (AIADMK). Eventually, he became Tamil Nadu's Chief Minister, and was in office, till his death. He was known to be a Philanthropist and active social developer. He was posthumously decorated with Bharat Ratna, the highest honour in India.

This is a compact and comprehensive account of the above mentioned great life, which is bound to attract the attention of scholars, researchers, students and the general readers, alike. Let's hope this humble effort would receive a warm welcome and due applause.

— ***Editors***

Contents

1

An Eventful Life

Eminent politician and veteran film star, Maruthur Gopalan Ramachandran (January 17, 1917 – December 24, 1987), popularly known by his initials MGR, was Chief Minister of Tamil Nadu, actor, director and producer. In his youth, MGR and his elder brother, M. G. Chakrapani became members of a drama troupe to support their family. Influenced by Gandhian ideals, MGR joined the Indian National Congress. After a few years of acting in plays, he made his film debut in the 1936 film *Sathi Leelavathi* in a supporting role. In the late 1940s he graduated to leading roles and for the next three decades dominated the Tamil film industry. He became a member of the Dravida Munnetra Kazhagam (DMK) and rose rapidly through its ranks. He successfully used his popularity as a film hero to build a large political base. In 1972, he left the DMK to form his own party the Anna Dravida Munnetra Kazhagam (ADMK). In 1977 he became the chief minister of Tamil Nadu — the first film actor in India to become the chief minister of a state. He remained chief minister till his death in 1987.

In Tamil Nadu, he had a reputation for philanthropism and was considered to be one of the great political leaders and actors in the state. He was idolised by his followers as *Puratchi Thalaivar* (lit. Revolutionary leader) MGR was posthumously honoured with the Bharat Ratna, India's highest civilian award.

In his films M. G. R. represented the lower class. As a the honest hero fighting against corruption and injustice and rejecting alcohol and tobacco he became an idol for the lower class people of Tamil Nadu. He appeared in the first Tamil colour movie *Alibabavum Narpatha Thirudargalum*. He had joined the DMK (Dravida Munnetra Kazhagam), one of Tamil Nadu's most important political parties, in 1953 and started to represent it in his movies. In 1962 he started his political career in the DMK, supported by its leader C. W. Annadurai. In 1967 he was shot at when delivering a speech, but survived. When Annadurai died and Karunanidhi took over the lead of the DMK, a process of alienation between M. G. R. and the DMK began. Finally M. G. R. founded the ADMK, which was later renamed AIADMK (All India Anna Dravida Munnetra Kazhagam). In 1977 the AIADMK won the state elections and M. G. R. became Tamil Nadu's chief minister. He was re-elected thrice and remained chief minister until his death in 1987.

While for some people M. G. R. was a god - others strongly criticised his way of running the state, claiming that the poor, who by their vote enabled him to rule Tamil Nadu, would not at all benefit from his rule. In his movie *Iruvar* the Tamil director Mani Ratnam told the story of a film star entering politics. The plot of *Iruvar* was strongly influenced by M.G.R.'s life.

The Backdrop

The Birth Place: Kandy (formerly Candy), a town of Sri Lanka and the administrative centre of Central province and Kandy District, is situated near the centre of the island on the Kandy plateau 75 miles North-East of Colombo by rail and 1,602 ft. above sea level. Known to the Sinhalese as Senkadagala Mahanuwara, it became the capital of a kingdom about 1480. It was temporarily occupied by the Portuguese in the 16th century and by the Dutch in 1763; but the Sinhalese Kings maintained their independence protected by an encircling ring of heavily forested hills, until the British occupation in 1815.

Kandy lies in a district renowned for its beauty, amid bills round the margin of an artificial lake constructed by the last King of Kandy in 1806. Of a number of important Buddhist temples, the best known is Dalads Maligawa or the "Temple of the Tooth" where the sacred Tooth Relic of the Buddha is supposed to be preserved. This relic is the centre of the well-known annual *Esala Perahera,* a torchlight procession of dancers, dignitaries and richly decorated elephants.

The Royal Botanic gardens and part of the University of Ceylon are situated at Peradeniya, 3 miles distant, and two Buddhist temples, Lankatilaka Vihare and Gadaladeniya Vihare, are quite close to Peradeniya. Kandy is an important administrative, commercial, cultural and educational centre, and attracts many tourists. The Pavilion of the Governor General was located there. Round it lies a hilly region filled with densely populated Sinhalese villages whose inhabitants grow paddy in skilfully terraced fields and also produce tea, areca nut and other crops. There is much estate production of tea, though Kandy remained less of a centre than formerly for European planters. The administrative district of Kandy had a population of 8,40,382 in 1953. Sinhalese are in a majority, but there are a large number of Indian Tamils. The district has an area of 914 square miles and contains most of the tea estates of Sri Lanka as well as "cacao plantations" on the banks of the Mahaweli Ganga, a few miles below Kandy town. Its northeastern part is still largely covered with jungle.

Kumbakonam (formerly Combaconum), a town in the Tanjore District of the State of Madras, stands on the delta of the Cauvery river, 194 miles from Madras city (now, Chennai) on the Southern railway. Kumbakonam is the home of some of south India's most celebrated lawyers. It is also an industrial centre noted for silk weaving and the manufacture of brass vessels. It was a subsidiary capital of the Chola dynasty and possesses a famous monastery, the Kashi math, founded by the Hindu philosopher Sankara Acharya. There are several temples including the Nagesvara, which dates from Chola times, and the great Vishnu temple, built in the Vijayanagar period, whose gopuras or monumental gateways are richly decorated. The nearby Mahamakam tank is believed to have direct subterranean connection with the Ganges, especially so during the Mahamakam (Mahakumbh) festival celebrated once in 12 years.

Family Background

Marudur Gopalan Ramachandran (MGR) had lost his father Gopal Menon, a magistrate at the hill town, at an early age. He along with his elder brother M.G. Chakrapani and mother Satyabama crossed over to India. Although they hail form Kerala, they chose Kumbakonam in Tamil Nadu to settle down. MGR was of Malayali parentage, but he was the object of adoration of the Tamil masses.

Early Life and Career

Marudur Gopala Menon Ramachandran, popularly known as M.G.R and Puratchi Thalaivar MGR (means, Revolutionary Leader), was born on 17th January 1917 at Kandy, Sri Lanka, to Maradhur Gopala Menon and Satyabhama who were of the Nair caste from the state of Kerala in Southern India. After his father's death, M.G.R along with his mother Sathyabama and brother Saranga Bani, settled with his family at Kumbakonam in Tamil Nadu. He could not pursue his studies beyond the primary stage due to poverty and hence joined a drama troupe named Boys Company.

A Painful Childhood

Subjected to abject poverty, neither MGR's elder brother Chakrapani nor he could afford education. He had to cut short his schooling at the tender age of seven while in the third standard. Shortly thereafter, Ramachandran joined the Madurai Original Boys Drama Company owned by Kandaswamy Pillai. For another ten years he was with the theatre group which toured even faraway places like Burma.

Marriage

MGR married a former actress V.N. Janaki (born in 1923) who paired with him in a film called "Marthantattu Ilavarasi".

An Illustrious Career

As describe earlier, he made his film debut in 1935, in the film *Sati Leelavati*, directed by Ellis Dungan, an American born film director. Generally starring in romance or action films, MGR got his big breakthrough in the 1947 film *Rajakumaari,* written by M. Karunanidhi. Soon he rose to superstardom in the 1954 blockbuster *Malaikallan.* He acted as hero in the Tamil film industry's first ever colour movie, the 1955 blockbuster *'Ali Baba and the forty thieves'*. He rose to become the heart throb of millions of Indians with movies such as 'Anbe Vaa', 'Aayirathil Oruvan', 'Mahadevi', 'Panam Padaithavan', 'Ulagam Sutrum Vaalibhan', 'Adimaippenn', etc. He won the National Film Award for Best Actor for the film *Rickshakaran.*

His film *Nadodi Mannan,* which was a tamil version of the interpretation of the Prisoner of Zenda, was produced and directed by himself and released in 1956, ran to full houses. His 1973 blockbuster' Ulagam Sutrum Vaalibhan' broke previous box office records. It was one of the few movies shot in abroad in those days. It was shot in nations like Singapore, Malaysia, Thailand, Hong Kong and Japan. The DMK unsuccessfully tried to curtail that movie. His acting career ended in 1978 with his last movie, *Madurai Meetta Sundara Pandian,* which he acted when he was the Chief Minister of the state. He was awarded the Bharat Ratna, India's highest civilian award, in 1988 (posthumous).

Screen Life

Gaining considerable experience on stage, he entered the world of cinema through the film *Sathileelavathi* where he played the role of a police officer named Ramanathan with negative shades who planned to execute the hero M.K. Radha and gradually rose to enviable positions by persistent efforts and endurance. He sang a few lines in the film and tried his hands in playback singing. He acted with his third wife V.N. Janaki in films *Marutha Naattu Ilavarasi, Mohini,* and *Naam.* After strenuous hard work he tasted success and portrayed his first lead role in the film *Rajakumari.* He portrayed an excellent anti hero role in *Panakkaari.* In 1954, he acted along with his on screen rival Shivaji Ganesan in *Koondukkili.* It was the film the two had acted jointly. It was during the shooting the film *Kavalkaran,* he was shot in his throat by his fellow actor M.R. Radha. After his recovery, he came to continue with the popular song *"Ninaithaen Vanthai Nooru Vayathu..."*. His star power did not diminish even after he was shot, affecting his ability to speak clearly, but rather he became more famous after this incident and people ordained his tamil as "Mazhalai Tamil" and called him "Engal Veetu Pillai" (our own son). *Madurai Veeran,* one of his most popular films, is based on the legend of Madurai Veeran, a popular deity of Southern Tamil Nadu. He continued with his memorable performances in films like *Gulaebaghavali, Thaikupin Thaaram, Chakaravarthi Thirumagal,* etc. He acted in the first colour film in Asia, *Alibabavum Narpathu Thirudarkallum* with actress Bhanumathi.

He produced and directed his first film *Nadodi Mannan,* a film which was partly made in Black and white and colour. It was the debut film of actress Saroja Devi. He celebrated the success of he film in Madurai Thamukam grounds, where he was honoured with a golden sword of 110 pounds. In return to the love of his fans and well wishers, he offered the sword to Kollur Mookambiga Temple. The onscreen pair continued with their successful performances in films like *Thirudadhe, Paasam, Kudumba Thalaivan, Thaayai Kaththa Thanaiyan, Parisu, Periyaidathu Pen, Padakotti, Enga Veetu Pillai,* etc. He was a highly health conscious person, after he met with a minor accident in his leg during one of his shootings, he acted in the mega hit film AVM's Anbae Vaa.

He exhibited his physical strength by lifting a 300 pound weighing villain Nelloore Kantharao. His fight sequences proved that he was at his pink of health. His second phase started with glamorous on screen pair with Jayalalitha. Together they worked in 28 films. She made her debut with M.G.R. in *Kanni Thai.* Together they continued in notable films like *Mugarassi, Kudiyiriruntha Kovil, KavalKaaran, Ragasiya Police115, Pudhiya Bhoomi, Kanavan,* and more. His 100th film *Olivilakku* was a big hit. He received a remuneration of 45 lakhs for director C.V. Sridhar's film *Meenava Nanaban,* he was the first actor to receive such a huge amount. In Engal Thangam for example, MGR playing a truck driver Thangam, fought, sang and cared for the poor and preached against smoking and drinking.

Mother tongue, motherland and motherhood were what he based his popularity on... He played dual role in the film *Maattukara Velan* with actress Lakshmi and Jayalalitha and latter with a triple role in Naalai Namathae with actress Latha. His second directorial hit film was *Ullagam Sutrum Valliban,* which was shot mostly in foreign locations. The film was a runaway hit for more than 200 days. After his successful political career, he quit film industry with a hit film *Maduraiyai Meeta Sundara Pandiyan.* He worked in other languages including Hindi - *Ek tha Raja* (1951), Telugu - *Sarvathikari* (1951), Malayalam - *Jenova* (1953). His legend has been the subject of various ballads and plays and this was the second filmed version of the story. In the 1960s MGR turned to more 'realistic' fantasies mostly in a contemporary setting often playing someone from the oppressed class — a peasant, taxi driver or fisherman. For millions of fans, his image as the knight in shining armour, saving damsels in distress and being totally dutiful towards his mother was in fact a reality.

He is known for his white fur cap and dark spectacles. The white cap he wore was gifted by a poor old Muslim shop owner, who gave this cap to him during his campaign for Indo China relief fund in 1962. As a film hero MGR chose his roles carefully with an eye on building his own image. Starting with mythological, he moved on to social themes where he picked up the roles of the poor underdog who stands up to the might of rich oppressors and gets the better of them. This gave him the image of a modern day Robin Hood and a fan base which eventually turned into a huge vote bank sustained by more than 10,000 fan clubs that M.G.R took care to nurture and promote.

Reaching Stardom: He became a great actor, director and producer. He rose to stardom by playing characters that portrayed him as the saviour of the poor. He would take a keen interest in the theme of the song, its musical composition and its exact appearance in the movie. *"Acheham enpathu madamaiyadah Anjaamai Dravidar udamaiyadah.... "Thoongathe Thambi Thoongathe Nee somberi enra peyar vaankaathey...", " Chinna payale Chinna payale Chethi keladah...", "Thaayillamal Naanillai Thaane evarum piranthathillai....* M.G.R would also make sure that he will teach good manners and discipline to the masses through the movies. Therefore, in the characters he played in 120-odd movies, he would never smoke or take alcoholic drinks. On top of that, he would never physically or mentally abuse women. This self-imposed rigidity restricted the character roles he would play and movie critics ridiculed him for this 'unnatural style' of his characters. But MGR would have the last word. Ultimately, he claimed the respected honorific 'Vaathiyar' (teacher) in its proper sense.

His Own Studio

He was the owner of Sathya Studios and Emgeeyar Pictures (willed to charity) which produced many of the films he acted in. He gifted a golden sword weighing half a Kilogram to Mookambika temple in Kollur, Udupi district.

Political Flavour in Movies

His movies were the medium of communication for the Dravidian movement. For the next twenty-five years he remained one of the biggest celebrities in Tamil cinema. MGR presented himself as a man of the masses, selecting reels that projected him as a champion of the deprived. It did not take the reel hero much time to become a real-life hero. This filmstar-politician, who came from Sri Lanka, came to be adored by millions of Tamils like an icon and grew to be the most powerful man in Tamil Nadu.

In Political Arena

In 1953 MGR joined politics through Dravida Munnetra Kazhagam, a prominent political party and became a member of the state legislative council in 1962. In 1967 MGR was elected to the Tamil Nadu Legislative Assembly for the first time. MGR added glamour to the Dravidian movement which was sweeping across Tamil Nadu as a storm.

Always the first to personally offer relief in disasters and calamities like fire, flood, drought, cyclone, etc., he was the first donor during the war with China in 1962, donating Rs. 75,000 to the war fund. After the death of his mentor, Anna Durai in 1972, he had a fall out with the DMK leadership as he wanted the financial results of the party publicised and so he was treated with slipper garlands when he entered the assembly hall.

M.G. Ramachandran, who dominated Tamil filmdom for "well over a quarter of a century, was an unwary transgressor into active politics until 1972. He took a plunge when efforts were made to project a rising star and son of the then Chief Minister Karunanidhi, Mu Ka Muthu, to overtake him. Ramachandran mobilised his followers and fans and raised a banner of revolt on the cry of corruption in high places. Within five years he was swept into power.

In politics, Ramachandran was an ardent Congressman and used to always wear *khadi,* even while he was attracted by the rationalist ideals of Periyar E.V. Ramaswamy and his Chief lieutenant C. N. Annadurai who later founded the DMK.

Ramachandran resigned from the Congress and joined the DMK in 1952. He took over from Sivaji Ganesan as Chief propagandist of the DMK through the medium of film, after the latter quit the party in 1954. From then on, every film which Ramachandran acted in was a box office hit and this earned him the title "King of collection" (vasool mannan).

The Magnum opus of his films was "Nadodi Mannan", a Tamil version of *Prisoner Zenda* which starred Ronald Colmen and Stewart Granger. It was a story of a young peasant's revolt against a despotic ruler and his eventual elevation to the throne. In the film, Ramachandran propounded several welfare schemes for the common man. Ideals set out in Nadodi Mannan were considered the directive principles of the All India Anna Dravida Munnetra Kazhagam (AIADMK) Government and the State Government officials were asked to see the film for proper guidance. As Ramachandran was reigning the film world, a number of film clubs sprouted throughout Tamil Nadu. These clubs had served as sword arm of the party.

Ramachandran was elected to the Legislative Council in 1963, but resigned his membership after two years as he was disinterested in active politics. However, he actively campaigned for the party in the civic elections in the city in 1959 and 1964 and also in the 1959 and 1962 Assembly polls. The response was so phenomenal that C. N. Annadurai remarked at the party's conference at Virugambakkam before the 1967 elections that he would value Ramachandran giving audience to the countless admirers than his donation to the election fund.

Area of Operation

Concentrated in a small area, Tamil Nadu houses one of the best forms of history, culture and religion, Here are the ancient capitals of once proud kingdoms. Like magnificent Madurai, its temple, one of the wonders of India, and ancient Thanjavur, its Brihadeeswara temple, a tribute to the splendour of Chola builders, are amongst the greatest the world has ever known. Here are the ruins of historic Poompuhar, the Chola port and planned city known to Ptolemy and Pliny. Here are the Pallava towns of Kanchipuram and Mamallapuram, the former one of the Hinduism's seven sacred cities and the latter famed for its sculpture but now becoming better known as one of India's finest beach resorts. Here are Tiruchirappali and Kanyakumari where ancient legend lives on in rock,·plaster and woods. Here are hill stations that waft the aroma of tea and coffee, eucalyptus and pine.

Madras (Channai) —a tiny fishing village that has mushroomed leisurely into a sprawling metropolis in the 350 odd years since it was founded in 1639—is the capital of Tamil Nadu. A spacious city of distances, beaches, parks and historic landmarks, Madras, free of most of the ecological problems of the major cities of today, is the point beyond all others for one who sets out to enjoy the south.

Escape from Death

On 12th January, 1967, Ramachandran escaped an attempt on his life. He was shot at by a fellow actor M.R. Radha who used to don the villain's role in MGR films. Ramachandran suffered a bullet injury in his neck and was hospitalised. His picture with a bandage on the neck happened to be the biggest vote catcher in the 1967 elections for the DMK. He got elected to the State Assembly from the suburban St. Thomas Mount constituency by a big margin of 26,000 votes from his hospital bed.

Rise in Politics

During the first DMK Government, he was appointed Vice-Chairman of the State Small Savings Advisory Board. After Annadurai's death in February 1969, there was a war of succession between Karunanidhi and V.R. Nedunchezhiyan in which

Ramachandran threw his weight behind Karunanidhi and got him elected leader of the DMK Legislative Party. For his part, he accepted the post of party treasurer vacated by Karunanidhi.

Ramachandran actively campaigned in the 1971 midterm poll and enabled the DMK to score a landslide victory by capturing over 180 seats in the 234-members Assembly. The Congress (O) led by Kamaraj was reduced to a mere 13 seats.

When the second Government was formed by Karunanidhi, friends of Ramachandran had suggested that he should be given a birth in the Cabinet. However, Karunanidhi firmly stated that Ramachandran should choose between his acting career and a minister post, contending that it would be ludicrous for a Cabinet Minister to act in films. Then came attempts to bolster up Karunanidhi's actor son Mu Ka Muthu.

Simmering at the insult inflicted on him, Ramachandran fired the first salvo against Karunanidhi on 8th October, 1972, while addressing a birth anniversary meeting of the late Annadurai at Tirukalukundram. Ramachandran demanded that party functionaries should give accounts for their assets and newly acquired wealth. His demand was suspended by the party executive on 10th October, 1972. An unrelenting Ramachandran reiterated his demand following which the party general council, at its meeting on 13th and 14th October ratified its executive's decision to suspend Ramachandran from the DMK.

Undaunted and cashing in on the mass upsurge in his favour, Ramachandran launched a new political party called the Anna Dravida Munnetra Kazhagam (ADMK). The party flag had the same colours of that of the DMK, with a portrait of Annadurai at the centre.

Ramachandran prepared a list of charges against the DMK Minister and led a massive march to the Raj Bhavan to present it to the then Governor K.K. Shah in November, 1972. As the Governor said he would refer the charges to the Chief Minister for his comments, Ramachandran took back the memorandum of charges and later presented it to the then President V.V. Giri in New Delhi on 6th November and demanded a judicial probe into his charges. More than three years later, in February 1976, the Union Government appointed a commission of enquiry headed by Justice R.S. Sarkaria to probe into the charges.

The first test for Ramachandran came in the form of a Lok Sabha by election at Dindigul in May 1973. His candidate, K. Maya Thevar, trounced the Congress (O) by a margin of over 1,40,000 votes. The ruling DMK party's candidate came poor third. Ramachandran has cashed in on the sympathy of women who were the victims of the relaxation of prohibition. After the by election, the DMK Government re-imposed prohibition.

On 29th September 1973, Ramachandran announced that the policy of the ADMK would be called "Annaism" on the lines of Leninism, Maoism and Gandhism. He described it as a blend of capitalism and socialism. In February, 1974 the AIADMK. in alliance with the Communist Party of India (CPI), was voted to power in the Assembly elections to the Union Territory of Pondichery. When Ramachandran formed the ADMK, only a few Members of Legislative Assembly (MLAs) had chosen to join him, only ten MLAs and three Members of Parliament (MPs) left the DMK to join the ADMK. The mass exodus from the DMK to the AIADMK began after the former was defeated in the 1977 polls and Ramachandran came to power. When the emergency was declared in 1975, Ramachandran was the first to welcome it. He also supported the 20-point programme, but criticised the five point programme as he considered it superficial. When there was talk of banning regional parties, Ramachandran changed the party's name to "All India Anna Dravida Munnetra Kazhagam' (AIADMK and imposed a rule that all party members should tatto the party symbol on their forearm.

In the 1977 poll, the AIADMK aligned with the Congress led by Indira Gandhi and won 18 Lok Sabha seats. However, when the Janata Party came to power MGR offered unconditional support to the then Prime Minister Morarji Desai. This he latter extended to the Charan Singh Government in 1979 and allowed his Parliament members, Bala Pajanor and Madam Sathiavanimuthu to join the short-lived Lok Dal Government. When the DMK struck a deal with the Congress for the 1980 Lok Sabha poll, the AIADMK had to seek the company of the Janata Party. The alliance proved disastrous as the AIADMK was able to retain only two seats and the Janata Party drew a blank. The AIADMK won the Assembly election in June 1977 and MGR offered the first Government. But it lasted less than three years.

After Indira Gandhi returned to power in January 1980, the AIADMK Government was dismissed on 17 February, 1980. But in the subsequent elections held in June, Ramachandran was swept back to power with increased strength. After the return to power Ramachandran started building bridges with the Congress Government. Although he attended the first conclave of the opposition parties convened by Andhra Pradesh Chief Minister N.T. Rama Rao at Vijayawada he refrained from criticising Indira Gandhi. He also expressed himself against any blind opposition to the Centre.

Stint as a Journalist

He was the founder and editor of *Thai* weekly magazine and *Anna* daily newspaper in Tamil.

End of Film Career

Ramachandran's film career, which had been the starting block for his political achievements, came to an abrupt end after he came to power. Although he had stated he would continue his acting career and even recorded a song for a new film on 1st April, 1978, he could not pursue it due to pressure of work. The last film he had acted in was "Madurai Meeta Sundara Pandivan", released in 1978.

Formation of AIADMK

He went on to form the ADMK (Anna Dravidian Progressive Federation) the only powerful opponent of DMK. In the 1977 state Legislative Assembly elections, MGR\'s ADMK won a resounding victory over the DMK. MGR and his political offspring, the ADMK never looked back after that. Until his death in 1987, MGR comfortably won the two subsequent state Legislative Assembly elections He became Chief Minister of Tamil Nadu in 1977, a post he kept even after he suffered a paralytic stroke in 1984. He was the first film actor to be a Chief Minister in India. He enjoyed unending support during his time as Chief Minister. He placed great emphasis on social development, especially education. He founded the Tamil University, The Tamil Nadu Dr. MGR Medical University and the Women's University in Tamil Nadu.

One of MGR's most successful policies was the re-introduction of the "Mid-day meals" in Tamil Nadu, which encouraged underprivileged children to attend schools. Through this scheme Tamil Nadu was able to achieve rapid literacy rates. The response was so successful that in 1995 the then Finance Minister Manmohan Singh had this scheme introduced all over the country. Efforts taken by him and the subsequent Tamil Nadu governments ensured the development of Primary and Secondary education in the State. In October 1984, MGR was diagnosed with kidney failure and was rushed to the US for treatment, and his niece M.G.C. Leelavathy donated kidney to him. When MGR died on December 24, 1987, the city of Madras saw the biggest ever funeral in its history. Over two million persons followed his mortal remains, more than 30 of his followers committed suicide and thousands had their heads tonsured as a mark of mourning. He was affectionately referred with many titles Makkal Thilakam was honoured on him by Late Tamizhvannan who was the editor of the magazine *Kalki*. Religious person Kirubananda Vaariyar gave him the title of Pon Manach Chemmal, owing to his Philanthropic activities.

He was titled Puratchi Nadigar by M. Karunanidhi. Last but not the least, he won the coveted title Puratchi Thalaivar from K.A. Krishnaswamy, after he started his own political party (A.D.M.K). He constructed the following education centres: MGR Memorial Charitable Trust MGR Higher Sec. School and home for the Speech and Hearing impaired. MGR-Janaki College of Arts and Science for Women Dr. MGR Educational and Research Institute. (It is a Deemed university has an offshore campus in Sri Lanka.

Political Career

MGR was a member of the Congress Party till 1953 and he used to wear Khadi. In 1953 MGR joined the Dravida Munnetra Kazhagam (DMK) with the help of M. Karunanidhi. He became a vocal Tamil and Dravidian nationalist and prominent member of the DMK ("Dravida Munnetra Kazhagam" a.k.a. *Dravidian Progressive Federation*). He added glamour to the Dravidian movement which was sweeping Tamil Nadu.

He became a member of the state Legislative Council in 1962. He was first elected to the Tamil Nadu Legislative Assembly in 1967. After the death of his mentor, Annadurai, MGR became the treasurer of DMK in 1969 after Karunanidhi became the chief minister. On the 12th of January 1967, he was shot in the neck by fellow actor M.R. Radha. The bullet was permanently lodged in his neck and his voice damaged. Within hours of the shooting, some 50,000-odd fans had gathered at the hospital where MGR had been taken. People cried in the streets. For six weeks, he lay in the hospital as fans awaited each report of his health. He was visited by a steady stream of commoners and luminaries of film industry, polity and bureaucracy. From his hospital bed, he conducted his campaign for Madras Legislative Assembly seat. He won twice the number of votes polled by his Congress rival and the largest vote polled by any candidate for the Assembly. In 1972, DMK leader Karunanidhi started to project his first son M.K. Muthu in a big way in film industry and also in politics. Understanding the tactics played by Karunanidhi to corner him, MGR started to claim that corruption had grown within the party after the demise of Annadurai and in a public meeting asked for the financial details of the party to be publicised which enraged the leadership of DMK.

Consequently, as expected, MGR was expelled from the party, and floated a new party named Anna Dravida Munnetra Kazhagam (ADMK), later renamed All India Anna Dravida Munnetra Kazhagam (AIADMK), the only powerful opponent of the DMK. He mobilised the period between 1972-1977 to spread and preach his party ambition with films like *Netru Indru Naalai* (1974), *Idhayakani* (1975), etc. He became Chief Minister of Tamil Nadu on the 30th of July 1977, remaining in office till his death in 1987. In 1979, members of his party Satyavani Muthu and Aravinda Bala Pajanor, became the first non-Congress politicians from Tamil Nadu to be ministers in the Union Cabinet. The AIADMK won every state assembly election as long as MGR was alive. Although Anna Durai as well as Karunanidhi had acted in stage plays in trivial roles, in their younger days, before becoming chief minister, MGR was the first popular film actor to be a Chief Minister in India.

Chief Minister of the State

Once he became Chief Minister of Tamil Nadu, he placed great emphasis on social development, especially education. One of his most successful policies was the introduction of the "Mid-day Meal Scheme" introduced by the popular Congress Chief Minister and Kingmaker K. Kamaraj to a nutritious Mid-day Meal Scheme in the Government-run and aided schools in Tamil Nadu, which encouraged underprivileged children to attend schools. He also introduced Women's Special buses. He set up a free school for the Cinema Technicians children in Kodambakkam called MGR Primary and Higher Secondary School which provided Free Mid-Day meals in the 1950s. He led the ADMK to victory in the 1984 assembly elections despite not taking part in the campaigning. At that time he was undergoing medical treatment in America and his images were broadcast in Tamil Nadu through cinema halls. This was an effective campaign tactic and ADMK won the elections, indicating the depth of his popular support. He was instrumental in setting up the Tamil University and the Mother Teresa Women's University in Tamil Nadu.

Graph as Member of Legislative Assembly

Year	*Elected/Re-elected*	*Place*	*Party*
1967	Elected	St. Thomas Mount	DMK
1971	Re-elected	St. Thomas Mount	DMK
1977	Elected	Aruppukottai	ADMK
1980	Elected	Madurai West	ADMK
1984	Elected	Andipatti	ADMK

Achievements as CM

During his two terms as Chief Minister Ramachandran made several far reaching reforms in the State administration. He abolished the Revenue Board and the system of village officers. He made prohibition very rigorous but later virtually scrapped it and now excise revenue on liquor fetches more than Rs. 200 crore per annum to the State exchequer.

Ramachandran had imposed a Rs. 9,000 income ceiling for grant of concessions to backward class students for admission to professional colleges but later withdrew it and also increased the backward class quota for admission to 50 per cent from 32 per cent. He introduced massive feeding scheme for children and destitutes and now about 80 lakh people are getting free midday meal.

Every move of Ramachandran came in for strident opposition from Karunanidhi. He was accused of corruption in the "Shipping scandal" relating to purchase of Bulgarian ships and the "Spirit Scandal" relating to export of rectified spirit to Kerala. The Ray Commission to enquire into the spirit scandal, appointed by the Central Government in June, 1981, is still in existence, although its operation has been stayed by the Supreme Court.

Ramachandran had received several honours/awards for best acting in his film "Rick shawaran" in 1971. An honorary doctorate was conferred on him by the Madras University in January 1987.

Ramachandran was also known as a great philanthropist and his beneficiaries were innumerable. During one rainy season he had distributed raincoats to rickshaw pullers.

Of late the monolithic AIADMK had to face internal squabbles. After his party's debacle in 1980 Lok Sabha poll his chief lieutenant K. Manoharan had left the party to join the DMK. The latest was Food Minister S.D. Somasundaram, who founded his own party.

Despite the exit of some members Ramachandran continued to be the supremo of the organisation. He appeared to be an enigma to the people and a puzzle to his detractors as his thoughts and actions were unpredictable. But to his followers Ramachandran was the messiah.

Honours and Awards

- National Film Award for Best Actor for the film *Rickshakaran* in 1972.

- Honorary doctorate received from University of Madras and The World University (Arizona).
- Bharat Ratna was conferred by the Government of India (posthumously) in 1988 for his reformation activities and support from Tamil Nadu.

Refused to Padmashree

One famous incident was that MGR was nominated for the Padmashree award by the Government of India but he refused to accept as the wording was in Hindi and not in Tamil in 1960.

The nation's highest honour of Bharat Ratna has been conferred on the late Tamil Nadu Chief Minister M.G. Ramachandran by the President of India, R. Venkataraman on January 25, 1988 on the occasion of the Republic Day celebrations. M.G. Ramachandran dominated the Tamil Nadu political scene for more than a decade as the leader of the AIADMK after having won the hearts of the masses. MGR had richly deserved (the honour) as a humanist, as a champion of the poor and as a political leader and statesman who had worked for the cause of national integration. The conferment of the national award on MGR is a matter of pride and honour for the people of not only of Tamil Nadu but the whole nation. Leaders of various political parties in the Tamil Nadu Assembly, including local Administration, Minister R.M. Veerappan, on January 26, 1988 thanked the Union Government and notably Prime Minister Rajiv Gandhi, for conferring posthumously the nation's highest civilian honour of "Bharat Ratna" on M.G. Ramachandran.

After moving an official condolence resolution in the State Assembly, the leader of the House, Veerappan, in his speech said, honour such as this came to the late leader without asking since he proved that he was a national leader. Others who welcomed the Centre's decision included D. Vasodha (Cong-I), K. Ramani (CPI-M) and A.S.A. Arumugham (Janata).

The Government of India honoured him with the national Award for the Best Actor for his acting in the film Rickshakaran in 1972. In 1983, the Madras University conferred on him, Honoris Causa, the degree of Doctor of Laws.

Illness and Recovery

On 5th October, 1984, Ramachandran was rushed to the Apollo Hospital when he developed breathing trouble. Doctors said that he had asthmatic trouble, and two days later he developed kidney trouble. He was given a peritoneal dialysis. On 13th October he suffered a stroke on the left side of his brain. His speech was impaired and his right limb was affected. He was put on haemodialysis. The then Prime Minister Smt. Indira Gandhi flew to Madras on 16th October to call on him. Ramachandran was able to recognise her.

Three American medical experts led by Dr. Eli A. Friedman from the Downstate Medical Centre, Brooklyn, were brought to Madras and they examined him. A few days later Japanese neurologist Dr. Tefsuo Kano visited Ramachandran and recommended treatment in New York. Ramachandran was flown by a chartered Air India plane to New York on 5th November. He was in semi-conscious state and was not aware of what was going around. He did not know the assassination of Smt. Indira Gandhi on 31st October. At the Brooklyn hospital Ramachandran made a remarkable recovery. He had kidney transplanted at the hospital. The donor was his niece Madam Leelavathi. He started to sit up and later walk about. He was given a speech therapy side by side. When the elections were announced, he signed the nomination papers at the hospital bed. In his absence, the administration was being carried on in Tamil Nadu and decisions were dictated by him from the Brooklyn Hospital.

During the campaign, some opposition parties raised the question of his ill-health and questioned his capacity to run the administration. To rebut, the AIADMK screened the video pictures of Ramachandran and it boosted his popularity and evoke public sympathy. The AIADMK in alliance with the Congress won a landslide victory in the polls.

M.G. Ramachandran returned to Madras on 4th February and was sworn in as Chief Minister on 10th February for the third consecutive time. He started attending public functions and made his first speech at the inauguration of Anna District at Dindigul. In 1986 he went to Japan and America for a check up. Although his speech was incoherent, people were able to understand it. Mentally he was alert throughout finding groupism and factionalism growing in the Party. Ramachandran threatened to quit office on 28th October. The Ministers submitted their resignations and asked him to reconstitute his Cabinet but not to quit. Ramachandran relented and did not carry out his threat to quit.

Ramachandran had announced that he would throw out the corrupt Ministers, and later, said that 10 to 11 Ministers would be dropped and asked to undertake party work. According to his close associates they found nothing wrong with the functioning of Ramachandran except the inability to speak fluently as before. He had attended Cauvery talks with Karnataka Chief Minister Ramakrishna Hegde twice, and met Prime Minister Rajiv Gandhi on several occasions.

He had held crucial talks with Sri Lanka Tamil militant groups and Central Ministers. Earlier, he had attended the State level conference of his fans at Madurai and drew big crowds which he used to get in olden days.

The Last Will

M.G. Ramachandran, left movable and immovable property worth Rs. 10 crores, which includes his residential bungalow and garden at suburban Ramavaram, shares in Sathya Studios Private Limited and buildings in and around Madras city.

According to MGR's "Will" which was released on January 9, 1988 by its sole executor and senior advocate, N.C. Raghavachari, MGR had created a trust for setting up an "MGR deaf and dumb home" in a portion of his residential Ramavaram gardens.

MGR, who suffered a speech impairment following a stroke in 1984, had bequeathed the 8.3 acres Sathya Garden in suburban Saligramam village for construction of sheds to house the poor deaf and dumb. The 23 page "Will" in Tamil was written on January 18, 1987, after revoking an earlier one written on April 28, 1986.

The late Chief Minister has willed most of the property to the AIADMK, which he founded in 1972. The shares owned by MGR in the Sathya Studio (about 95 per cent) have been left to his party.

MGR said all the shares in Sathya Studio Private Limited should be bequeathed to the ruling party subject to the following conditions. The conditions include all buildings and articles in the studio should be taken over by AIADMK and they should utilise the income for party expenses, provided 80 per cent of the present members of the party continued as members. He said if there is a split in the party, Sathya Studios should be taken back by my executor for MGR deaf and dumb home.

His wife Janaki Ramachandran was to take over the motor cars, furniture, silver utensils, cow, cow cattle, according to the will. The will should be implemented within six months by his executor and legal adviser N. C. Raghavachari and S. Rajendran.

Janaki Ramachandran who stepped into the shoes of her husband, had been bequeathed only their residence and gardens at Ramavaram, besides movable property. Janaki Ramachandran whom he described as his "only legal heir" does not have the right to sell, mortgage or lease the property received from him. The property would be enjoyed by her brother's relatives after her life time, according to the will.

The valuable items gifted to the late Ramachandran during his long film career had been given for exhibition in his house which is to be converted as a memorial. MGR has not willed any property to the family of his brother, the late M.G. Chakrapani.

MGR had said that his valuable gift articles and books should be housed in his home at Thiagaraya Nagar in South Madras, which he wanted to be converted into a memorial building. The executor of the will should make arrangements for its maintenance, the expenses of which could be met using the income from the building he owned at suburban Alandur, and to enable people to see all his gifts. He had made this arrangement to avoid money being spent by the State to buy a house as a memorial, he said pointing out that memorial houses of the late Chief Ministers K. Kamaraj and C.N. Annadurai were established at the expense of the State.

Last Phase

In October 1984, MGR was diagnosed with kidney failure and was rushed to the Downstate Medical Centre, Brooklyn, United States for treatment, undergoing a kidney transplant. MGR died on December 24, 1987 after his prolonged illness. His death sparked off a frenzy of looting and rioting all over the state of Tamil Nadu. Shops, movie theatres, buses and other public and private property became the target of violence let loose all over the state. The police had to resort issuing shoot-at-sight orders.

Tamilians from Bangalore rushed to Madras in trains to see the mortal remains of MGR. Govt. had announced free train facility for this visit. The violence during the funeral alone left 29 people dead and 47 police personnel badly wounded. This state of affairs continued for almost a month all over the state of Tamil Nadu. Around one million people followed his remains, around 30 followers committed suicide and people had their heads tonsured. After his death, his political party, the All India Anna Dravida Munnetra Kazhagam, split between his wife Janaki Ramachandran and J. Jayalalitha; they later merged in 1988. In 1989 Dr. M. G. R. Home and Higher Secondary School for the Speech and Hearing Impaired was established in the erstwhile Residence MGR Gardens, Ramavaram, in accordance with his will dated January 17, 1986. His film studio, Sathya Studios has been converted into a women's college. His official residence at 27, Arcot Street, T. Nagar is now MGR Memorial House and is open for public viewing.

After Death

Death laid its icy hands on M.G. Ramachandran, the matinee idol of the millions and one of the most eminent makers of modern India. He has been defying disease and doctors for quite a long time to serve the people whom he loved so much and who in return lavished their affection upon him. The last public function in which he addressed his people was on Monday the 21st December 1987 when he presided over a meeting at Madras where Prime Minister, Rajiv Gandhi unveiled a ten-feet bronze statue of Jawaharlal Nehru as a fitting tribute to the architect of modern India, which he said was the fulfilment of their long cherished desire. The leader who is now no more had just reached the Biblical three score and ten with many years of service to the people laying ahead of him. But "life's fitful fever" decided that he should be called back to his Maker at this time. His untimely demise has left his State and the country poorer; but infinitely richer for all the mighty contribution he made to the greatness of Tamil Nadu and India.

Loss of a Great Patriot

With the departure of M.G. Ramachandran, India has lost one of the greatest patriots, one of the few of those who enjoy the admiration and respect of political friends and foes alike. Now-a-days when sole aim in life is to join the race for grabbing as many labels of luxuries and affluence as it may be possible and in this process one is willing to over run and crush thousand of the weaker people, the younger generation in India may not understand why MGR chose the life of sacrifice and suffering after bidding goodbye to his prosperous film career. MGR continued to serve the neglected masses all his life. In all his deeds and words his concern for the good of the Indian Nation as a whole had been in evidence.

Legacy

In the death of Ramachandran a unique phenomenon passed away in Indian politics. The void caused by his demise in Tamil Nadu will be difficult to fill. In any case, the politics of Tamil Nadu will never be the same again. MGR, as he was known to millions, died on the fifteenth anniversary of his avowed mentor Periyar E.V. Ramaswami, the rationalist leader. There is more than mere coincidental significance in this. MGR's death marks the end of the second, and more prolonged phase of the rule of 'Dravidian politics' which came to stay with the ascent to office of the DMK under the late C.N. Annadurai in 1967.

MGR ruled for more than half of the two decades in which the Congress-I was kept out of governmental power in Tamil Nadu, winning three successive elections to the State Assembly, in 1977, 1980 and December 1984. Even before he launched out on his own, under the banner of the Anna DMK, 1972, Ramachandran was the biggest vote getter for the DMK. The late Annadurai had paid a tribute to his vote-catching abilities when he said that Ramachandran could fetch more votes, than himself.

His only political debacle was in the 1980 Lok Sabha election when the AIADMK was allied with the Janata Party and his party won a mere two seats to the Lok Sabha. Except for this Ramachandran suffered no major political reverses. MGR switched from the world of films in which he had totally dominated in his over 136 films, to politics with effortless ease, though it was five years after his exit from the DMK that he became the Chief Minister, with the blessings of the Congress party ruling at the Centre.

His total support to the National Emergency in 1975 was decisive in the Congress party backing him in the initial stages, though he had the knack of keeping on the right side of any party ruling at the Centre. He had an excellent rapport with Smt. Indira Gandhi as well as Janata Party Prime Minister, Morarji Desai. He took care to maintain good relations even with the lame duck Government led by Ch. Charan Singh. These, briefly alienated him from Smt. Indira Gandhi though he was a consistent supporter of her and her policies. His alignment with the Janata Party in 1980 led to a virtual breakdown of relations with her and the Congress. But he persisted and returned to be counted upon as a reliable ally in 1983.

2

Political Backdrop

Tamil Nadu's Situation

Situated on the eastern side of the southern tip of the Indian peninsula, Tamil Nadu is bounded by Andhra Pradesh in the North, Karnataka in the North-West, Kerala in the West, the Indian Ocean in the South and the Bay of Bengal in the East. Sri Lanka lies to its South-East.

Tamil Nadu covers an area of 1,30,069 sq. km. It is the eleventh largest State and occupies 4 per cent of the country's total land area. It represents the nucleus of Dravidian culture in India, which dates back to some 6,000 years. It is generally held that the Dravidians were the earliest inhabitants of India, and founded the Indus Valley Civilization of the 4th millennium B. C. With the coming of the Aryans into northern India they receded to the South. The Pallava, Pandyas, Cholas and Cheras were the earliest dynasties of this State.

At the time of independence, the Madras province (Tamil name Chennai which comprised Tamil Nadu, Andhra Pradesh and part of Kerala) continued as the State of Madras. In 1953, it was divided into two-Andhra Pradesh, comprising. Telugu-speaking areas and Madras, comprising Tamil-speaking areas. In 1969, the name of Madras was changed to Tamil Nadu.

Dravidian Movement

The Dravidian movement is confined to Tamil Nadu. Attempts to extend it to the other States have failed. There is a historical reason for its prevalence in Tamil Nadu alone and not elsewhere in the South. Tamil is an ancient language far older than Telugu, Kannada or Malayalam. It has had a fine literature from ancient times. Till recently, there was a happy blend of the so-called "Aryan" civilization with the Dravidian. Many perhaps most scholars were familiar with both Tamil and Sanskrit. There was no question of any cultural conflict. But a few features of the "Aryan" civilization have failed to stand the test of time. The most notable of these is the caste system. In Tamil Nadu, as in the rest of India, the Brahmin was held in regard and respect as the scholar. But with the advent of the British, when conditions changed diametrically, it became merely the holder of many of the important posts in the administration. That invited resentment. Out of this grew the Justice Party, the predecessor and, in some respects, the forerunner of the Dravida Munnetra Kazhagam (DMK).

The British rulers actively encouraged the Justice Party as a counterblast to the Congress, most leaders of which were Brahmins. But the Justice Party had no roots in the masses, and it led an artificial life for a few years. It formed the ministry on one or two occasions. It was regarded as a party of zamindars and other landed gentry and had no future.

C. Rajagopalachari was a different kind of "rebel". He rose high in national service, becoming the last of the Governor-General. He headed the Government in Madras twice once before and once after Independence. But his policies diverged from those of the Congress.

While he accepted state socialism, he tended to become a rightist, and believed in private enterprise. As the tone of Congress administration in the country as a whole degenerated, he took up the cause of anti-socialism and founded Swatantra Party. He was particularly vocal against the "Licence-permit Raj" of the Congress. Much of this was in the future, but when he resigned the Chief Ministership, the position he held after the 1952 general elections, he gradually turned against the Congress and worked for its overthrow.

Backward Caste Movement

It is not at all surprising that the backward castes movement should have started in South India at the beginning of the century. It was an anti-Brahmin movement. That, of course, would not have sufficed if two conditions were not fulfilled. These were fulfilled. The Brahmins had, if anything, acquired greater power and prestige as a result of the spread of Western education. And yet they were vulnerable on account of their numerical weakness and the British Government's distrust of them in view of their representation in the freedom movement which was then acquiring new militancy and organisational capacity. Indeed, a third condition had also to be met for the backward castes movement to arise and grow. This was the rise of a Western-educated elite among these castes. This condition too was met by the twenties. Thus the movement expressed the ambitions and frustrations of a second wave of Western educated people who found that nearly all prestigious offices and lucrative posts had been carried off by the Brahmin first wave.

As is well known, Western education had become the principal route to success under the Raj; it is equally well known that in view of their literary tradition, high caste Hindus were the first to take to new education, the Brahmins occupying the top position. Thus, is Madras, though the Brahmins comprised about three per cent of the total population of the presidency, they accounted for 71 per cent of the total number of graduates between 1886-1910. In 1921 the literacy rate among the Brahmins in the presidency was 28 per cent as against two per cent for the Vellalas. They had also taken over a large number of Government jobs. In Madras in 1913, 350 out of the 478 Hindus employed in the Government were Brahmins.

Because of their early exposure to Western ideas, the upper castes were also the first to espouse the cause of freedom. Almost half the Hindu participants in the freedom movement in the first two decades of the Indian National Congress were Brahmins. This could not but have alienated the British from the upper castes, especially the Brahmins. New education inevitably spread to lower caste groups with the passage of time. In Madras, for the first time in 1916-17, the total number of non-Brahmins in High schools outnumbered the Brahmins. So the State was set for an effective anti-Brahmin movement of which the backward castes movement was to be one expression. Facts speak for themselves. A committee, first of its kind, appointed by the Maharaja of Mysore in 1918 to recommend measures for adequate representation of "backward communities" in Government services identified as backward "all communities other than Brahmins".

On the basis of the commission's report, he provided special facilities for non-Brahmins in education and recruitment in Government service in 1921. The pattern had now been set. A Bombay Government resolution in 1925 declared as backward all communities other than Brahmins, Prabhus, Marwaris, Parsis Banias and Christians which means over 90 per cent of the population, and provided reservations in Government services for them. In 1928 the Hartog committee defined backward castes as "castes or classes which are educationally backward", that is, it ignored the economic factors such as possession of land. The State committee, set up by the Bombay Government in 1930 to identify the backward classes, divided these into three groups — "the depressed classed" (i.e., untouchable), aboriginal and hill tribes" and "other backward classes". It recommended special educational facilities and recruitment in Government service for the three groups.

During the hearings of the Indian Franchise Committee in the United Provinces, a memorandum presented by the Deputy Collector of Faizabad recommended that the "depressed classes should include all Sudras other than the Kayasthas. The United Provinces Hindu Backward Classes League submitted list of 115 "backward" castes (more than 60 per cent of the population) which included untouchables as well as those above them. "All of the listed communities belonged to non-Dwijas (non-twice-born, that is those who did wear the sacred thread) or degenerate or Sudra classes of the Hindus" A list presented by the Madras Provincial Backward Classes League to the Government in 1944 included among the Backward Classes more than two -thirds of the non-Brahmins of the presidency. In 1947 these "Backward Hindus', were provided reservations in the Madras Government. With preparation of list of scheduled castes, the term backward classes was no loger used for untouchables. The term "other backward castes" came into vogue and it referred to the strata above the untouchables. All in all peasant castes of various descriptions constitute the core of the OBCs. Generally they have a low ritual status, but with the decline of the in importance of rituals its society has ceased to be a significant factor in the lives of the people. More pertinently, the OBCs are dominant force in the political and economic life of the countryside and cannot qualify for positive discrimination in their favour, especially in the context of the phenomenal increase in agricultural output, the enormous investment the Government has made in agriculture and rural development, and the growth of their influence in the administration at the State level. But the OBCs movement is not an exercise in rationality. It is precisely because these communities have acquired enormous power and that they are well placed to press the demand for reservations.

When on the achievement of independence, the national leadership took up the task of framing the Constitution, it was inspired by the concepts of equality and justice. So the Constitution empowered the Government to make special provisions for the advancement of socially and educationally backward castes. This referred primarily to scheduled castes and tribes but included others as well. This reflected a mix of idealism and inadequate understanding of the rural society on the part of the leadership. Southern States, with their long history of backward castes movement, took the lead in making special provisions for the OBCs in respect of reservations for them in Government services and professional institutions.

In these States powerful dominant castes such as the Lingayats in Mysore and the Ezhavas in Kerala were included in the earlier lists of the OBCs. By 1964 Tamil Nadu had reserved 25 per cent of State Government jobs for the backward castes. This was in addition to the 16 per cent reservations for scheduled castes and tribes, On the basis of the Sattananhan commission report of 1970, reservations for the OBCs were raised to 31 per cent and finally in 1980 to 50 per cent. This did not include 18 per cent reservations for scheduled castes and tribes. The inference is obvious. The upper castes, especially the Brahmins, were to be eliminated from both higher education and Government services. The courts have tried to check the drift towards higher and higher reservations for the "other backward castes, but without much success. In 1966 the Andhra Pradesh Government had provided reservations in Government services and professional colleges for 112 OBCs. The list was struck down by the State High Court on the ground that the Government could not produce evidence of social and educational backwardness of these communities.

But on the basis of the Manoher Pershad Commission Report (1970) the government ordered 25 per cent reservations for the OBCs. In the 1950s the Karnataka High Court had struck down the Government's attempt to prepare lists of backward classes. The Government order of 1961 based on the recommendations of the Naganna Gowda Committee was also declared illegal by the Supreme court in the famous Balaji case. But finally under Devraj Urs, all communities with the exception of the Lingayats, Bunts and Brahmins were included in the backward class category and given reservations. What could be a more patent demonstration of discrimination against certain communities.

No news from the States indicate normality. When things go wrong, newspapers become over active, as they are in reporting the surprising developments in Tamil Nadu. The ruling party there, the All-India Anna DMK has split into two within a week of its leader's death. Much of the legislature wing has gone over to the dead man's wife and much of the organisational structure to the crowd puller, Madam Jayalalitha. This is today's equation and given the ideological vacuum in which the AIADMK exists, and it is not safe to rule out a brisk trafficking in MLAs in the days to come. There are people who like to be surprised by the splintering of the party. Actually, even they realise that a regional party is not a political entity in the text book sense, but only an appendage to a leader who articulates, in the most effective manner, one or the other urges of his people.

Almost always such a leader tends to be autocratic (not in the wholly negative sense but in the sense that he does not respect consensus methods), charismatic demands and easily secures unquestioning loyalty from followers. The leader's departure almost always signals the setting of the sun on the party as a whole. His second-in-command, if ever there exists one, suddenly finds that he has many rivals; in fact everyone becomes a second-in-command. What is tragic is that these "stalwarts in sycophancy" are not even aware of the political ways settling a dispute, and they like submitting their claims to a well-recognised and established committee. A fierce battle ensues among these faceless men, who have never tried to — or, never had a chance to acquire an identity of their own. Prolonged exposure to thoughtlessness renders them political featherweights and utterly helpless in dropping ideological anchor.

In Tamil Nadu, the Dravidian movement spawned a string of charismatic leaders who lived deep into the post-Independence era. (The Congress corps of such individuals started leaving the scene almost immediately after 1947.) First there was the lovable non-conformist, Periyar Ramaswamy Naickar, who fathered the self-respect movement which soon flowered into a quizzical amalgam of a separatist campaign, radical posturing and exaggerated love for Tamil and its heritage. Once Periyar's idea caught on many young adherents, first thronged him and then undercut his standing and soon parted ways, carrying the mass base. C.N. Annadurai was the most mature and articulate of them all and he became the totem pole of the resurgent but as yet delightfully undefined Dravidian identity. When "Anna" died in 1969, there was an intense tussle among his many heirs but crafty politician as M. Karunanidhi snatched the mantle by virtue of his control over the organisation and propaganda organs.

A few disappointed men strayed away but loneliness drove them back to the partyfold. When M. Karunanidhi decided to promote himself to the position of a latter-day Annadurai, M.G. Ramachandran revolted and, in due course, cut the former to his size. The idea behind recapturing the cavalcade of popular leaders is not to test one's memory but to emphasise that not one of them ever talked of ideology or a carefully worked out programme of action but merely asserted his individual merits over the demerits of his detractors.

In this rarefied political atmosphere, mental foot-touching became not merely a fashion but the basic requirement. All "thambis" (younger brothers) eagerly surrendered their identity, self-respect and even the capacity to think to the "anna" (elder brother) of the day. His word became law and politics was reduced to a pantomime. There was a culpable lack of thinking and this deficiency was sought to be made us by resorting to social welfare measures. Likely, longterm effects were ignored in striving for short-term popularity. The State's potential for growth in the real sense was systematically undermined in this process of pursuing a mindless distributive egalitarianism.

Congress in Power

The Congress formed the ministry in Madras Presidency in 1946 under T. Prakasam. But, after about eighteen months, he was replaced by Omandur Ramaswami Reddiar. Meanwhile the linguistic Andhra State had been formed in November, 1953. Ramaswami Reddiar himself gave way to P.S. Kumaraswami Raja. He held office till the general elections in 1952, when he was defeated. In the new Assembly the Congress held only 152 seats out of 375. Yet Rajagopalachari, who, a few months earlier, had resigned the Union Home Ministership, formed a Government and in a short while mustered an absolute majority in the State Assembly. A gifted politician, he soon created a favourable impression, particularly when he removed food controls through the Presidency. But a conflict was developing with Kamaraj.

Kamaraj had been a Congress volunteer, with a few advantages of birth or influence. By 1952 he had become President of the Tamil Nadu Congress Committee. He and the Chief Minister fell out partly because the latter was not consulting him in affairs of State. Rajagopalachari had introduced an educational reform scheme. Kamaraj opposed it, and enjoyed the support of E.V. Ramaswami. Rajagopalachari resigned and Kamaraj succeeded him as Chief Minister.

In the years immediately before Independence, some Congress leaders in Tamil Nadu were apt to take an independent line. The most prominent of these was Srinivasa Iyengar, a leading lawyer who became Advocate-General. He was what would now be regarded as radical in politics. He presided over the Guwahati session of the Congress, but later drifted away from the official leadership. He could cross swords with Mahatma Gandhi himself, and fully supported Subhash Chandra Bose.

The political scene in Tamil Nadu has undergone a sea change in the last 25 years (1963-1987). The State was a Congress bastion a quarter century ago as were the other States in the country. In the elections in 1962, the Congress repeated its victory and K. Kamaraj formed the Government only to make way to M. Bhaktavatsalam. Kamaraj stepped down under the "Kamaraj plan". Both the leaders, who gave a stable Government to Tamil Nadu, are no more. The Congress is no longer in power.

Birth and Rise of DMK

The end of the Congress rule in Tamil Nadu marked the beginning of the ascendency of a regional party in the State. It was the Dravida Munnetra Kazhagam (DMK) under the leadership of the late C.N. Annadurai, popularly known as "Anna" (Brother). It humbled the Congress in the 1967 poll. The DMK was swept to power with 138 seats out of the expanded Assembly's strength of 234—a feat which even the DMK leaders had not expected to achieve. A feat it was for the DMK considering that the Congress had won 139 out of 206 seats in the assembly in the previous poll. A significant political development had taken place between the two elections. It dealt a severe blow to the Congress in Tamil Nadu from which it has yet to recover. This was the anti-Hindi agitation led by Annadurai. The DMK rode to power on the anti-Hindi sentiment of the Tamil speaking people. The Hindi issue still stalks this southern state.

The DMK's position improved further when, in 1971 Karunanidhi, who succeeded Annadurai, opted for a midterm poll. It won 184 seats. Annadurai did not complete the first term as Chief Minister, owing to his premature death. With the massive mandate it received from the people who were angered over what was termed as imposition of Hindi on the non-Hindi speaking people", the DMK should have been able to solve the irksome language issue, or so one thought. But the issue remained. Worse, it became a weapon, as it were, in the hands of some political leaders. When the DMK was in power, the Tamil Nadu Assembly adopted a resolution recommending to the Centre to bring forward an amendment to the Constitution to enshrine in it India's first Prime Minister late Jawaharlal Nehru's assurance on the continuance of English as long as the non-Hindi people wanted it.

Later, the All-India Anna Dravida Munnetra Kazhagam (AIADMK) Government led by M.G. Ramachandran introduced a similar resolution in the present assembly and it too was passed. The DMK Government was in office for five years. The period saw a clash of personalities in the party and it came into the open. The party was split when "MGR" then treasurer, came into conflict with party supremo, Karunanidhi, on the issue of accounting of the party funds. Many DMK stalwarts, who had joined the party when Annadurai formed the DMK as a splinter of the Dravida Kazhagam, founded by his mentor, E.V. Ramaswamy (Thanthai Periyar), went over to the AIADMK and were ministers in the "MGR" Ministry. Karunanidhi, who wielded a powerful pen as a writer of stories and scripts for Tamil films, had for once underestimated the crowd-pulling power of his film actor-political adversary, MGR.

In 1957, the DMK contested the General Election for the first time and secured fifteen seats in the Tamil Nadu Legislative Assembly. Annadurai won from the Kancheepuram Assembly Constituency with a thumping majority. His speeches in the Assembly House as leader of the opposition made a great impact and embarrassed the ruling party.

However, in 1962 General Election he was singled out for defeat and with all the means at the disposal of the then ruling party, Annadurai was defeated. But he was elected to the Council of States whereby his brilliant exposition and performance conquered the hearts of his listeners. In the Fourth General Elections held in February, 1967, the DMK won all the Parliamentary seats of Tamil Nadu and a single party with the majority of 138 members in a house of 234 members in the State Legislative Assembly. Annadurai was elected leader of the DMK Legislature party and on March 6, 1967, he became the first non-Congress Chief Minister of Tamil Nadu. He resigned his membership of the Parliament and was elected to the Tamil Nadu Legislative Council from the Madras Local Authorities Constituency. His assumption of office as Chief Minister marked the beginning of a new epoch.

Roots of AIADMK

The AIADMK has its roots in the movement nurtured by Periyar E.V. Ramaswami and C.N. Annadurai. A new social order, where everybody were not just born equal but were also treated as equals, was the heartbeat of that movement. The Government put its heart and soul and even the first year of its existence came out with schemes that gave quality to the life of the people. A glance at the progress gives an idea of the efforts of the Tamil Nadu Government to bring into reality the ideals of the Great Annadurai.

AIADMK on Scene

In the elections in 1977, the AIADMK led by the latter romped home, winning 130 out of the total of 234 seats. The AIADMK has been in power since then. It is the rivalry between the two Kazhagams, one going all out to regain power and the other trying to retain it through populist measures that makes the Tamil Nadu political scene interesting. Even the once-popular Congress party has been able to play only a peripheral role. The two Kazhagams miss no opportunity provided by political developments in the State to show to the people that are really concerned, be it the "Hindi imposition" issue or the more recent Sri Lankan Tamil problem.

The Congress has been aligning itself with either of the Kazhagams during the polls, its latest poll ally being the AIADMK. Though it could not put up an impressive show by itself, it has helped its allies significantly. The DMK for instance, fared well in 1980 when it had an alliance with the Congress led by Late Prime Minister Indira Gandhi and bagged all the seats it contested. This was a better performance than in 1977 when its ally was the Janata and the AIADMK's Partner was the Congress. The Indira-wave is said to have worked in both cases. MGR's break with Indira Gandhi was deemed to the chief reason for the AIADMK's debacle in the Lok Sabha elections in 1980. His miscalculation provided Karunanidhi with a golden opportunity to halt the sinking fortunes of his party.

Following the AIADMK defeat in the Lok Sabha election, the Centre dissolved the State Assembly on the ground that the party no longer enjoyed the confidence of the people, but AIADMK led by Ramachandran inflicted a crushing defeat on the Congress-DMK alliance in the midterm poll to the State Assembly held subsequently. During the next Assembly elections in December 1984, the Congress and AIADMK were poll allies, and Ramachandran being away in the US for the treatment of kidney ailment generated a sympathy wave for the party. So its winning streak continued.

Political Skill of MGR

The political situation in Tamil Nadu underwent a swift change after MGR's sudden departure from the scene. MGR left his imprints on fields as diverse as politics, economy, diplomacy and films. His strategy and leadership were comparable to those of the best politicians like Nehru, Churchil, Macmillan, Suharto, Nassar, Tito, etc. His was the brain that masterminded the victory of All India Anna Dravida Munnetra Kazhagham (AIDMK) in 1977 in Tamil Nadu. Asked by his political mentor late C.N. Annadurai (he defeated the Congress Party in 1967 and became Tamil Nadu Chief Minister) to command and reorganise the DMK cadre, MGR silenced all those who had raised the question: "After Annadurai, Who?" He was a man of indomitable spirit and courage and always had the good of the country at heart. MGR had not ruled only Tamil Nadu but ruled in the hearts of the Tamil masses.

Annadurai, the Mentor

Canjeevaram Natarajan Annadurai, dearingly called and popularly known as Anna (the elder brother) was born on September 15, 1909 in a lower Hindu middle class family of the weaver community at Canjeevaram and died on February 3,1969. Canjeevaram known as city of temples, is 45 miles away from Kancheepuram, the capital of the Pallava Kings. Short statured, soft-spoken and broad fore-headed Annadurai was as versatile, scholarly and fluent in English as in Tamil. He wrote articles, stories and dialogues for films. As a matter of fact, he is considered to be the doyen among dialogue writers, well-established for his catchy and ornamental and descriptive passages and impressive talks.

Besides, having been a dramatist, he had acted on the stage as well. He was deeply interested in social reforms and was a champion of liberty, equality and fraternity. He highlighted the cause of the poor, spoke and wrote on the anguish and misery of the exploited, unprivileged and have-nots. These were the themes of his plays as well as the film stories. Even if Annadurai had not entered politics at all, he would still have been recognised and adored as a writer of the first-rank in Tamil. All through his writings he projected his social conscience and presented the burning problems of the day courageously. Annadurai has to his credit more than 200 publications — speeches, plays, short stories, novels, etc. Annadurai first met Periyar E.V. Ramaswami in 1934 at Tiruppur in Coimbatore District at a Youths Conference and was immediately attracted to him.

Annadurai started the Dravidian Progressive Federation in 1949. He remained an ardent campaigner for the Justice Party candidates. He was also associated with the Tamil Weekly, *'Kudi Arasu'*. His editorials and articles were read with great interest. In 1942, he started his own weekly — the *"Dravidanadu"*. He was the Editor of *Malai Mani,* a Tamil Daily started on August 10, 1949, to present the cause of the Dravidian Progressive Federation. He edited the Tamil weekly *'Kanchi'* till he was elected leader of the DMK Legislature Party in 1967.

In 1957, he started an English Weekly, *the Homeland* which ceased publication after some years. In 1966, he founded another English Weekly the *'Homerule'*. By relentless efforts Annadurai under the guidance of Periyar provided a mass base for the Justice Party which had been suffering from a lack of mass contact. They infused the party with revolutionary ideas. Annadurai felt that the Justice Party was considered a pro-British party and maligned as a party opposed to the freedom struggle. So in 1944 he resolved to rename the Justice Party as the Dravidar Kazhagam.

He proposed that titles like 'Sir' and 'Dewan' or 'Bahadur' conferred by the ruling British should be surrendered and the proposal was adopted without dissent. These changes had its positive effect on youths and students. His message of Dravidar Kazhagam spread like wild fire throughout the State. His way to counter and propagate his point of view was logical, unaggressive and persuasive. His cultured and civilized way and amicable approach paid rich dividends. He was appreciated and respected by people of all shades of opinions.

He was quite independent in his personal point of view and ready to dissent any person however dear and respectful he might be. Though a follower of Periyar he did not hesitate to differ with him in 1947, when power was transferred and the independence Day — August 15 was to be celebrated. Periyar declared that it was a day of mourning for the Dravidians. It was because Annadurai loathed and hated colonialism and he declared that it was a day of as much rejoicing for the Dravidians as it was for others in any part of India. It was too much for Periyar and there came the split in the Dravidar Kazhagam in 1949. As a result, the Dravidar Munnetra Kazhagam (Dravidian Progressive Federation) was started on September 17, 1949 by Annadurai. Surprisingly enough, majority came into the fold of Annadurai's party.

After Anna

After the death of C.N. Annadurai and after splitting away from Karunanidhi, MGR had to begin a new among his people, large sections of whom had been fed on separatist slogans, the alluring politics of North-South confrontation and anti-Hindism. He did not even have a full-fledged party setup of his own. A lesser leader would have garbled any opportunity to breathe fire at his enemies, real and imaginary, to drum up support for himself. He would have stoked the fires of discontent which is always brewing in poor communities. But he did not succumb to this temptation. He remained his low-key, sober, and dignified self

3

Rise in Politics

Entering Politics

When M.G. Ramachandran joined the DMK, the party was already a force. He did not have to suffer for the cause which the party represented. Others who had been in it from the beginning had to go through suffering. MGR's sole claim to influence in the party was his mass film following. But it must be admitted that he had tried to combat evil through his films. People took his pronouncements on the screen seriously and followed him into politics. MGR came to power only because DMK leader M. Karunanidhi was charged for corruption.

Years ago MGR firmly made up his mind that he was going to become an actor. He became a charismatic film-star and turned politician. "My blood brothers and sisters" was how M.G. Ramachandran used to begin his public speeches. The reference to blood was due to the liberal blood donation by scores of his fans when he was hospitalised after being shot in the neck by M.R. Radha, another famous actor who played the villain role in films starring Ramachandran.

Called "purachi thalaivar" (revolutionary leader) Ramachandran had several titles, but to his fans he was simply "vaadhiyaar" (the ustad) who in his film roles fought against tyrants, wiped out the evil and restored good.

Mass Popularity

With his mass popularity Ramachandran could get away with anything. Although he belonged to the Dravidian movement with its original concept of atheism, he went to Kollur in Dakshina Kannada District to worship Sri Mookambika. With a stroke of the pen Ramachandran at one time asked all the officials to sign their names in Tamil in all the official files. Although the files and circulares and orders were in English, they bore the signatures of ministers and officials in Tamil language.

Gentle but Short-tempered

Ramachandran was known to be short-tempered, and rarely spared the rod when angry. He would sometimes strike a blow he could hit really hard at those who angered or displeased him but he would quickly assuage their feelings, invite them to his house, and provide them a lavish meal. That was his way of saying sorry. One of Ramachandran's admirers accidentally touched his cap while garlanding him at a railway station. Ramachandran who was sensitive about his cap, lashed out the youth, a hard slap landing on his cheek. He went sprawling. Even those who were very close to him had received blows at times, they recounted with pride.

A Hero for All Times

As a matinee idol MGR played in the role of a good Samaritan. He lived as a hero in the hearts of people for all times. He was the first star who entered politics with a bang, and with his star image he occupied the political stage like an unconquered giant till the last breath of his life. In one of his 136 films, when MGR sang "if I can be the ruler, these poor people will not suffer" transformed him from man to God in Tamil Nadu. He dominated Tamil filmdom for well over a quarter of a century. He did the role of a do-gooder in most of his films. His dialogues and songs had ideals of the DMK and these contributed significantly towards popularising the party and its eventual capture of power in 1967. The mascot of MGR films had the DMK flag held aloft by a man and woman. MGR made his debut in Tamil films in 1935 when he was given a minor role in "Sathi Leelavathi" scripted by

Mr. S.S. Vasan of Gemini Films. For the next decade he had to be content with secondary roles as the Tamil screen was then dominated by veterans like M.K. Thiageraja Bhargavathar, P.U. Chinnapa and K.R. Ramaswamy. The real break came in 1945 when he was given a lead role in "Rajkumari" which was instrumental in his meteoric rise to stardom.

On Top in Films

MGR, who resigned from the Congress and joined the DMK in 1952, took over from Shivaji Ganesan as Chief Propagandist of the DMK through films after the latter quit the party in 1954. From then onwards, every film in which MGR acted was a box office hit and this earned him the title of "King of Collection".

The magnum opus of MGR films was "Madodi Mannan", a Tamil version of the "Prisoner of Zenda". Ideals set up in that film were considered the directive principles of AIADMK Government and the State Government officials were asked to see the film for proper guidance.

It was not a question of a good actor enacting the politician's role; in any event, his acting abilities in films were an arguable point, and other actors had come to grief by launching themselves into politics. MGR had the uncanny ability not only to marry films to real life but also to use his political powers to good effect by keeping the various factions in his party at bay while forcing the only real opposition he faced the DMK on the defensive. His decision to forge an alliance with the Congress ensured that there would be a sympathetic Centre viewing the State's needs.

A Democrat

It must be recognised that MGR was acting within a democratic framework, despite the peculiarities of the Indian system. There have been dictators in the world who have held absolute sway in their countries — Stalin and Peron, to name two. In the short term, the dictator's task is easier because he has the engine of repression at his command. To be able to carve out a supreme position in a democratic framework requires greater political acumenship. But in probing the MGR phenomenon, a few nagging questions remain. To begin with, can his phenomenal popularity be ascribed to a particularly Tamilian or southern temperament? Second, if such popularity is divorced from achievements on the ground, how is one to correct the imbalance? Third, granted that films are the opium of the masses in India, is it wise to increase the dosage? It would seem that the MGR phenomenon happened in Tamil Nadu, rather than elsewhere, because the climate was favourable for it for a variety of local reasons. It can be duplicated in the rest of the country, given the right circumstances and the emergence of an MGR. The very fact of the popularity of the mythological soap opera on television *Ramayana,* is testimony of how an MGR phenomenon can emerge in the north provided the right ingredients are present.

The answer to the second question is obvious. The end of a phenomenon such as MGR's must be followed by the regime of a man or woman who can look at the nuts and bolts issues and get on with the task of paying attention to all the neglected areas in administration and the development of. Again, this is not peculiar to India. West Germany needed a Helmut Schmidt to follow the charismatic leadership of Willy Brandt, who played a historic role in reconciling his country to its communist neighbours and the rest of the world. It was left to Schmidt to tie the loose ends left by Brandt.

Power of Celluloid

Films occupy a place in Indian life out of proportion to other forms of entertainment. This is so for the simple reason that the people do not have access to other forms, except for the middle class now being increasingly hooked on to the idiot box. There is no reason why we should deny the people their fantasy world of films since we cannot provide all of them the basic necessities of life. The popularity of Indian commercial films in other developing countries bears testimony to the fact that, whatever the Government's edicts, Indian producers know what their audiences want.

Grief, joy or any other emotion has to be depicted in song, and the good guys must win in the end, but only after epic battles between good and evil and a bit of history thrown in to bring in colourful costumes. And in a country full of politicians making speeches by the yard, there must be moralising, something to make us feel good at the end of it all to enable us to lead our mundane lives. MGR knew how to tug at the emotional heart strings of his people better than any producer. He was besides, his own best script writer, and, after having dispensed with the services of his old script writer, M. Karunanidhi, he worsted him in the field of politics. The danger in the MGR phenomenon lies in the fact that others in the acting fraternity might be tempted to enter the world of politics.

There is no bar to actors, in common with members of any other profession, trying their hands at politics. Some of them have already discovered the pitfalls and have resumed their primary activity. Others are persevering, in the hope of winning political rewards. Indeed, actors would be missing the essential point of the MGR phenomenon if they equate their profession with success in politics. An MGR is a rare occurrence, and the fact that he was able to use his acting talents, such as they were, to create unique waves in the political firmament is an indication of his populist genius. He filled an emotional need of his people and in the process gained a stature in Tamil Nadu history which will defy posterity.

Source of Inspiration

MGR was a source of inspiration for many of the younger heroes of the Tamil screen from Kamal Hassan to Rajnikanth and Bhagyaraj. If Kamal Hassan learnt gymnastics, Rajnikanth and Bhagyaraj were inspired by MGR in moulding their image. While MGR left the centre stage of politics and cinema in Tamil Nadu, his carefully cultivated image was likely to Persist as a great crowd puller.

MGR's fame crossed national boundaries and he was Perhaps one of the few privileged star in the country to have 'All World MGR Fans Association' which later became a Powerful political arm. The Fans Association has branches in London, South-East Asia, America and in countries with Tamil settlements.

In line with the national perspective that inspired all his actions including the advice he gave from time to time on the vexed question of Tamils in Sri Lanka, is the pioneering welfare work that he initiated for the weak and vulnerable sections of society whose pulse he could unfailingly feel. The midday meal scheme for the school children is an instance of the many imaginative ones that he got implemented. Doubting Thomases were many. But Ramachandran persisted with remarkable vigour till those who came to scoff stopped to pray. If he was a revolutionary actor, as he was, he was also a revolutionary administrator who reached instinctively to the troubles and travails of the simple annals of the poor. The constructive role that this Colossus played in Indian politics will be remembered for long and will remain as an inspiration to those on whose shoulders his mantle will fall.

Historic Role

One of the many outstanding features of the role played by this film star turned politician (recalling the instances of the US President Ronald Reagan and Andhra Chief Minister N.T. Rama Rao) is that with all his passionate pre-occupation with promoting the interests of the people of Tamil Nadu, he never lost sight of the national perspective and ever kept the interests of the nation above everything else. With the formation, many years earlier of the Dravida Munnetra Kazhagam (DMK) there came the distant echoes of the demand for a separate Dravidistan.

Forces of history including the emergence of the film star as a politician dissipated. These fissiparous tendencies and the separatist echoes died away. The founding of the All India Anna Dravida Munnetra Kazhagam (AIADMK) by MGR dealt a fatal blow to those centrifugal tendencies. This is no mean achievement against the background of the mighty influence of the DMK and is a monument to his enlightened leadership which steered for the last ten years the ship of the State in Tamil Nadu as an integral part of a united India.

Tamil Identity

Seldom can it be said of an individual that his end marks that of an era as well. That, however, will only be an accurate summing up of what the demise of M.G. Ramachandran signifies. This is certainly true as far as Tamil Nadu is concerned. MGR effected a sharper break with the State's past in some respects than many may have thought possible when he took office 1977. The decade since then, during which he has held three terms' as Chief Minister, has witnessed remarkable changes of a social character — though it remains to be seen how deep, extensive and durable these have to be the biggest and most conspicuous change has consisted in an unmistakable dilution of what has imprecisely been called the 'Dravidian' temper of the variety of politics that emerged victor in the State under the leadership of late C.N. Annadurai in 1967.

Even the political adversaries of the departed leader will perhaps agree that this transformation has meant a longer spell of stability as well as a larger degree of freedom from sectarian conflicts for the populace than seemed indicated by the earlier surge of a movement that sought to divide the nation as also the State. This was indisputably no mean achievement, and the mystery of how he achieved this, the methods he employed, does not make it any less so. The starpolitician, who attained virtual sainthood in his people's eye, was a living legend with an appeal that was never adequately explained, but nonetheless potent for that reason.

Tamil, the principal language of Tamil Nadu, is one of the oldest and most developed of Indian languages, as is the State's culture. Relatively free from foreign influence the people have preserved a continuous tradition of classical dance, music, art and architecture in their purest forms. "Bharata Natyam" is the famous classical dance of Tamil Nadu which has been in vogue here for several centuries. Karnatic music, as the south Indian style of classical music is called, is dominant here. The typical south Indian instruments found in this State include the *nadawaram* (a wind instrument), the *mridangam* (a percussion instrument), the veena, the flute and the violin.

Tamil literature, like its art, reflects the culture, civilization and outlook of the Tamils. The most important among ancient literary works are *Thirukkurae, Silapathikaram* and *Manimekalai.* The first written by Tiruvalluvar, deals with the various requirements of an ideal code of conduct for Kings and commoners alike. *Silapathikaram,* a great epic, tells the story of a devoted wife, while *Manimekalai* is a Buddhist classic which narrates the story of a great lady ascetic. These classics have been hailed as the three bright gems in the diadem of Tamil literature. Some renowned

Tamil literatures of old are Sekkitar, the author of *Periapuranam* Kamban who wrote the Tamil version of the *Ramayana* and Villiputhur Alwar who wrote the *Mahabharata* in Tamil. At the turn of the century came Sri Ramalingaswami and Subramanya Bharati and in recent times, the outstanding literary figures have been C.N. Annaduari. Thiru V. Kalayanasundara Mudaliar and Kalki Krishnamoorthy, among others. The age-old architecture of Tamil Nadu is reflected in the countless temples found in this State. These temples are the symbols of a great period of building activity that lasted from 500 to 1600 AD.

Thomas Carlyle and Ralph Waldo Emerson believed in representative men and heroes. I think that the idea is relevant in the Tamil context more than in that of other Indian regions, one might call the Tamils backward in that respect perhaps but they believe in heroes and representative men. None, absolutely no one, was more representative of the Tamils in these years and decades than M.G. Ramachandran. It was both his strength and his weakness perhaps. He was representative of the confusion of culture that the popular film especially the Tamil variety, shows. He was representative of the non-elite quality of culture and art emanations of today. He was a movement away from intellectually at all levels — including the pseudo and the real intellectuals of the left, the right and the middle.

Whether one considers him a wholesale influence or not is according to one's own convictions. That too is very much in the tradition of non-intellectuality. But he was an epitome of all the bourgeois virtues that have sustained human life in its history inspite of being called a revolutionary leader. His death leaves a vacuum in the hearts of the people. Though alien press correspondents tended to make fun of him for not knowing social reform as distinct from socialism in his earlier days in office they have remained to wonder at a phenomenon that is so Indian and so Tamil in the last analysis. Though born a Malayalam speaker, he was a Tamil in his heart and that was that mattered. In the larger analysis, E.V. Ramaswamy too was a Kannada speaking Tamil. It will take a long time for the Tamil Nadu and the Tamils to recover from the life and death of this Titan of a man whom his people deified so naturally. In death, as in life, he remains a Titan.

Tamil identity has clashed with the dominant ethos that characterised India's nation-building crisis even before Independence. The ethos was that of the middle class of the populous Hindi-heartland as it is now. The Tamil's search for an identity began when the Justice Party, promoted by the British as a conscious policy of "counter-poise" (to deepen the cleavages or to create them where none existed) metamorphosed into the Dravida Kazhagam in the 1940s. The Justice Party was for the non-Brahmin movement, an anti-imperialist orientation and democratised it.

The 1949 split in the Dravida Kazhagam (ostensibly over a subjective reason; the 70 year old leader marrying his secretary still in her thirties) was in fact the result of a lack of understanding between the younger crop of workers and senior party leaders. The Dravida Munnetra Kazhagam (the Dravidian Progressive Party) as the break-away was secessionist and populist. M.G. Ramachandran, not a Tamilian, was a small town boy who made good in Tamil films (there was no Malayalam film industry worth the name then) but even when he was struggling in films he was involved in Dravidian politics.

He cast his lot with the new party founded by C.N. Annadurai who had no ideology but had a vague vision of Tamil identity — the search for which found expression over the language issue when the Constitution made Hindi the sole official language. People of non-Hindi areas accepted Hindi with reservations and though there was elation over the success of a long-struggle for freedom there was also despair stemming from the uneasy feeling that the country lacked the linguistic unity thought to be so vital for a new republic but how did the Hindi-speaking people view it? T.A. Ramalingam Chettiar, a Tamil member from the old Madras Presidency told the Constituent Assembly when it debated the language issue that it was a matter of life and death for the people of the south. "Sir, coming here to the capital and feeling ourselves strangers in this land, we do not feel we are a nation to whom the whole thing belongs. It is not even the things that are said-we have given up our language in favour of Hindi but the way in which the Hindi speaking people treat us and the way in which they made demands is more galling".

The Hindi-speaking populace attitude to other languages scarred the Tamil psyche more than any one else's. The DMK jettisoned its secessionist plank but the Hindi issue remained and found devastating expression in the 1965 language riots in Madras State and saw the end of Congress domination in the state. Dravidian politics had arrived but long before 1965 the screen image of M.G. Ramachandran swashbuckling film star was that of a friend of the underdog and the chivalrous hero of damsels in distress. He transcribed this image to real life too.

When there was heavy rains in Madras, one year, the hero spent his own money to feed the poor and to distribute rain coats to rickshaw pullers. The DMK needed MGR because celluloid was its main medium of communication. Thus every leader of consequence wrote film scripts. The party cultivated Ramachandran the filmstar, not only because he donated generously to the party coffers but also because his cinematic role mattered and in his turn the "Ideal actor" used the party to promote his cinematic image. Soon it was not the party machinery that really mattered the many MGR fan clubs became the thing. It was a parallel setup perhaps more structured and organised than the DMK cadres.

The 1971 split in the DMK was brought about by M.G. Ramachandran protesting against the growing corruption in the party. This move enhanced MGR's image — here was one who was above it all and though he continued to act in films he was particular not to hold any office even in the new party he founded. He bowed out of acting only after he became the Chief Minister. To the underdog Ramachandran was the model to emulate, the symbol of their aspiration from humble beginnings to the most successful filmstar and yet he was one with them.

When he came to power the image perpetuated itself — politics to MGR was secondary. Outside his populist flourishes M.G. Ramachandran had little ideology, and even less of politics, not even the sheer instinct which gave a grassroots leader like Kamaraj his political acumen. The line between film acting and his political role was thin, if, even though he had traded films for power. The dangerous political vacuum resulting from the primacy of charisma over issues inevitably led to corruption and psychophancy. But in MGR's case charisma obliterated everything else. He was more a myth than a reality. The heady brew of Tamil nationalism and charisma were a bizarre permutation that gave the people a folk hero in him. The poverty of the state's politics is an indication of the harm charisma can do to a volatile, sensitive people. The phoney confrontations Tamil Nadu has had with the Centre concealed political co-option. The Congress which accepted one kazhagam or the other as their ally — indistinguishable politically in its parliamentary opportunism was unable to provide an alternative focus even after the DMK split.

The English-educated elite of Tamil Nadu lament the fact that the State Government has gone into the hands of politicians who know only Tamil. This is a perverse approach. It is not necessary to know English to be a democrat and a good administrator. The late Kamaraj knew only Tamil but is still remembered for his honesty and dedication. Conversely we have had many examples of "well educated" Chief Minister turning out to be most corrupt, inefficient and high-handed.

Whatever they may say in public, politicians in Tamil Nadu are at heart really thankful to the Central Government for its so-called Hindi promotion policies. It was the Hindi issue which helped the undivided DMK to come to power with a little imagination and fact, then Congress Government at the Centre, could have defused the anti-Hindi agitation. All that needed to be done was to give a firm and clear constitutional guarantee that English would have the status of associate official language of the country, while Hindi continued to be the main official language. Mere verbal assurances were not considered enough and the DMK hotheads skilfully exploited the misgivings of the public.

Once again, the Central Government had gone to the help of linguistic fanatics in Tamil Nadu. Can anything be more foolish than trying to promote the use of Hindi by directing Government officials in the South to sign letters and files in Hindi Most amusingly, this ritual was to be observed only during the "Hindi Week": After that the officials would revert to the old practice of signing letters and files in english. There could be no better way of insulting Hindi.

The two main rival parties in Tamil Nadu the ruling AIADMK led by late MGR and the DMK headed by Karunanidhi were really waiting for this latest move on the part of the Central Government. They fully knew that the circular about signing letters and files in Hindi was a routine one but it provided them with an excuse to persuade the people of Tamil Nadu that something terrible was happening and that the monster of North Indian linguistic imperialism was about to strike the South once again. Interestingly, it was the Tamil Nadu Congress (I) which was the first to rake up the "issue" by sending a telegram to the Prime Minister protesting against the circular on Hindi. Enquiries in New Delhi show that neither Rajiv Gandhi nor the Home Minister were even aware that a "Hindi Week" was being observed till the storm broke in Tamil Nadu.

Understandably they were busy grapping with the grim problems in Punjab and trying to understand what exactly is happening in "Gorkhaland". It took them quite some time to comprehend the nature of the tragic-comedy in Tamil Nadu. Mean while, politicians there were preparing the funeral pyres on which they were to immolate themselves for the great glory of Tamil. While the anti-Hindi outbursts took a violent turn in several places in Tamil Nadu, the State's Minister for Commercial Taxes announced his readiness to join a "suicide squad" which would lead the holy war against Hindi. Another Minister said: "We are all Tamils first and then only Indians." Yet another Minister, known as the knife wielding firebrand of the AIADMK threatened to walk out of the Government Secretariat to lead the Tamils. As if this were not enough, one of Chief Minister Ramachandran's senior Cabinet colleagues warned the Prime Minister that a "Sri Lanka type" situation would arise in Tamil Nadu if the Hindi circular was not withdrawn.

I am sure that Prime Minister Rajiv Gandhi's assurance that Hindi will not be imposed on non-Hindi speaking peoples must have come as a disappointment to the politicians of Tamil Nadu. This was evident from the fact that many politicians continue to speak of the danger of Hindi imposition. They say that if Jawaharlal Nehru's assurances to non-Hindi-speaking peoples be ignored by the Central Government the fate of a similar pledge by

Rajiv Gandhi will not be any different. So the agitation has somehow to be kept going and DMK President Karunanidhi has promised his followers that a "regular programme" will be chalked out.

Now, while Tamil fanaticism deserves to be condemned it must be conceded that those in the North who pretend to be champions of Hindi are in fact its real enemies. Take a very simple example, Can anything be more irritating than to send a Government communication to a non-Hindi State in Hindi even if it is accompanied by an English translation How would the Chief Minister of Uttar Pradesh or Haryana react if he had received a letter from MGR in Tamil ? They would just throw it into the waste paper basket. Mind you, this was the reaction of Kamaraj, a staunch nationalist and a pillar of the Indian National Congress, when, as the Chief Minister of Tamil Nadu he started getting official letters from Delhi in Hindi. "Just throw them away" Kamaraj advised his officials.

All linguistic fanaticism is bad but Hindi fanaticism is particularly so since Hindi-speaking people in the country are in a huge majority. Hindi enthusiasts should try to understand the fears and susceptibilities of non-Hindi people. These are not always imaginary. According to the Hindustan Times in November 1985 the Union Home Ministry issued a directive making the grant of financial aid to autonomous bodies and societies conditional on their use of Hindi in official work. (It appears that subsequently the directive was quietly withdrawn). Could there be anything more provocative ? Doordarshan's reckless enthusiasm for Hindi is also providing to be counter-productive. In the name of the "national programme" viewers in the South and West Bengal are forced to stomach an over dose of Hindi features.

It is elementary commonsense that no one would like to witness or hear a programme which is in a language he cannot understand. Just show a Kannada or Bengali programme over Doordarshan during peak viewing time and see how people in Haryana or Uttar Pradesh react. They would just switch off their sets and they cannot be blamed for doing so because television is meant for entertainment and is not an instrument for punishment. What Hindi lovers in the north - especially those in power-fail to realise is that Hindi can be spread only through persuasion. At the national level only Hindi and English are going to matter. There is absolutely no Deed to force Hindi on non-Hindi people. Hindi alone has the potential grow into a national link language. This is already happening. More and more people in Tamil Nadu are beginning to understand Hindi and this is not because of the so-called promotional efforts of the Central Government. This is a natural process which Hindi bigots are trying to reverse through their impatience. During freedom struggle Hindi was among the symbols of nationalism. In the South, including Tamil Nadu, to learn Hindi was considered a patriotic duty. Now, people in the South talk of "Hindi imperialism". Who is responsible for this tragic transformation? Certainly not the non-Hindi people.

The disqualification by the speaker of the Tamil Nadu assembly of seven DMK members for burning Part 17 of the Constitution in protest against the "Imposition" of Hindi by the Centre raised grave constitutional issues. The speaker's feelings on the matter shared by those who believed that, whatever the strength of their resentment on the Hindi issue, the DMK Members of State went too far in publicly setting fire to a section of the Constitution. This was no ordinary document but a potent symbol of nationhood and collective identity by their action, the offenders, who were in jail custody and against whom criminal cases had been filed, were repudiating this identity and challenging national cohesiveness. As the speaker saw it, they had violated the oath they took under Article 188 and as set out in the Third Schedule to "bear true faith and allegiance to the Constitution of India as by law established". They had, as a result, invited disqualification, and he claimed to be empowered to disqualify them under Article 208 of the Constitution and under rule 312 of the Tamil Nadu legislative assembly rules.

The speaker appeared constitutionally to be on shaky ground. Article 191 (1) of the Constitution sets out the reasons for which a State legislator may be disqualified, but these do not include violation of the oath taken under Article 188 and whether the seven MLAs had violated the oath must itself be established. The speaker had claimed that Article 193 expressly provides for a penalty for non-compliance with the obligation to uphold the Constitution. In fact, it says that a legislator who sits or votes as a member before complying with Article 188, or when he knows that he is not qualified or has been disqualified or is prohibited from sitting or voting by a Parliamentary or State legislature law, will be liable to a fine of Rs. 500 for each day on which he sits or votes. Nor does Article 208 provide for the disqualification of a member by the Speaker on the ground that the former has failed to "preserve and protect the Constitution." Likewise, Article 192 requires the question of whether a member has become subject to disqualification under Article 191 (1) to be referred to the Governor whose decision "shall be final".

The Governor, moreover, "shall obtain the opinion of the Election Commission and shall act according to such opinion". Not only did there seem to be no clear-cut provision under which the Speaker could disqualify a member, but it was not also clear whether the disqualification was for the duration of the House to which a member belonged on whether it permanently disallowed him from seeking future membership. Even, as the Tamil Nadu Assembly Speaker had referred his ruling to the Governor and the Election Commission for "appropriate follow-up action", these issues would have to be carefully sorted out.

The arguments in the language issue in Tamil Nadu appeared to be contrived in the face of the assurances given by Prime Minister Rajiv Gandhi that Hindi would not be imposed on the Non-Hindi-speaking States. It was an extension of what Jawaharlal Nehru had said in 1959 about the continued use of English as the Jink language. However, the DMK's agitation and the ruling AIADMK's resolution in the State Assembly seeking a Constitutional amendment to give English the Status of the official language were retrograde steps meant to prevent an emotional integration of the nation by harping on a divisive theme, While the DMK leader Karunanidhi's agitation which culminated in the burning of portions of the Constitution and slips of paper containing the words "the official language of the Union will be Hindi Devanagari script" and horrendously, a bombing of the office of the 'Hindi Prachar Sabha', the AIADMK's resolution would take the country back to colonial times because in the midst of self-generated hysteria fit was being sought to obfuscated that English was a colonial language.

Instead of trying to seek a via media between the demands of improving the usage of local language and creating the linkages that give meaning to the concept of unity in many splendoured diversity the attempt to permanently ensconce English as the official language of India runs contrary to everything that is enshrined in the Constitution of a free and independent India. True, English has its uses and because we were colonised it managed to creep into our psyche as well. English is a *lingua franca* for the reason that it was a vehicle for the British rule just as French is in certain other parts of the globe and also Portuguese. It is time that we got out of this Raj mentality and understood the requirements of so diverse an entity as India and seek solutions accordingly.

There are valid arguments against the imposition of Hindi just as there is obsolute justification that the local people must be adept in their mother tongue. Neither of these objectives is served by the demand to maintain English as the nationwide link. It is tragic that the adherents of Tamil do not see the retrograde effect of the continuance of English on Tamil itself. This is also appropriate occasion to warn the adherents of Hindi that over-assertion and dogmatism will be counterproductive and damage the very spirit and intent of the founding fathers, and Jawaharlal Nehru who is so copiously quoted today without trying to understand what he was trying to say: unify India.

With no sanction in religion, custom, tradition frowned upon by the law the recent practice of self-immolation, a new variant of the medieval *sati* (suicide) with new motivations prompting it, is largely restricted to Tamil Nadu. Apparently an extremely emotive genre of political statement, it has in fact a host of functions. Not least of these is insurance the extraction of compensation for one's survivors as a material reward for one's supreme sacrifice.

During 1984 at last 25 persons in Tamil Nadu reportedly burnt themselves on hearing of the serious illness of M.G. Ramachandran or the assassination of Indira Gandhi, in various parts. Two years ago, also an occasion, when the DMK leader Karunanidhi was arrester, seven youth burnt themselves. At the height of the anti-Hindi agitation in 1964-65 three youths used kerosene to achieve a fiery death. All this was love for their native language or their inability to bear the shock of the illness or death of a person whom they revered deeply — the real or only motive?

This writer discussed the issue with top police officials, psychiatrists, academics, philosophers and classical scholars. They were agreed that it is the politicians who portray the immolation as a sacrifice for their own end. When an individual commits suicide because of poverty or privation, or acute sickness, politicians give it the colour of sacrifice. The family of the deceased also play the game by conniving with the politicians for pecuniary gains. When a Andhra Pradesh Chief Minister N.T. Rama Rao fan immolated himself near Madras, during the Andhra Pradesh crisis in 1984, Rama Rao, after his reinstallation as Chief Minister visited the family and announced cash compensation of Rs. 50,000. It is difficult to judge if the man really killed himself for the sake of love for NTR or for any other reason. The press and police perhaps relied upon the statement of the family members to arrive at that conclusion, said one police officer.

He however, added that in a few cases, particularly during anti-Hindi agitation, emotion may have prompted such extreme action. What is intriguing is that neither the DMK which claims the maximum fiery sacrifices from its cadre, nor the police have full address of the families of the deceased. Official records too, have no consolidated date on these incidents. The first known modern Indian case of suicide for a political cause was that of Potti Sriramulu who fasted to death for the creation of a separate Andhra Pradesh out of the united Madras State, in the early 1950's. But the spark of self immolation in Tamil Nadu can be traced to the anti-Hindi agitation in the mid-sixties. During the stir, which lasted seven weeks, two students and one party worker (in the undivided DMK) burnt themselves. One of them, according to contemporary reports, had written to a friend that he was sacrificing this life to preserve Tamil. When the fire was reducing the 25 years old Chinnaswamy to ashes on the eve of the 1964 Republic Day he raised the slogans "Long live Tamil" and "Down with Hindi."

With Ramachandran gone, the Tamil people face their moment of truth. Charisma undercut issues though Tamil Nadu could get a few lollypops from the Centre because of the strategic alliance the Congress had with the DMK or the AIADMK in the State. The result was a depoliticised milieu. The impending power struggle in the name of a legacy would prove this. When C.N. Annaduri died as Chief Minister of Tamil Nadu in 1969, the encomiums for him from outside were patently hypocritical. His contribution to the assertion of the Tamil identity was played down or just ignored. He was praised for his conformism while in office. MGR owed his political success to the Tamil identity, which he stressed, though not himself of Tamil origin, but all that has merited praise at his death was his charisma and his concern for the underdog.

Champion of National Unity

What impressed every one was that behind the glamour there was a man intensely patriotic, humane and full of compassion for the poor million people of Tamil Nadu. Only MGR's glory survived. He has become a great national hero of India. His idea of a United India was at the top of his political programme. Unity, integrity and independence of the country are being threatened by forces of disintegration and separation. Proper tributes to MGR could be paid only by working unitedly and single-mindedly towards social equality, regional harmony and prosperity.

M.G. Ramachandran had always advocated a strong and stable Government at the Centre. Stressing this view in a letter to Karnataka Chief Minister Rama Krishna Hegde in July, 1983, Ramachandran had said that the unity and integrity of the nation should be preserved at all costs.

On another occasion, Ramachandran had stated that a weak Centre was not in the interest of the States. It was this reason, he explained that he had supported the Morarji Desai and Charan Singh Governments despite his constant support to Indira Gandhi.

He defended his support to Desai saying the Janata Government implemented the food-for-work programme, pushed through the Kanyakumari rail link and liberal financial assistance to Tamil Nadu. His support to Charan Singh was because the latter had agreed to provide reservation for the backward classes. Two of his party MPs, Madam Sathiavani Muthu and Arvind Bala Pajanor, had served in the Charan Singh Government for a few months.

On November 11, 1983, Ramachandran told the State Assembly that his Government did not believe in the blind support or blind opposition to the Centre. Ramachandran, who had attended the opposition conclave at Vijayawada, Andhra Pradesh on May 29,1983, boycotted the subsequent conclaves. Even at Vijayawada Ramachandran had refrained from attacking the then Prime Minister Indira Gandhi. He was against opposition to Indira Gandhi for the sake of opposition.

At the same time Ramachandran asserted the rights of the State. He opposed Indira Gandhi in 1980 Lok Sabha poll, on the ground of her reported statement against regional parties. He said regional parties were necessary to preserve the separate cultural identity and self-respect of States.

Ramachandran relentlessly opposed the imposition of Hindi. He was able to persuade the *Doordarshan* to drop relay the Hindi news bulletin by the Madras Kendra. He was also able to shift screening of Hindi films on Sunday to Saturday at Madras centre while all other centres have Hindi films on Sundays. It was the synchronic adherence of the Tamils in the guise of political strategy which he met successfully.

Ramachandran went on a eight hour hunger strike on February 9, 1983 to urge the Centre to allot more rice for the drought stricken State but for a short period, Ramachandran had always supported the leadership of Indira Gandhi. She was the only leader who enjoys the support of the majority of people of India and she deserved to be Prime Minister much more than anybody else, he had stated once. Ramachandran had opposed the JP (Named after Jayaprakash Narain) movement and also supported national emergency in 1975.

To the particular charisma radiated by the Nehru family we are accustomed but the spell in which in India, Ramachandran held not only Tamil Nadu but all other parts of India and even outside where the Tamil speaking people live was of a special brand.

Because, Ramachandran charisma emanated form the pit of poverty, from the hardships of life, from the school of bitter experience, from a hero on the silver screen he became a hero in real life.

No bright particular film star stands over the head of an infant when it is born into this world and hardly anyone, in fact, no one at all could have visualised the fantabulous progress of Ramachandran from the depths of poverty to glamorous filmdom and from the latter into successful, even triumphant national politics.

Unlike, many others, Ramachandran not only acted with realism, his roles depicting suffering humanity on the screen, but his heart went out to the distressed and the suffering the real world. His philanthropy reached out to the innumerable poor, and during one season when "it rained and the wind was never dreary", he distributed raincoats to rickshaw pullers.

Like the screen hero who drives out all before him. Ramachandran was imbued with the ambition of doing away with the ills of his people, and so he entered active politics.

Ramachandran had noted his mass popularity as an actor and he saw no reason why he should not earn mass popularity as a doer. He knew that he had a personality that could launch a million votes, and so they did when he entered the political arena.

His ideas for achieving public welfare were simple. Take care of the women and the children and the men will take care not only of themselves but of their family.

Thus, in his bid to wipe the tear from every eye, Ramachandran reimposed prohibition while the earlier DMK Government had relaxed it. His free mid-day meal for school children heralded a new deal wluich was later taken by other States.

MGR was a sincere and staunch crusader against corruption, unhealthy means, narrow mindedness and regionalism, while trying for regional interests. While fully identifying himself as the most powerful, dynamic and dedicated regional leader, he never allowed himself to be meant as controversial figure by the Centre in his dealing with the latter, especially in terms of financial help.

He always wanted stable and strong government at the Centre in the interests of unity and integrity of the nation at large and in the interest of the groins concerned. MGR never wanted to be at longer heads with the Centre whichever party was there in power too because MGR earned State's interest, more that his personal political ends. He had no mean mentality to make. Tamil Nadu and its poor millions suffer, for his own sake. That was why he enjoyed the affection and support from his people at large.

In any fundamental sense, MGR's AIADMK was not a new party. What was new was MGR's leadership. MGR's AIADMK sans in ideological terms was the same old DMK sans Karunanidhi's leadership but the lables were confusing. And until his death MGR never missed an opportunity to claim that he, in fact, was the true political heir of Annadurai and that his party faithfully adhered to the original Dravidian ideology. He meant what he said and the majority of the electorate in Tamil Nadu still believe that as far as Tamil Nadu is concerned only this ideology would deliver the goods.

In its first election manifestos in the year 1977 as well as in the subsequent election manifestos, MGR's party did not move away even by a fraction from the original DMK ideological positions, from the Annadurai path (whatever it means) and from the DMK policies. At times he diluted these policies to suit his convenience and at times he was just politically expedient in compromising with the party that ruled at the Centre.

Of the DMK's package of anti-Brahmin, anti-Hindi, anti-Centre and linguistic/regional chauvinism, MGR's AIADMK buried the anti-Centre platform unceremoniously. It is difficult to say whether this was done just for the sake of political survival or it was a question of evolution of MGR's mind. Let us say MGR evolved it, MGR grew. As the nation progressed, he also progressed with progressive forces. Let us err on the right side.

But for this progression from the anti-Centre to national unity, the original package is still intact in the new package, perhaps as a diluted version. And in MGR's passing away, the new package has lost its illustrious leader. It remains to be seen whether AIADMK will remain All-India Anna DMK in MGR's absence or disintegrate into pieces. In the last three years of his rule, MGR, rendered ineffective with his debilitating illness, contributed neither to an efficient State administration nor to a cohesive party organisation. His party is faction-ridden and weak. The powerful DMK in opposition is well organised with a well-oiled party machinery to face election challenges.

But Karunanidhi's leadership is its asset as well as liability. The people are still afraid of Karunanidhi's men and his political apparatus. Whether the majority will re-examine Karunanidhi's credentials to rule is a question that cannot be answered at the moment. It all depends on Rajiv Gandhi's Congress.

4

Great Personality

A Born Fighter

A born fighter Ramachandran fought grimly with the relentless reaper and kept him at bay against heavy odds with the indomitable courage characteristic of the man. It is customary to pay ritualistic tributes to the great departed soul. But all that is being said to honour his memory from the President downward has a ring of sincerity and sadness, for MGR had endeared himself by both the classes and the masses alike. His success story was literally from '*rags to riches*". An obscure figure born in poverty, he did not allow "chill penury to repress his noble rage". Showmanship was in his blood. Starting literally from the bottom rung of the ladder in the theatrical art he climbed to the dizzy height of stardom.

A Fearless Person

God, they say, always takes away such persons whom he loves most. When Mahatma Gandhi died, India's first Prime Minister Jawaharlal Nehru declared in these moving words: "The light that has illumined this country for these many years will illumine this country for many more years and the world will see it, and it will give solace to innumerable hearts". Nearly four decades later Mahatma Gandhi's principles of service to the daridranarain (the poor) were to take root and flourish hundred of miles away, in a completely different environment, in a manner that vindicated Nehru's words that "the light represented some thing more than the immediate present: it represented the living truth the eternal truth."

Forthright, outspoken, M.G. Ramachandran feared no one. "Don't look at a man's feet. Look him between the eyes. Don't be a worm, be a man". He had always practised what he had preached.

Great Charm

The matinee idol stole everybody's heart with his ineffable charm and yet to be excelled histrionics as an actor. To millions he appealed as a deity, a veritable god not only on screen but in real life. He was a trendsetter that way. N.T. Rama Rao another star who followed him in Andhra and became Chief Minister of his State like his counterpart in Tamil Nadu, attained godhood with charismatic skill. MGR and NTR between them opened the sluice gate for the entry of actors and screen stars who flooded the political arena in their wake.

Mark in Politics

Ramachandran made his mark in politics after struggling for years. His arch rival was Karunanidhi, the D.M.K. Chief Minister. Ramachandran mobilised his followers under the banner of AIADMK and raised the banner of revolt on the cry of corruption in high places and was swept into power within five years. Such was the popularity for the 'Puratchi Thalivar' (Revolutionary hero) the honorific that MGR was better known by that the AIADMK wiped out all opposition for a long spell. But infeuding within his party and his failing health brought about a partial eclipse of this charismatic figure in his later years.

Charismatic Leader

President R. Venkataraman in his condolence message struck the right note when he described Ramachandran as "charismatic leader", whose life pulsated with the common people. He thought and felt with the masses and for the masses. Whether in the world of art or of politics he enjoyed a unique rapport with the people. The masses in turn gave him their spontaneous "love and trust". Ramachandran's passing away is particularly unfortunate at a time when his restraining hand was needed to prevent an angry upsurge of millions of Tamil Nadu spearheaded by the DMK President Karunanidhi who had denounced "the killing of Tamils by the Government of India in Śri Lanka" and is agitating for the reversal of the Centre's policy on this ethnic issue. Ramachandran was a staunch supporter, and a most faithful friend of Rajiv Gandhi (Prime Minister). But whatever shape politics may take in this strategic state, it's a safe bet that MGR will be gratefully remembered and even worshipped by millions as a demigod for generations to come.

A Revolutionary Hero

Styled as a revolutionary hero, the virtues MGR held up were all non-revolutionary, except, bourgeois virtues. Helping the poor, a Reynoldsian melodramatic belief in virtue triumphant, above all his respect for the mother clan were parts of the image of MGR culminating in the final unfading image that became the common property of a vast majority of the Tamils. His approach to life and living was uncomplicated, simple, and non-intellectual. He had no use for ideologies or isma of alien, or native manufacture. And in this he was quite the traditional Indian, the prototype of a vast majority of the conservative Tamils who sought instead of an Aryan conservatism a Dravidian conservatism. MGR fitted into this ideal role both as hero in his films and in his real life activities.

Tamil Identity

MGR embodied the true Tamil identity, for which the State had been searching for six decades with the initial thrust provided by the British-sponsored Justice party. That party was anti-Brahmin and stood for upliftment of the non-Brahmins who were discriminated against in education and jobs. The Justice Party later gave way to the Dravida Kazhagam and the Dravida Munnetra Kazhagam, which spawned the All India Anna Dravida Munnetra Kazhagam. The Justice ideology was fully vindicated with the elevation of MGR, born poor, uneducated and faced with stark deprivation for a major part of his life. He fulfilled his "mandate" when he ruled the State for over a decade (1977-1987) with a firm hand as its undisputed leader with unquestioned authority. Despite his birth as a Malayali, who lived his life as a Malayali, despite the theoretical bows he grandiloquently indulged in to stoke Tamil chauvinism, MGR proved that there could be no better man than he to uphold the Tamil identity that the Justice Party and his and his own political mentor C.N. Annadurai, had struggled to establish. He espoused the Tamil identity with the enthusiasm of a neo-convert.

His image, assiduously cultivated and sustained, and his charisma, helped him to be the Chief Minister of Tamil Nadu. He had little of political acumen or understanding. There was no ideological conflict between his AIADMK and the DMK but the common people associated MGR with a totally different set of values they assigned for his arch-rival M. Karunanidhi or the DMK. The AIADMK that he set up is no more than a confederation of the MGR Fan Clubs that littered the villages and towns of Tamil Nadu from it, he drew his political sustenance. The party is today bereft of the charisma of its towering leader. Many things were done and connived at under the blanket of that charisma.

MGR was a screen actor before he entered politics, as was indeed the US President Ronald Reagan but MGR was remarkable in how he managed to buttress his political career through films, and achieved the almost impossible task of transposing his film roles to the Tamil Nadu Chief Minister's office. Fantasy became reality and although such gestures as mid-day meals and plastic pots for the poor helped, it was MGR's ability to transform reality into fantasy that made him into the most extraordinary phenomenon Indian politics has known. Like a consummate actor, MGR knew that fantasy must have more than a whiff of mystery, and he created the fur cap and dark glasses as symbols of the mystery surrounding him.

He was, of course, helped by a rival actor's foolishness attacking a pot shot at him, as by other factors, but the symbols proved powerful enough to survive his rather recent serious illness and impediment in speech. Whatever his physical condition, it was taken for granted by all that no one else could rule Tamil Nadu during his lifetime and it is futile to berate MGR for non-grooming a successor because there can be no real successor to MGR. Does India then require a father (or mother) figure it can look up to?

There can of course be no gainsaying the assurance such a figure provides a nation, but India is not peculiar in this regard. The names of Churchill and de Galle readily come to mind. Nor it is unique in Indian characteristic that saints and sages attract blind devotion. Even in the jaded West, a Reagan phenomenon has existed, and the very success of Indian swamis in the western world would indicate that they are filling a need. Self-immolation as the ultimate form of expressing grief or making a personal statement is admittedly an easter, rather than western trait; in the East, it is not unique to India. Leaving aside the rationality of such acts, a leader's death provoking them is an indication of the magic he had woven round his people for many in Tamil Nadu, MGR's death was a personal loss, and the reactions have varied from weeping and wailing to acts of self-immolation or pure hooliganism. MGR went beyond launching a *garibi hatao* programme after the fashion of Indira to indentify himself with the poor. He simply had people to believe that he was enacting in real life his film roles as the hero perennially fighting for the poor and he received adulation of a kind not showered on any Indian politician although his constituency was largely restricted to the State of Tamil Nadu and the Tamils outside it.

Growing up in an underdeveloped region in the midst of poverty-striken people, participating in their struggle to eke out their livelihood under harsh conditions, fighting against social injustices traditionally imposed on Scheduled Castes and Tribes and championing their cause for better living conditions, MGR was the only political leader in Tamil Nadu who developed a unique empathy with the poor. This feeling dominated his thinking and actions throughout his political life and this was the secret of his overwhelming popular support, particularly amongst the poor millions.

Social Service

MGR personally offered relief in disasters and calamities like fire, flood, drought, and cyclones. He was the first donor during the war with China in 1962, donating Rs. 75,000 to the war fund.

Dream Unfulfilled

Although he did much for the poor during his two tenures as Chief Minister, his main regret was that he was unable to realise his ideal of transforming the poor of Tamil Nadu, fraught with economic deprivation, endemic hunger and malnutrition, and grave social inequities, to one of a fuller life for the poor and downtrodden the increased opportunities to the undergo by widening education to reach the grassroots level, introducing more dynamism into agriculture and by putting an end to economic exploitation of the masses by the elite who are not just the industrialists and the rich commercial farmers but also include lakhs of business people, office workers, land owners and educators.

MGR fought successfully the stranglehold of dominant castes and vested interests in the field of political power by his masterly political strategy.

Undoubtedly, every politician is convinced that bureaucracy just cannot be expected to have that necessary rapport with the masses and cannot possibly secure their active participation in the regeneration of underdeveloped society, once he is inducted into power, he becomes a prisoner of the bureaucracy. It has happened everywhere, at the Centre and the States, and the MGR Government was no exception.

A Great Man in History

The problem of the present age is the problem of leadership. History of what man has accomplished in this world is at bottom of the history of great men. When circumstances allow little men to abound and to control, words drown actions and leadership sinks into chatterings of apes miscalled debates in Assemblies, committee and legislatures, in short talking shops. Shops in which words are sold and where verbal swindlings become the measure of man's worth.

MGR strode like a colossus the political arena in Tamil Nadu. It will be a long time before we see the like of him again. The little men who have emerged as leaders by invoking his name and his policies are political pigmies who do not have hit great love and sympathy for the poor and the downtrodden and who certainly do not have his courage and ability to fulfil the aspirations of the people. His invaluable assets as the leader were his transparent sincerity, his rapport with the poor and the downtrodden, his winning manners and his unfailing courtesy to one and all including his bitter political opponents. Whoever in need went to him never returned empty-handed even when he was out of power. When people sought his help in official matters, he would ring up the official concerned requesting his intervention and the official would respect his word as if he was still in power.

The universal love and respect he commanded publicly and privately from the common man, the politicians of all hues, the civil servants, the police and the people from all strata of society was amply demonstrated during that memorable State funeral, so far unsurpassed in not only Tamil Nadu but in the "whole world".

In the beginning, the regional party showed a degree of sensitiveness to the administration but soon even senior officers came to be treated as Ministers-that is, they were curtly asked to carry out orders. Many demurred and paid the price in terms of humiliation and worse. From being one of the best administered States, Tamil Nadu slipped to a position where unseemly dramas became the order of the day. The concern for the urban poor took such flippant forms as free distribution of plastic buckets to slum dwellers who anyway had no water to keep in those colourful containers. Chappals were presented to pregnant women who had nowhere to go. Districts were carved up in a convulsive effort to honour E "great" men of yesteryear.

Universities came up in the name of honoured men, even as the standard of education slipped alarmingly. Decades of efforts to insulate Tamil from the impurities of other languages, including English, stunted its growth; in the claustrophobic atmosphere of the State today nothing grows, certainly not new ideas. It would be comforting to think that the sad story of Tamil Nadu is peculiar to itself and it will not be replicated outside its borders. This is myopic. The State's misfortune stems essentially from the fact that first the DMK and then the AIADMK presided over its destiny both are archetypal regional parties. They have no economic policy, except to maintain the status quo. In practice it works against the larger and long-term interests of the State. Their social policy is to stabilise the pre-eminence of the land-owining castes and push down the lower castes. There is a method in this seeming madness. Only a vast reservoir of the poor will enable them to "buy" a vote with a plastic bucket (in Tamil Nadu) or a cheap Rs. 15-worth sari (in Andhra Pradesh) both at the State's expense.

Their political policy is to fashion a glittering cardboard sword to clash with the Centre or seek unviable and opportunistic alliances to pump up their hurt vanity with borrowed muscles. It is their exclusivist cultural policy that has actually planted a time bomb with a long and cleverly hidden fuse. Their full-throated and oft-repeated allegiance to regional or sectarian sensibilities is in conflict with the fundamental urge in everyone to be different and yet be part of the whole. The regional parties demand conformity, regimenting, particularly the youth, into barrent channels and condemning those yearning to be different. Self-criticism is the very seed of growth, and self-criticism is the first casualty of regionalism. This is understandable; a critical and clinical look at oneself does not go well with the basic assumption behind all regional parties that they are superior to others, more just and caring than others. Regional parties look back in terms of time rather than look ahead.

This is what sustains them and this is what set the State on the backward march. A narrow outlook, focused on past achievements, does not fertilize social cohesion. Tension is the natural order and State repression the answer. When regional parties identify a social enemy they are brutal in dealing with him. The so-called anti-Naxalite operation in Tamil Nadu and Andhra Pradesh attests to this. The Tamil Nadu melodrama acquires meaning or becomes meaningless only in this light.

There is no regional party which has not split and split again. There is no regional party which has not capitulated somebody to the top of the head and equally abruptly cast him aside. All this is not to say that regional parties carry the germ of underdevelopment economically, socially, politically and culturally. All these entities, as they are organised and functioning today, find it difficult, if not impossible, to fit whatever ideology they profess into larger perspective of national development. There are two contradictory features in this. One, barring the National Conference of Kashmir and the Akali Dal, other regional parties are post-1947 phenomena. Most of them came into existence by striking a posture to the Congress. This has in effect resulted in the disowning of not only the Congress legacy of democratic functioning but its policy framework. The ascendancy of regional parties has therefore, brought about a break in the course of development, in the broadest sense of the term, in all these States since each one of them was ruled by the Congress at one time or the other. There is the transformation of the Congress itself.

It is no more the nationalist monolith it was at one time. It is more like an agglomeration of regional tendencies. At one time this trend was expected to subsume the regional parties or atleast make them that much less relevant but the opposite has come about. The late seventies and eighties have witnessed the strengthening of the State level political groups rather than their diminishing importance.

With his great qualities of leadership, personality and tireless energy, he would have reached the top anywhere, as he did in films and politics.

A most endearing quality of MGR was his intense loyalty to his friends. Many so-called friends betrayed him after swearing their loyalty to him and taking full advantage of his generosity and trust. After the mass betrayal of self-seeking Ministers and legislators, when he was about to region as Chief Minister, his trusted lieutenants deserted him one after another. When some one approached him on his selection of friends, his reply was characteristic, "You are abusing the word friendship when you refer to them as friends. They are just political weather cocks ready to change their loyalties for immediate personal gain, ever avaricious and unprincipled."

One Minister who professed life-long friendship and loyalty to MGR, said, "What is my political future if I remain with MGR? I am responsible, for my constituency which elected me." He joined another party like many others but missed the ministerial berth he seemed certain to get and, after his self-same constituency rightly threw him out, he was repenting and licking his wounds out in the wilderness.

To MGR filthy lucre never had any attraction for its own sake and later, when politicians used to come to him begging for money, ha gave them freely but with ill-concealed contempt.

MGR's main contribution is that as a natural corollary of the change that came about in the outlook of the parent DMK when Annadurai accepted the Chief Ministership of the State in 1967, MGR brought about the confluence of Tamil aspirations into the national mainstream and, thus, he rose to be, as Veerappan has said, "a national leader whose loss has affected the country as a whole". Veerappan was wholly justified in claiming that "MGR became an exemplary model in serving the people."

Amazing Phenomenon

The amazing phenomenon of MGR is a telling comment on the Indian political system we must take to heart for it shows us how a leader can succeed in India, quite apart from the achievement he may or may not have to his credit. The 40-years old tree of Indian democracy has been nurtured by a phenomenon variously described as charisma, dynamism or great qualities of leadership; let us call it the "x" factor. Jawaharlal Nehru came to lead the country with the halo of the independence struggle and the Mahatma's blessings, and his daughter Indira came to acquire a larger-than-life image, through a combination of political astuteness and populism. The reigns of the other Prime Ministers have been too brief to lend themselves to a historical judgement.

Apart from possessing the "x" factor, both Jawaharlal and Indira had considerable achievements to their credit, the former more than the latter. Nehru was the builder of modern India and set his seal on the country by establishing it on the democratic path and weaving a fabric that has ensured the nation's integrity, despite tensions and problems. Indira proved equal to the challenge posed by the events in erstwhile East Pakistan by carrying out a surgical operation to protect the country's interest. MGR represented the "x" factor in its purest form.

His popularity bore little relationship to his achievements and the kind of frenzied devotion he attracted was remarkable by any standards. Ronald Reagan has been given the sobriquet of a "taflon present" but the taflon has worn out in the wake of the Iran-Contra affair. In MGR's case, no disability, physical or otherwise, affected his flaming popularity with the people of his State. It is the task of leadership in any country to inspire people and give them the hope of receiving more than it can possibly deliver. It is immaterial in this context how posterity will assess a particular leader's achievements. But in India's case, as in that of any developing country, the "x" factor is of crucial importance because the gap between promises and fulfilment is tragically wide and it is only this factor which can keep people's belief in the system alive.

It is said that hero worship is a human trait. It is more than under Indian conditions. The large identification of late Prime Minister Indira Gandhi as Mother-India or even Mahishasuramardhini in artistic work of M.F. Husain is understandable in the context of India. Romans are also said to have had this complex and tend to identify the mother-country as the Madonna, I hear on the authority of a European psychoanalyst was MGR a father figure, or a mother figure, will be a moot question. He seems to have been both in turn and there is nothing wrong or limiting in this identification. While a body of his opponents claimed that he was inactive, others the larger majority, believed in his activity.

Even as late as in 1987, when he was approached by a pop novelist saying that he would have to commit suicide if he did not receive a cash award conferred by a university (his debts were so overwhelming) MGR is said to interfered personally to see to it that the writer got the award. His concern about what his opponent and erstwhile friend and colleague DMK leader, Karunanidhi was saying led him to fund an academic researcher from the same university to find his own Tamil antecedents. Literature, the arts and other precious things have been too long the property of the elite, the intellectual disciplined few, current American and, expectedly, Soviet, attitudes seem to indicate that all the arts, including literature should be rescued from the hands of the intellectual high-brow, the elitist practitioners of them and should go "pop" in a mass sense. If this contention were accepted in its full implications, MGR represents the mass mind of the Tamil which has had no image like him in its annals. His hold on the public cannot be explained away in any other way.

His Charisma

Charisma, like existentialism, means what you want it to mean. But MGR had something more than charisma. Living he was almost a deity. Tamil tradition has a native story of how a woman becomes a goddess in the epic *Silappadhikaram*. The Roman caesars had the will to be defied by their people. Julius Caesar started the process which continued for 12 generations, all of them short-lived. MGR was naturally defied. No Government orders were needed, no rule by fiat was needed, no proclamations were necessary, no consequences were expected. It assumed natural proportions. The Tamil felt that all was well in the world in which MGR ruled. He refused to be deflected from the belief.

In life as in death, faith in MGR is long likely to sustain, the Tamils. Masti Venkatesa Iyengar, speaking on Valmiki Ramayana in Madras, once observed that Valmiki, like a modern engineer, had marked the high flood level of human behaviour in his Rama. The Tamil's high flood mark was M.G. Ramachandran. Others might succeed him as naturally they will in the course of circumstances but no one will replace him in the hearts of his lovers. Of whom there are millions as was demonstrated both in the spontaneous grief that his death evoked in the Tamil public. That his death gave rise to some goondaism is in the nature of Indian events — Tamil Nadu too is inclined to go the way the rest of India inspite of claimed differences.

Last Speech

Only two days before his death, MGR presided over the function at which Prime Minister Rajiv Gandhi unveiled the Statue of Jawaharlal Nehru. For the first time in several months and for the last time in his life, MGR spoke on that occasion. He said: "We are all proud of that our great Prime Minister Rajiv Gandhi is following in the footsteps of his mother and grandfather. He devotes his entire attention to the development of the country, working tirelessly to create a new India in which unity, integrity and casteless egalitarian values would be cherished and promoted further."

Thus, he carried forward his political mentor Annadurai's legacy by giving up chauvinism and merging Tamil aspirations into the effort to build a new India with "casteless egalitarian values". That is his legacy. Veerappan's statements since the death of MGR suggest that he is anxious to carry forward the legacy of MGR. If that is so, he need not split the AIADMK and can count on the support of the Centre and the nation in fighting disintegrative forces by strengthening the State's unity with the rest of India.

Notwithstanding who wins the race, AIADMK is not going to be the same as it was when MGR was alive. It was his legendary personality which was able to keep the party together. There were many revolts during his time but none succeeded. Even when he dropped Veerappan from the Cabinet the party remained intact. The cementing element is no longer there.

The chances are that the party may split in more than two directions. It would not be surprising at all if in addition to the two factions rallying round the two women, the conservatives members prefer to join Karunanidhi. The politics in Tamil Nadu is fraught with many imponderables and regardless of who is able to grab the reins of power, the situation in the State is going to be uncertain. This was inevitable considering the type of leadership MGR provided to Tamilnadu. It was not based on any ideology. Although he inherited the Dravida ideology, whatever its merits or demerits, from the founder leaders late Naicker and Annadurai, he had dispensed with it long ago.

He had personalised the electoral game and reduced complex political issue to the charisma of one individual. Indeed, with this background, that is the only thing he could have done. Although the transition from a movie idol to Chief-ministership and transformation of fan clubs into a support base came easily to him, the change was accompanied by the unrealities of the commercial films. In the harsh world of politics he used the soft option of the screen. Distribution of vests or providing subsidised midday meals is no substitute for developmental policies.

It is no surprise that during his regime, the State slipped from the third position in the developmental ladder to almost the bottom rung. All this has a lesson for all of us, the leaders and the people alike.

Demise at a Crucial Hour

MGR's passing away could not have come at a more critical hour. Long past capability for effective functioning due to ill health, he seemed able to his mere physical presence to preserve an uneasy status quo. His death could unleash a power struggle to fill the void at a time when the Sri-Lankan crisis-has created an explosive mood in Tamil Nadu. The prospect of wild populism fuelling a struggle for power among the contending rivals is giving sleepless nights to the saner elements of the Central Government. Competition in populism could not only split the AIADMK, it could destroy Tamil Nadu's relations with the Central Government. It is in this background that New Delhi is viewing prospects in Tamil Nadu, What are they?

A taste of things to come was provided immediately after MGR's death. The police in Madras stood idly by as vandals were allowed to loot shops and spread terror in the city. New Delhi must have got the message. The Centre had better behave or else. Veerappan is the strong man controlling the AIADMK legislators and the administration but Jayalalitha controls the major chunk of the All-World MGR Fans' Association. In the long run, the influence of that body should not be underestimated but nursed for long on an ideology relying heavily on caste, how far will be AIADMK rank and file trusted to Jayalalitha, who is a Brahmin?

Post-MGR Era

The transition to the post-MGR era in Tamil Nadu is a matter of all-India interest, not the concern of the State alone. There are many reasons for it. One, the vastness of the void left by MGR, on account of his stature and charisma. Two, the relevance of the Congress, the ruling party at the Centre to the game of numbers in the wake of the split in the legislative wing of the AIADMK. Three, the interest in the course adopted by Government, S.L. Khurana, which could not but become a precedent for other States. Both the Centre and the States, including Tamil Nadu, faced the problems of transition in the past and though the circumstances of no two cases were similar or identical, the yardstick applied by those entrusted with taking decisions under the Constitution are of interest now. To take the latest example—

the change at the Centre after the sudden assassination of Indira Gandhi on October 30, 1984—the role played by the President of the day Giani Zail Singh, was decisive. Cutting short his trip abroad, Zail Singh rushed back to intensive but informal discussions with R. Venkataraman, then Vice-President, and senior Ministers and in the process, made known his preference for Rajiv Gandhi then not even a member of the Union Cabinet. Zail Singh wanted Rajiv Gandhi to take over not as a caretaker Prime Minister but in a full-fledged capacity. While the discussions were on G.K. Moopanar handed over to Zail Singh a copy of the resolution adopted by the Central Parliamentary Board of the Congress, a nine-member nominated body, not of the Congress Parliamentary Party. Feeling fortified, Zail Singh went about with the formalities of administering the requisite oaths to Rajiv Gandhi and at his instance to three or four other members.

Zail Singh even prevailed upon Rajiv Gandhi to include Buta Singh in the first batch on the plea that his exclusion might be misunderstood in the communally surcharged atmosphere. The endorsement of Rajiv Gandhi's choice by the Congress party—which really mattered in the situation-came later. As Zail Singh explained to his callers he wanted to avoid the uncertainties of an interim arrangement. However, different courses were followed after the death of Prime Minister Jawaharlal Nehru in May 1964 and of Lal Bahadur Shastri in January 1966. On both these occasions, Dr. S. Radhakrishnan, the President, appointed the senior most Minister G.L. Nanda, pending the election of a leader by the Congress Parliamentary party. Nanda performed the duties of the head of Government during the interim period though in strict constitutional terms, he was tot an interim Prime Minister.

There is one case from the States. What happened in Jammu and Kashmir after that colossus Sheikh Abdullah was no more in 1983 was notable in many ways. Dr. Farooq Abdullah was sworn in within a few hours after the Sheikh's demise—as part of an arrangement, blessed and supported by New Delhi. Dr. Abdullah was not even number two in the Sheikh's Cabinet-the senior most Minister D.D. Thakur did not press his claim while a serious aspirant for the top post G.M. Shah, the Sheikh's son-in-law, was sidelined. Dr. Abdullah was inducted in the Ministry a month before the Sheikh's death when he was struck by serious illness and the problem of succession became real. Of course, the Sheikh had designated the young medico as his successor and put him in charge of the ruling party, the National Conference. The party legislators met later formally to elect him as leader. The consideration that weighed with the Central Congress leaders was that G.M. Shah, known for his capacity for manoeuvring was not to be allowed an opportunity to upset the Farooq applecart.

That the same Central leaders later used Shah to out Dr. Abdullah from power was a different story. The circumstances in which the succession issue was required to be settled in Tamil Nadu were different. What stood out in the case was the speed and the manner with which the Governor went about with the job of verifying the claim of one faction of the AIADMK and the manner adopted for this purpose. Opinions differ on it as also on the criterion applied by him. The report of the Committee of Governors, which considered norms and conventions governing the role of gubernatorial heads in 1971, used the case history of several developments in the States to enunciate principles for future guidance for Governors.

The present Tamil Nadu case does not have a close parallel to any of the episodes examined by the Committee, but one of the principles outlined by it has a validity in the present case. The Committee saw no reason for giving sanctity to the claims of the 'largest single party' when no party has a clear majority. This is what it said 'Must' the leader of the largest single party in the Legislative Assembly be called upon to form a Government by the Governor even without satisfying himself that leader will be able to command a majority in the Legislative Assembly ? The answer of this question is simple. The test for the choice of a Chief Minister is not based necessarily on the strength of a party except when it has a majority of seats in the Assembly.

The leader of the largest single party in the Legislative Assembly may be invited to head a government if he is able to satisfy the Governor that, in combination with other parties or with the support of other members in the Assembly, he is in a position to command a majority in the Legislature. He has, however, no absolute right as leader of the largest single party or group to claim that he should be entrusted with the task of forming a government to the exclusion of all others. The relevant test is not the size of a party but its ability to command the support of the majority in the Legislature. It may be that a party, even though leading in relative strength in a Legislature, may not be able to obtain the support of other members in contrast, a numerically smaller party may command majority support with the help of other parties or groups.

The Governor has thus first and essentially to satisfy himself that the person whom he invites to form the Government commands majority support in the legislature. Obviously, he must satisfy himself only on the oasis of an informed and objective appraisal of the prevailing situation in the Assembly. For that purpose nothing prevents him from consulting the leaders of different parties or groups; in most circumstances, it may be necessary for him to do so. The Congress leaders, both at the Centre and in the State, proclaimed-in conspicuously loud voices-their neutrality in relation to the AIADMK tussle. It, thus, was on neither side for a time. But when the Governor, Mr. Khurana, accepted the claim of the faction favouring Mrs. Janaki Ramachandran and invited her to form the government, the congress was quick to send a message of congratulation to her.

The simultaneity of the Governor's action in Madras and the welcome accorded to the prospective Chief Minister in New Delhi could not have gone unnoticed. The Congress will act as a 'responsible, responsive and constructive Opposition', senior Central leaders said in New Delhi, adding that each of these words has a specific connotation. They seemed to recognise the need for continuous review because of the emerging nature of the political situation.

The idea appeared to be not to close the options finally, as one of them said: 'We do not want to look fools if tomorrow, both the factions get together or if there are large scale desertions from the majority faction to the other side'. There was nothing to suggest that the Governor had taken into account the tentativeness of the Congress stand.

Significant Facts

- Devar films produced the maximum number of 17 of his films.
- Director P. Neelakandan directed a maximum of 17 of his films.
- He is also referred as Chinnavar, Mudalali, Thalaivar in the entertainment Media.
- He was very fond of his blue ambassador car TMX4777.
- His mentor in the theatre world was Kaali N. Rathnam.
- He had a habit of taking a black box in his car which contained money to help the poor and needy.
- The only person to call M.G.R. by name was his friend and fellow actor M.N. Nambiyaar.
- He used to call affectionately K.R. Rajagopal, A.V.M. Saravanan, and K.N. Varatharajan as Mudalali (meaning: Owner).
- He acted as a woman in *Devar* films Kadhla Vaganam, it was the only film that he had acted as a woman.
- He was the first man to use an Air-conditioned Make up room and it was during the film *Enga Veetu Pillai.* The films Producer Nagi Reddy constructed a special A.C. room for M.G.R.
- An unknown fact is that he never knew cycling before entering the film Industry.
- A stamp was issued in memory of him on 17/01/1990.

5

At the Helm in the State

An Unassuming Chief Minister

M.G. Ramachandran was one of the most unassuming Chief Ministers that Tamil Nadu had produced. He was easily at home in any company and his fingers were always on the pulse of the people. He was a phenomenon. Over 4 million of mourners on the occasion of his funeral clearly demonstrated that his popularity was unprecedented in Tamil Nadu and elsewhere. It is virtually impossible to find out his substitute. But the political party (All India Anna Dravida Munnetra Kazhagam) which he had founded and nurtured virtually with his blood has come to stay. Just as during the life of MGR, so after his demise, the Congress, with 64 legislators, will remain in a position to have its presence felt in the AIADMK affairs. After throwing out the DMK regime led by M. Karunanidhi in June 1977, MGR had sent the DMK packing from the hustings thrice in a row, a feat unrivalled by even the redoubtable late Chief Minister of Tamil Nadu K. Kamaraj.

The Dravida Munnetra Kazhagam President Karunanidhi had been literally rescued from oblivion with the decisive victory of his party in the civic elections held in Tamil Nadu on February 23, 1986. The DMK led Opposition front which had been humbled in the general elections just a year ago made a triumphant comeback in the civic elections. The debacle of the All India Anna Dravida Munnetra Kazhagam and Congress combine had been attributed to the corruption and nepotism in the State administration and incidents of police excesses there. From the time the election dates were announced, the AIADMK and the Congress had bungled. Hectic and high pressure bargaining went on between the two electoral allies and precious time was lost in haggling during which time the Congress tried all the tricks of the trade to armtwist the AIADMK into conceding more seats than it could rightfully claim. Finally a ratio of 62: 38 was forged between the AIADMK and the Congress.

Then began the process of selection of candidates in which both parties made a mess. The Congress leadership lost control of the situation. Finally it openly announced that all the Congress candidates could file their nominations and that after the finalisation of the official candidates the other candidates would have to withdraw their papers. This was obviously wishful thinking for having filed their papers, nothing could make the Co-Congressmen withdraw. Hence, the party had to contend with more than its usual harvest of rebel candidates.

In the case of AIADMK the five-member selection committee comprised elders who did not have much contact with the party rank and file. They included S. Raghavanandam (the new General Secretary of the AIADMK), Finance Minister V.R. Nedun-Cheziyan, Kallimuthu, K. Madhavan and Information Minister R.M. Veerappan. All those who were associated with the Jayalalitha faction were systematically weeded out and only those candidates who owed personal allegiance to Veerappan were selected. The defeat of the AIADMK had however been caused not so much by the sidelining of pro-Jayalalitha candidates as due to the fact that adequate pains were not taken to ensure that the candidates selected were worthy of the seat.

Unlike in the Lok Sabha and Assembly elections where the reputation of the party or leader is of overriding importance the individual merit of a candidate is perhaps the most important factor in local elections. So while it is rare to have Independent candidates winning a Lok Sabha election the proportion increases in the Assembly and other localised elections. This fact had been borne out by the civic election results. For instance, while five Independents won in the municipal elections, 29 won in panchayat union and 173 in town panchayat elections.

The AIADMK erred grievously in not paying adequate attention to the reputation of the candidates chosen. The Congress which continues to be in a state of disarray in Tamil Nadu of course, was, in no position to examine the background of each candidate. In striking contrast to this was the choice of candidates in the DMK led Opposition front particularly in the DMK and the CPI (M). The local units of the DMK chose the best candidate which was later endorsed by the party high command.

The AIADMK-Congress combine was replete with dissidents. Although Jayalalitha had issued a statement urging her loyalists to remain faithful to M.G. Ramachandran, pro-Jayalalitha rebel candidates took some of the votes that would have otherwise gone to the official AIADMK candidates. In several places, the erosion entailed the defeat of the official candidates. Indiscipline which was a hallmark of the Congress in Tamil Nadu resulted in a large number of rebel candidates. Sivaji Ganesan who had been sulking in the wings because of being ignored by the Moopanar faction, after a few desultory campaign excused himself from electioneering on health grounds.

Other factors that accounted for the miserable performance of the combine was the utter neglect of the urban areas by the AIADMK Government. During the nine years of the AIADMK regime, the small and medium-sized towns had been sorely neglected, no attention had been paid to water and power supply, sanitation and housing. Tamil Nadu is the second most urbanised State in the country, second only to Maharastra. The State has the largest number of towns with population of over one lakh. This obviously accounts for the trouncing of the AIADMK in the municipal elections it won only 11 seats while the DMK won 64 seats, its allies bagging six more.

Another reason cited for the poor performance of the combine is the AIADMK's systematic dilution of its prohibition policy in blatant contravention to what it professed. This had alienated a sizeable section of women voters who used to be MGR's most ardent supporters. In fact one of the first things that Karunanidhi announced on hearing the election results was that his councillors would see to it that the arrack shop would be removed from near places of worship and educational institutions.

A major issue that turned the voters against the AIADMK was its unpardonable mishandling of the teachers agitation. About 60,000 teachers had been arrested which provoked a mass upsurge all over the State in protest against such high handedness. The whole issue could have been effectively defused if only MGR had met the representatives of the teachers associations. But what was most surprising about the civic elections was the drastic change in attitude of the people within a span of two months. In the Cheyyar by election held in December, 1985 the AIADMK candidate had won.

As an ebullient, Karunanidhi said, shortly after his party's decisive victory, the difference was that Cheyyar had been pampered to an extraordinary extent by the AIADMK. It was flooded with drinking water facilities and new bus routes. All the ministers had campaigned and MGR had also gone to the constituency albeit for a private function. Money was poured in—the victory was bought not won. But when it came to administration, the people wanted the DMK which they felt could handle their local affairs better since it had a reputation for efficiency. More than anything else, the result was an indictment of the inefficiency, incompetence and mal-administration of the AIADMK Government.

Another reason that could have contributed to the DMK's success was that the local elections which were held after 16 years, came to be identified as a demand wrested by the Opposition from a reluctant AIADMK Government. By their dilatory tactics, the AIADMK earned the reputation of being inimical to the elections and thereby to grassroots democracy.

The municipal election results proved in no uncertain terms that devoid of charisma and glamour, the AIADMK collapsed like a house of cards. This was the first election in which MGR did not personally campaign barring the 1984 elections when the picture of the Chief Minister struggling for his life made a greater impact than even his presence. The myth of Ramachandran's invincibility had taken a severe beating. His charisma was beginning to dim, but AIADMK partymen of course stoutly denied this. They pointed out that if fresh Assembly elections were to be held now, the AIADMK would sweep the polls.

The Food Minister, S. Thirunavukkarasu said: "If you analyse the results you will find the independents have done very well, even better than the AIADMK. But does that make them a powerful new phenomenon. If we have Assembly elections now very few independent candidates will win. These results in no way prove that the DMK has become powerful than the AIADMK".

The results had been a big disappointment for the Congress. Using the AIADMK as a crutch, the Congress had banked on winning an adequate number of seats at the grassroots level in the State so that it could lay the firm foundation for a good organisational network in Tamil Nadu, which would have come in really useful in the next general elections. The Congress was confident that it would surely be elected by the people to succeed Ramachandran's AIADMK as it had looked upon the DMK as a spent force.

For the DMK, the victory had come as a tremendous shot in the arm. Veerappan had confidently declared that with these elections the DMK would have to pack up and retire. But this victory was a tribute to the DMK's staying power, the commitment of its party cadre and its organisational strength, all of which remained intact despite a series of crushing defeats. It was also a tribute to Karunanidhi's leadership that despite his inability to lead the party to a victory for a decade his hold over the party had never weakened.

Political Corruption

Political corruption has been having unbridled sway over the body politic ever since political leaders tasted power, particularly at the level of States administration which affected the people immediately. With the style and functioning of democracy in our country and the blatant disregard for the directive principles of the Constitution to ensure justice, social and economic, and the vested interests in full cry, corruption has no doubt become a way of life.

MGR could not escape blame and responsibility for the proliferation of such corruption although he had the will and power to cut it down to manageable proportions. He ignored, though reluctantly, the corrupt practices of his trusted political satraps and turned a Nelsonic eye towards those otherwise close to him. This was what eventually disillusioned the people and shook their faith in him. However, after the openly admitted his mistakes with characteristic and disarming candour, the people forgave him and once again rallied to his support. Had he lived, he would have come back with a resounding victory and a thumping majority during the 1989 General elections.

The irony of the MGR decade (1977-87) was that not withstanding repression, corruption, nepotism, maladministration, and religious obscurantism, he continued to be the only popular leader in the State. He had systematically eliminated all threats from within his own party by clipping the wings of future contenders like Jayalalitha and Veerappan, and the Congress had been unable to produce an alternative. Even though the AIADMK candidates for the 1985 elections were chosen when MGR was undergoing treatment in the US, none of them had the capacity or charisma to replace him. He had also succeeded in insulating the State from the mainstream of national politics and the crosscurrents of the southern state politics, where Government had changed in the past decades.

MGR had uniquely demonstrated time and again that a dismal performance in office need not have anything to do with a Chief Minister's hold over the masses. In 1977, he won 130 out of the 200 seats contested by the total votes polled. In 1980, share of votes polled rose to 38.74 per cent, but he won 129 out of the 177 seats contested. And MGR reached his pinnacle of popularity when a sympathy wave hit the State following his illness. While he was in the US, the AIADMK won 133 seats out of the 155 seats contested, including the 12 Lok Sabha seats it fought.

A trend setter in Indian politics M.G. Ramachandran was the first matinee idol to become Chief Minister of the highly politically conscious State of Tamil Nadu. His example was followed by N.T. Ramarao in Andhra Pradesh a decade later.

Ramachandran had donned the role of a do-gooder in most of the 136 films in which he had starred. His dialogues and songs had an element of the ideals of the DMK and these contributed for the popularisation of the party and its eventual capture of power under the leadership of his mentor and founder of the Anna DMK, late Annadurai in 1967, overthrowing the Congress which had wielded power for two decades since independence. The mascot of MGR films had the DMK flag held aloft by a man and a woman.

M.G. Ramachandran was a unique phenomenon in Indian politics. Having strayed into it from the glamorous world of films he initially showed little interest in active politics; indeed he quitted his seat in the Tamil Nadu legislative Council without completing his full term. Yet politics was to pull him back into its embrace and he had a leading role to play in the DMK and later in the AIADMK which he founded. Riding on the crest of an unprecedented popularity wave a decade ago, he was swept into the office of Chief Minister. He was thus the first matinee idol to become Chief Minister.

Although Ramachandran did not have the benefit of formal education having been brought up in dire poverty, he was obliged to quit school at the age of seven; he was, like Kamaraj, another great leader of Tamil Nadu State, gifted with a good deal of shrewdness and earthy common sense and therefore proved to be one of the most durable Chief Ministers of the State.

MGR was by no means a political thinker or even an able administrator. All power flowed from him; his authority was supreme and could not be defied. Yet for the common people he was a messiah, a charismatic leader, a politician who called them "blood brothers and sisters". He was the darling of the masses.

Ramachandran himself showed deep compassion for the poor and enacted the good samaritan role of his films in real life as well. As Chief Minister he ushered in several social welfare schemes such as the midday school meals. Even though he earned the ire of his critics for such populist measures which became a drain on the exchequer, the people simply loved him.

Record as Speaker

M.G. Ramachandran had created a record in the Tamil Nadu legislature by speaking for seven hours and 10 minutes. Replying to a debate on 18th February, 1982 he continued his speech for two days. He also created history, speaking without the mike for two hours in December, 1972 during the no-confidence motion against the then Speaker, K.A. Mathialagan.

Even though the mike was switched off, he continued his speech, which was not officially recorded.

It will be grossly unfair to M.G. Ramachandran to hold that as Chief Minister of Tamil Nadu he shone in the reflected popularity of the screen hero. Other screen gods and goddesses have realised to their chagrin that the road to political stardom was not that easy, with the exception possibly of Andhra Pradesh Chief Minister N.T. Ramarao, but the tenure of the Andhra Pradesh Chief Minister may not be as durable and smooth as MGR's. Stability was MGR's trade mark, and he reigned supreme in the two worlds of celluloid and politics as long as he lived. For more than a decade he gave Tamil Nadu a political stability known to few States. What marked out his regime from most others is his style of low-key administration; he did not seem to rule at all.

His political philosophy was free from cant and dogma. When he broke away from the DMK, the party founded by C.N. Annadurai, he gave his faction the name — Anna DMK — to proclaim that he was true and faithful follower of his departed leader. It is idle to speculate on what turn DMK politics would have taken had Annadurai lived long, but it stands to Ramachandran's credit that he smoothed the rough regional edges of DMK policies to fit them into national politics. He believed in the unity and indivisibility of India and no conflict between national and regional interests. He was ostracised for this by some non-Congress Chief Ministers, but he was not deterred.

The stability of Ramachandran's regime was largely dependent on two simple measures—rice at a price within the means of the common man and free mid-day meals for school children. His enormous popularity with the masses gave him a clout which he used, almost always unobtrusively, to hold the party together. No dissident dared to challenge his policies, far less his leadership, even when he was incapacitated by illness. Not everyone in the party liked his policy of alliance and collaboration with the Congress (I) at the Centre or his support to the India-Sri-Lanka alliance. He was the great conciliator of the party, and in the closing months of his life of a valuable and valued link between New Delhi and the Tamil militants of Sri Lanka over whom he wielded considerable influence.

When MGR formed his own All India Anna DMK (AIADMK), no one imagined that he would achieve the level of success which later became his. Of course, his spectacular success was due, in part, to the general disillusionment among the people with the graft and nepotism within the DMK Government and administration. Thus, MGR and AIADMK romped home and he became Chief Minister. It was, however, revealed quite some years ago (Andhra is just discovering the fact) that being a star on the silver screen need not necessarily make one a star administrator. For MGR, the situation became all the more difficult with rival factions forming around him. They vied for his favours and tried to pull down the others.

The real crunch came when advancing age and ill health began catching up with MGR. He suffered a massive stroke and had to be flown to the United States for emergency surgery and extended convalescence. During the long months that he was in the United States, all hell broke loose within the AIADMK. The various factions, whose rivalry had been guardedly convert until then, now unsheathed their knives and did not mind spilling blood. The one who came out worst off in the ensuing power struggle was AIADMK Member of Parliament (MP) and Propaganda Secretary Ms. Jayalalitha. The presentable, articulate and young Members of Parliament had generated a lot of envy by her reputation of being MGR's favourite. The backlash now came home to roost and Jayalalitha had to pay the price.

She was, for instance, not allowed to meet her guide and mentor in his New York hospital; she was removed from her post of Propaganda Secretary; then it seemed for a while that MGR might not recover, the other ganged up on her and made Jayalalitha's life difficult. She had to await MGR's recovery and return, and a subsequent long meeting with him before being reinstated. She was not doubtable to neutralise some of the poison that had been injected into MGR's mind about her.

Although MGR miraculously recovered, unfortunately for everyone he did not seem to have fully recovered all his faculties. It was a moot point whether he could any longer shoulder the heavy burden of Chief Ministership. For MGR, there was the further complication that the Congress, with which he had an alliance of shorts, was definitely getting more ambitious. With the DMK, AIADMK was hotting up, the electorate might well decide in the not too distant future to give a chance to the long-left-out Congress. Meanwhile, MGR's dilemma was real. Going by his record, he was not the kind of person who would cling on to power for the sake of power. But, even knowing that he was finding it difficult to cope, he dared not retire, for he knew that whenever he stepped down, factionalism would tear asunder all that he had built up with such great care. That was the eternal dilemma of MGR.

In fact the political circles in the State knew that it was primarily the matinee idol MGR who had become a byword for his benevolence on and off the screen and who had steered the DMK to victory even in 1967 with his photographs showing him with bandages around his neck as he was then recovering from a pistol wound inflicted on him by actor M.R. Radha and with the backing of the thousands of his Manram volunteers (MGR fan club members) throughout the State.

It is this success of MGR at the hustings that kept his aspiring Cabinet and party colleagues hopefully glued to their leader at any cost, waiting hopefully for the eventual day when they could become the second in command if not the top. And yet when the Chief Minister who fell ill in June 1987 and confined himself to the Ramavaram Gardens allowed the sharp, soft spoken but suave Panruti Ramachandran, said to be closer even to the Congress top, to look after his files, it is said that the Cabinet bickerings came to the fore with the hitherto No. 2 Finance Minister V.R. Nedunchezhian expressing his resentment understandably by sending even his resignation letter to the Chief Minister. While P. Ramachandran still continued to take action on the routine files of the

Chief Minister entrusted to him leaving the important ones for the latter to decide, political and knowledgeable circles seemed to think that the Chief Minister aware of the happenings during his absence abroad in the New York hospital in 1984-85 and the role played by Nedunchezhian and others then, had now shifted the responsibility of looking after his work during his likely absence again now to P. Ramachandran.

Populist Schemes

MGR was in the habit of coming out with some populist scheme or the other every year. Invariably, the opposition and the intelligentsia would howl that the ship of State would sink under the weight of populism. But at the end of it all, almost as it happens in his films, MGR would emerge victorious, having found the money from the Centre, somehow. During the financial year 1986-87, MGR Government received an outlay of Rs. 1,153 crores, involving a 20 per cent increase over the 1985-86 State plan outlay.

The possibility of Central assistance for the massive housing scheme was going to help MGR fight to retain his following among the Harijans. His standing among them was shaky, since Harijan leader V.A.J. Balasundaram had been arguing that without reservations, the Harijans would never get a fair share of seats in the local bodies and without adequate representation, the higher castes would simply trample them under their feet. The Harijans leader's efforts to secure a stay failed at the Madras High Court. The court felt that constitutionally the State was not duty bound to provide reservations for all elections. Whether Balasundaram won or lost MGR would have to contend with a slight erosion of credibility among the Harijans and he would have to mend the fences with them. The housing scheme should enable him to do that.

MGR had been preparing the ground for a victory in the February 23, 1986 polls very assiduously. When the Centre announced an increase in the prices of petroleum and petroleum products, the Tamil Nadu Government promptly came out with a statement that its public transport corporation would not increase their fares. The usual practice under such circumstances would have been to raise the fares and put the blame on the Centre.

At the end of January 1986, MGR Government announced the grant of two instalments of dearness allowance to its employees in a full year, this should cost the exchequer Rs. 28 crores. Many began to ask if such an announcement was necessary when the annual budget was due to be presented in a little over a month. The finance minister made an additional promise that the Pongal gift which MGR gave to the teachers and other Government staff during 1986 would become an annual feature. It would be some kind of a bonus which the staff had been wanting. This too was done, ostensibly with an eye on the forthcoming elections in which the teachers and Government servants could play a crucial role as grassroots level workers.

With the summer months round the corner, farmers and towns people were concerned about the possibility of power cuts. But the Chairman of the State Electricity Board had come out with an assurance that there would be no power cut during 1986. On his part, the Food Minister said that the prices in the fair price shops would not be increased irrespective of the Centre's position on the question.

MGR was also keenly cultivating the communal votes. He warmly welcomed the Pope, sought a private audience with him, presented him with and special gift and had the Pope hugging him at the end of it. With an eye on the Hindu vote, he had special prayers arranged in a number of temples thanking the Lord for his miraculous recovery from a recent debilitating illness. He had these pujas (worships) done even though as a follower of Periyar he was supposed to shun religious rituals. He could not care less for Karunanidhi's criticism that his regime was doing everything to perpetuate superstition, with a narrow political end in view.

Despite the feverish preparations for the elections, there was a feeling in some quarters that if he could help it, MGR might not hold the elections at all. "If MGR is keen on holding the elections, why did he not send the Advocate General of the State to argue the Government case in the writ appeal at the Supreme Court seeking an order against the elections. The Government had earlier sought the services of a leading lawyer (Ram Jethmalani) to pursue a case against some opposition leaders. Why can't it pursue the elections case with the same vigour," asked Karunanidhi, President of the Opposition DMK. Karunanidhi also wondered how the counsel for Tamil Nadu let the court fix February 21, 1986 as the date for the State to make its submission—barely two days before polling. This would keep the candidates on tenter hooks till virtually the last day. Many would be demoralised and if elections were called off everybody could have spent the enormous amounts in vain. The opposition candidates would be the worst sufferers having to fight the elections without the resources of the ruling party.

The AIADMK was in power at the State level and as such would not like other centres of power to develop in the various towns and panchayats. Though with all its populism and MGR's charisma, it would romp home victorious, it would have to concede to the opposition that it was able to cash in on local issues. If the elections were shot down at the Supreme Court level MGR would certainly not be an unhappy man. It is the Opposition including the Congress (I), the official opposition, which would be unhappy. While the DMK wanted to throw a challenge to the AIADMK to test and establish its strength everywhere, the Congress (I) wanted to use the power that might accrue to it as an ally of the AIADMK to build its grassroot organisation which was virtually non-existent now.

M.G. Ramachandran repeatedly kissed the hand of State Governor S.L. Khurana at their last meeting together and, despite poor health, waited to see him off, the Governor said in Madras on December 24, 1987.

Khurana said Ramachandran was in "frail health" when he last met him on December 22 at the airport to send off Prime Minister Rajiv Gandhi. Though Khurana had asked Ramachandran to go to his car, even jokingly putting it as an "order from the Governor", the Chief Minister had insisted on waiting to see him (Khurana) off, the Tamil Nadu Governor said.

The political drama in Tamil Nadu marked only one of the high points of the fierce infighting in the AIADMK that had been raging for quite some time, now, especially since the party's victory in alliance with the Congress in the 1980 Assembly election. And, obviously enough, the curtain had not been rung down on the affair with the submission of resignation letters by the members of the State Cabinet to Chief Minister MGR to enable him to reconstitute the Ministry following his threat to relinquish leadership of the State Government. The squabblings came out into the open when a faction led by Ministers R.M. Veerappan and K. Kalimuthu sought to capitalise on MGR's illness and absence from the country to settle scores with the group represented in the main by Miss Jayalalitha by divesting her of a party post. The same faces figured in the controversy following her reinstatement in the party post along with the demotion of Veerappan by MGR. The new factional war, that precipitated the AIADMK supremo's move, had the same participants, with a corruption scandal involving Kalimuthu being sought to be projected as a conspiracy of the Centre against the State Government with Miss Jayalalitha as its proxy.

The larger importance of the infighting, however, lied not in the personalities but in the policy issues that had come to be involved in it. The anti-Jayalalitha faction had quite stridently identified itself with a whole series of stances that were presumed to be the peremptory dictate of "Dravidian politics". It had been trying to raise a scare about attempts to impose Hindi on the people of the State, and made common cause with an ill-conceived agitation on the issue. It had also sought to ride the crest of the Tamil wave of sympathy for the ethnic minority in Sri Lanka and made an anti-Centre platform of it. And, besides pushing a similar line on other subjects of local interest, it had also been striving to its utmost to sour the AIADMK-Congress relations and break the alliance that had marked a wholesome change in the direction of Tamil Nadu politics, promising to end the monopoly of a fascist-type chauvinism over it. The clique, in other words, had been playing very much the same role as the Karunanidhi-led DMK, whose philosophy and policies could not have been rejected more unmistakably by the electorate.

MGR might have bought peace with his dramatic move, but the truce achieved now was too uneasy to endure long. The conflicting trends represented by the infighting could not be forced to coexist, though it could temporarily be subdued by the unwillingness of even the thinly disguised DMK lobby inside the ruling party to lose the advantage of MGR's charisma to which alone it owed its political power and influence. Whether the Chief Minister acted to end this untenable arrangement or allowed the drift continue under the facade of party unity remained to be seen.

The reversal by the all India Anna DMK of its earlier stand against the Muslim Women (Protection of Rights on Divorce) Bill would not surprise anyone. In fact, what should have been surprising was that it could gather the courage to oppose the Bill all along. Though AIADMK claimed to be a 'regional' party it had never hesitated to kowtow to any and every Government at the Centre. It had been a supplicant of the Congress-I, Janata Party and even the Lok Dal-Congress-S Coalition at the Centre.

The Deputy leader of the 11-member group of the AIADMK in the Lok Sabha announced in May 1986 on the eve of the Bill being taken up for consideration that the party would vote for it. This flied in the face of its earlier gyrations, when its leader P. Kolandaivelu joined a delegation of Opposition Members of Parliament on April 30 to plead with the Prime Minister for the withdrawal of the Bill.

What was surprising was not the AIADMK's vote face, but a stand against its own political interests, perceived from its narrow obsession for one-upmanship over the rival DMK. The Muslim League had always been closer to the DMK and Ramachandran's, as much as his opponent Karunanidhi's policy had been to remain at daggers drawn. Whoever was with one cannot be with the other. In this queer thrust of policies, one would have expected the AIADMK to oppose the Bill, if only because the DMK was with the Muslim League.

The Kazhagam, DMK and AIADMK, though ever at daggers drawn, were thus unfailing when it came to making quick and dubious political gains. A similar situation prevailed when Giani Zail Singh was contesting for President. Both the Kazhagam extended support to him, with the Giani addressing the rival parties in quick succession. No wonder he kept seeking the support of the AIADMK at the meeting of the DMK and vice-versa.

The stance that MGR adopted did not come from a later day change in his policy. It was in the making of his political personality. He was true to it from the very start, since he broke away from

DMK leader M. Karunanidhi, who had run away with the trappings of power. MGR was left to form a new party, the Anna Dravida Munnetra Kazhagam. At this time MGR faced several disadvantages. Born in Kandy, Sri Lanka, he was supposed to be of Malayali origin, though he had studied in Kumbakomam which is in the heart of Tamil Nadu. Try as they would, his critics attempt to paint him as an outsider, did not wash.

Image as a Good Doer

There was, of course, something that helped him something that is peculiar to politics in the South. He converted his cinema image of the doer of good deeds and rescuer of weaker persons into his real-life vocation. He continued his philanthropic deeds, sharing his wealth with those in need. His fans associations gave him great support. His image of a true follower of C.N. Annadurai helped too.

When he came to power, he continued on this very course. His midday meal scheme became a great social welfare measure. Sixty-five lakh meals were served to school students every day. In a State which cannot be said to be free of corruption and inefficiency in administration, the meals were of a uniformly good quality. Much later. N.T. Ramarao in Andhra Pradesh tried to do the same, but it did not have the same success, nor the same impact.

Not that this means that pampering people is what a leader should do to gain acceptance with his electorate. There have been other politicians who put additional burdens on his people and yet succeeded. At the other end of the country, in Jammu and Kashmir, Sheikh Abdullah, when he was back in power after the accord signed with Smt. Indira Gandhi, abolished the food subsidy. The measures resulted in higher food prices, but the people did not desert him. Sheikh Abdullah went on to win another election. The lesson is that a politician's measures, whether harsh or liberal, yield results only when the people have faith in the leadership. MGR's rapport with the masses was a great help to him.

MGR inspite of his affection for V.R. Nedunchezhian (he tookover as interim Chief Minister after MGR's death on December 24) did not rate him very high. He thought Nedunchezhian was indecisive and tended to falter at the time of taking a decision. This did not deter MGR from entrusting him later with the important ministerial portfolio of finance. Nedunchezhian on his part considered MGR wilful and domineering.

To all his political rivals, MGR used to say only one reply, i.e. as long as I live, I will be the Chief Minister and this greatest towering matinee-idol turned politician — MGR did it so.

MGR was the first ever Chief Minister of Tamil Nadu for having occupied the chair of Chief Minister on three occasions (1977, 1980 & 1984), but also created a record in meeting, discussing and receiving all the three Prime Ministers and three Presidents, i.e. Morarji Desai, Indira Gandhi and Rajiv Gandhi and Sanjeeva Reddy, Giani Zail Singh and Ramaswami Venkataraman.

MGR made his last appearance on a public platform to preside over the function at Madras on December 21, 1987 three days before his death. Prime Minister Rajiv Gandhi unveiled the 10-foot bronze statue of Jawaharlal Nehru at that function.

In his speech, MGR paid glowing tributes to Nehru family for its sacrifices and for its contribution to nation building. "Today the statue of our first Prime Minister and the light of Asia, Jawaharlal Nehru, is being unveiled. Our Prime Minister Rajiv Gandhi who is Nehru's grandson has come to unveil the statue and I extend my greetings to him"

"It was the persistent wish of the people of Tamil Nadu to have the statue of Jawaharlal Nehru in the capital city. I am happy that their wish is being fulfilled today. For generations the Nehru family has been playing a glorious role whether it was during the freedom struggle or after independence".

"Jawaharlal Nehru is the architect of independent and Modern India. He was a leader beyond compare in this century. With every fibre of his being he worked for a bright and glorious future for this country. The doctrine of non-alignment and the code of 'Panchsheel' were his greatest contributions to the nations of the world".

"It was Jawaharlal Nehru who laid the strongest foundation for science and technology and modernity. After Nehru his daughter Indira Gandhi took over the leadership of the country and pursued vigorously the policies evolved by her illustrious father. Under Indira Gandhi's leadership the country progressed enormously to surprise even the developed countries. We are all proud of that our great Prime Minister Rajiv Gandhi is following in the footsteps of his mother and grandfather. In his own right, he is the leader of the developing countries, the non-aligned world and the South Asian Regional grouping. He devotes his entire attention to the development of the country. He is working tirelessly to create a new India in which unity, peace, integrity and casteless egalitarian values would be cherished and promoted further. So long as this planet exists, the services and sacrifices made by the Nehru family not only in our national cause but also in the cause of the world would be remembered and cherished by the people. I wish the Prime Minister well being and further glory. I wish him more success in making our country the pre-eminent nation in the world."

Portrait in Assembly

Leaders of some other political parties in the House urged the unveiling of a portrait of M.G. Ramachandran in the Assembly House.

6

Great Achiever

Great Qualities of Leadership

As a party leader, ever since M. G. Ramachandran drifted to the Dravidian movement from the Congress, he had displayed great qualities of leadership. He emerged as a balancing force between the hardliners led by his arch rival M. Karunanidhi and the moderates in the AIADMK. If party has withstood strains and fissures all these years, it is in no small measure due to his charisma and leadership qualities. Ramachandran was a steadying force in the relationship between India and Sri Lanka. To the Tamil Lankans, he was a messiah. In his death they will feel orphaned. Political stability in Tamil Nadu is sure to suffer a setback with the disappearance of this stabilising force — M.G. Ramachandran. The best tribute his partymen can pay to him and all the ideals he stood for is by rallying round to the new leader with a singleness of purpose and dedication. The MGR charisma has ended but not without leaving behind the knotty problems for the party.

MGR was well known for giving obscurantist calls to his followers, often leading them in dangerous directions. In 1977, he had demanded of his loyalists to prove their loyalty by branding or tattooing the AIADMK party symbol on their arms. There are many in the State today who showed their subsequent disenchantment by wiping off the tattoo with acid. Earlier he had made another strange call by asking his followers to carry knives on their persons to protect themselves from 'enemies'. MGR said his police had become incapable of providing such protection.

The secret of his rise lies in the fact that he was an astute reader of the pulse of his men which he utilised them for the greater good of the society and nation. He had an unassuming appearance and personality. He never grumbled against his lot but had revolutionary temperament. His had been a uniquely successful political career enabling him to fulfil almost all his wordily ambitions, a high political office as also material prosperity. No political leader and screen actor earned so much fame, respect and goodwill from his countrymen as M.G. Ramachandran during a span of a decade of his graceful Chief Ministership of Tamil Nadu and 35 years of film career, scored.

MGR had strong likes and dislikes but managed to keep the flock together. He did not designate any one as his successor. The cap he wore is too big for any head in the party MGR chaired.

The death of six fishermen in police firing in Madras in December 985 underlined the confusion that had gripped the Tamil Nadu administration ever since M.G. Ramachandran took ill. Although Ramachandran staged a remarkable recovery, his effectiveness as the leader of the Government as well as the ruling AIADMK had been considerably weakened by his impaired health and advancing age. Without his effective leadership, the ministers and the bureaucrats had been found wanting in taking firm decisions not only on policy matters pertaining to the development of the State but also on issues like flood relief, fishermen's agitation and teachers' demand where crisis of management of a high order was called for to put it bluntly, the administration was just drifting, taking *ad hoc* decisions when it was forced to.

The Clashes between the police and the fishermen resulting in loss of lies and injuries to many could have been prevented if only the Government had been more alert. The trouble started as on November 4 when the official machinery, in an unprecedented show of strength, removed the fishermen's boats and catamarans from the sands of the Marina under the pretext of beautifying and cleaning up the second longest beach in the world. This created widespread resentment among thousand of fishermen rand their families who had been occupying the sea front for many years. Although a settlement was claimed to have been reached between the Government and the fishermen subsequently, it was plain to all that the simmering discontent among the fishermen was bound to erupt into a major law and order problem sooner than later and that was exactly what happened on that during. School teachers also had been on the warpath for more than two months, demanding the redressal of their grievances which pertain mainly to inadequate pay rise under the Pay Commission's formula. Teachers and their wives had been courting arrest almost every day throughout the State.

It was estimated that more than 35,000 teachers were behind the bars awaiting trial. The agitation had snowballed with college teachers and Government employees also rallying to their support, not to speak of the Opposition parties. The principal demand of the teachers was that Chief Minister M.G. Ramachandran, should personally discuss their problem with them. The agitating teachers were not satisfied with official level talks. The education system at the school level had been seriously disrupted by the absence of teachers to man the classes. The Government had been standing on prestige in dealing with the teachers' agitation. In an attempt to shatter the morale of the teachers, the Government had threatened to appoint new teachers. Large sections of students had expressed their resentment against this move and solidarity with the striking teachers.

Immense Popularity

As leader of the masses, MGR could draw a sea of audience. As a Chief Minister of Tamil Nadu, MGR dedicated himself to the upliftment of the downtrodden. He was one of those few Chief Ministers, who had made a deep impact on the minds of the people by endearing himself unparalleled in the contemporary politics. No head of any State had commanded so much respect and confidence of the public as MGR. Nor is anybody to take his place. Because of his personality and complete control over the AIADMK party and the State machinery, principles and ideology took a back seat.

Late C N. Annadurai said "Our aim is to achieve the welfare and happiness of each section of society. By achieving the happiness of each section, it is our aim to pave the way for the happiness of the entire society".

MGR pledged: "The Government of Tamil Nadu follows the approach of Anna. The Tamil Nadu Government has taken a pledge to remove any obstacles in its way while trying to realise the egalitarian society as conceived by Periyar and Anna".

For the 10 years MGR presided over the destiny of Tamil Nadu. M.G. Ramachandran conceived and implemented with a wide impact a number of social welfare schemes. But the one that had the biggest impact was the programme of supplementary feeding for over eight million children. Acknowledged as a very fargoing venture, an investment in human resources development, the Chief Minister's Nutritious Meal Programme (CMNMP) was the jewel in MGR's crown. There had been feeding programmes of different types in Tamil Nadu itself and a few are running elsewhere in the country but they do not match MGR's noon meal scheme in content and coverage. When introduced on July 1, 1982, it was to feed about 5.5 million children in the age group of 2-10 in the rural areas, soon its scope was enlarged to cover the urban poor also. Two years later the programme was extended to benefit students in high schools.

Today, in all, about 8.5 million children between the ages of 2 and 15 all over the State are getting nutritious food in about 65,000 school and pre-school centres, at an annual cost of approximately Rs. 200 crores. Another feature of the CMNMP is that the feeding is done on the 365 days of the year (although at the start it was limited to 200 days. It is worked out strictly according to the menu planned by nutrition experts at the "Avinashilingam Home Science College" for Woman in Coimbatore. The intake ensures that a child gets at least one-third of the daily nutritional requirement as recommended by the Indian Council of Medical Research-ICMR.

The implementation of the scheme also provides employment to nearly 2,00,000 people most of whom are women (including 40,000 widows). At the time of its launching, the measure was characterised by critics as nothing but a "political stunt' enacted by a film actor turned politician to stabilise himself in power. MGR's detractors were sceptical and questioned the wisdom of spending huge amounts on what they called an economically "unproductive" programme of feeding the poor.

Soon the critics were silenced by concrete results. It became obvious to experts and lay people alike that the programme was not a mere State-sponsored charity for mitigation hunger in a target group of the population.

Official and non-official studies have brought out the fact that although there have been certain lapses and irregularities in implementation, the noon meal programme has boosted the school enrolment and retention rates along with improving the health standards of the beneficiary pupils in standards 1 to 10. It has made more children from among the rural poor enter the portals of education. Even in the first year of its implementation, an additional 2,63,000 children were enrolled and in the next year a further 2,68,000 children. The tempo is kept up. At the end of 1986-87, the percentage of enrolment in the 6-11 age group was close to 100 and that of the 11-14 age group was around 75.

Surveys conducted by the "Avinashilingam Home Science College" spoke of a significant improvement in the health of participating children. Over a 12-month period, all the children examined showed an increase in their height and weight measurements and the increments higher than ICMR standards. Mothers have recorded the observation that better health has made their children more active and lively. The studies have also found a decline in the incidence of common diseases such as angular stomatitis, bleeding gums, dry skin, dental caries and mild anaemia. Appreciation for the project has come from not only nutritionists but also administrators from all over the country. The Centre too has come to realise, though belatedly, the effectiveness of the scheme as a direct intervention to break the vicious cycle of poverty-malnutrition-infection.

After sustained efforts by the State Government, the planning Commission agreed in 1985 to recognise it as a Plan scheme. Taking not of suggestions made by nutrition experts, the State Government recently decided to widen the scope of its noon meal scheme to comprise nutrition, pre-school education, health immunisation and medical care. With the estimated cost of the enlarged version of the project going up to around Rs. 400 crores, the State has approached the Centre for help in securing the assistance of the World Bank.

Neither his advanced age nor his faltering health seemed to have dimmed the heroic antics of MGR, Tamil Nadu's charismatic matinee idol of yester-year. The actor-turned politician made this amply clear when he confronted his party colleagues with his dramatic threat to quit the Chief Minister's office. MGR's stunning announcement on was clearly meant to shock the squabbling AIADMK ministers and party stalwarts into total submission. And, to be sure, the shock treatment had more than the desired effect. Like a faithful flock, the entire ministerial team had instantly bowed to the supreme leader, mindful of the fact that he had kept the AIADMK on the top of the political heap in the State ever since he founded it in 1972 after parting company with the DMK leader Karunanidhi. All the 24 ministers had submitted their resignations, individually and collectively, ostensibly to enable the Chief Minister to recast his Cabinet as he wished.

Some heads were bound to roll when MGR reconstituted his team. It was almost on the cards that the axe would fall on Kalimuthu, the controversial Agriculture Minister, who had been waging a better feud with Jayalalitha, the equally controversial propaganda secretary of the party. As a matter of fact, MGR's totally unexpected resignation threat itself was meant to end the open conflict between the two rival camps. Kalimuthu had charged Jayalalitha with quietly operating as an agent of the Central Government. Furthermore, he had accused her of nudging the CBI to enquire into his alleged role in the Rs. 60-lakh bank fraud case. On her part, Jayalalitha had stoutly denied these charges. She clearly suspected a conspiracy being hatched by her opponents in the party to politically cripple her.

Anyhow, there was no denying that Kalimuthu, Tourism Minister Veerappan and others in their camp had not reconciled themselves to the former movie star's rehabilitation in the party by MGR. Moreover, it was widely believed that by virtue of her proximity to MGR, Jayalalitha's rivals in the party might not succeed in their drive for her political eclipse, afterall. On the other hand, it might not come as a surprise if MGR found a berth for his one time movie co-star and later on his close political confidant in his reconstituted ministry.

There was no question that MGR's shock move had achieved its immediate political objective. But it was debatable whether the then enforced calm would endure once MGR, undeniably in failing health, disappeared from the scene, in the absence of a leader of MGR's stature and popularity, the squabbles and feuds.

Great Vote Catcher

M.G. Ramachandran had a promise to keep which went unfulfilled. He wanted to shift the State capital to a central place at Tiruchirapalli. But in view of the huge cost involved, it could not be taken up. Ramachandran was likened to Helan of Troy by his mentor C.N. Annadurai. Homer described Helan as the face that launched 1000 ships. Annadurai had stated the face of Ramachandran that could fetch one million votes.

Ramachandran had ready explanations for every act he did or undid. When he made prohibition very rigorous, he said he was doing it so to wipe out the tears from the eyes of women flok. Later when he relaxed it his ready answer was, he did so to stop the tears of housewives whose breadwinners were going to jail on dry law offences. Later in, January 1987, Ramachandran closed down toddy and arrack shops.

Honour of Doctorate

An unlettered man who made no bones of his educational background, MGR was conferred a Doctorate honour by an American university and later by the Madras University. In his frequent jousts with pressmen, MGR almost always successfully managed to have the last word.

Simple in Manners

On one occasion an agency correspondent rang him up late in the night for a reaction to a political development. As minutes ticked by and the correspondent anxious not to miss his last train to a distant suburb, rang up MGR's house and thinking he was talking to his secretary said "please ask the Chief Minister to hurry up, otherwise I'll miss my train."

"Don't worry, the statement is ready and you won't miss your train home". MGR himself on the line, comforted the correspondent.

If MGR was cautious and guarded in handling the press he was equally diplomatic and had a definite poise in handling their most tricky questions. If leading questions were put to him by seasoned journalists, MGR would brush them off with a smile: "You mischievous persons, you want to trap me."

MGR could successfully mollify pressmen hanging around for hours near his Sathya Studios, where he held most of his party meetings, first asking them if they had anything to eat. They could have their lunch or dinner before the press meet.

Beloved Leader

M.G. Ramachandran had earned the love and affection of the poorest of the poor and citizens from all walks of life. During Jawaharlal Nehru's period (1947-1964), MGR had contributed all his earnings from acting (more than one crore rupees) for the Prime Minister's Relief Fund.

A Phenomenon

MGR was a phenomenon, the like of which India has never seen and perhaps will never see again in centuries to come. He came to power on the issue of corruption, promising to provide a clean Government. During the decade (1977-87) that MGR held the reigns of power in Tamil Nadu, the State recorded an abysmally high economic growth rate besides free meals scheme covering seven million children and several welfare schemes fore women.

In June 1987, MGR completed a decade of his reign over Tamil Nadu. The region, which still exults in the vibrant memories of the legendary Cholas and Pandy as who excelled in military exploits, learning, and trade and commerce, was suddenly left, it seemed, without a moder legend. When he strode upon the political stage 10 years ago, MGR seemed to be a character right out of the history books-a sage-poet-politician in the mould of the famous 'Alvars and Nyauars' — who would fashion a new era for a region that prided itself as the crucible of indigenous Indian culture. Analysts of the MGR decade, even the most vituperative critics, would readily admit that, notwithstanding his glaring failures, the fur-capped Chief Minister still had an uncanny hold over the masses. Because of his welfare schemes—the public dole — they look up to him as the fount of all munificence.

But the MGR welfare formula, just about the only thing his Government was now associated with and which informed its very style and functioning had proved simply a disastrous short-term palliative in which efficient administration and economic development had been sacrificed at the altar of largesse. That hardly appeared to be the case when MGR captured power on the promise of eliminating corruption, fighting Brahminism and idol worship, ensuring speedy development and an open Government, and opposing the Central Government, and its language policy. But the only thing that MGR provided in the ensuing years, apart from state charity, was stability. But it was the stability of stagnation.

A decade ago, a change took place in Tamil Nadu. A change that has since ushered in growth in all spheres of life: cultural, economic and political. The people of Tamil Nadu voted the All India Anna DMK led by M.G. Ramachandran, known to the masses simply as "MGR" to power. Chief Minister MGR, on assuming office took a solemn pledge to provide a clean, corruption-free administration and to overhaul the administration. Tamil Nadu has come long way since then.

Successful Five Year Plans

Tamil Nadu enjoys the fine reputation of implementing the Five-year plan programmes effectively and has achieved all plan targets. As against the outlay of Rs. 3,150 crores for the sixth plan, the State had spent Rs. 3,675 crores.

In the first phase of the 7th plan for the State, the expenditure was anticipated around Rs. 1,050 crores as against an approved outlay of Rs. 960 crores. In the second year of the Plan, i.e. for the year 1986-87, the Annual Plan costed Rs. 1,153 crores.

The Annual Plan for 1986-87 had 'power' as a major thrust with an outlay of Rs. 387.36 crores. The break-up for the other sector of the Annual plan was: Water supply and Sanitation — Rs. 125 crores; Social Welfare and Nutrition — Rs. 110.42 crores; Agriculture-Rs.94.44 crores; Rural Development-Rs. 47.89 crores; Irrigation and Flood Control—Rs. 77.94 crores; Industry and Minerals-Rs. 54.38 crores; Transport-Rs. 57.75 crores; Science, Technology and Environment—Rs. 1.68 crores; General economic services—Rs. 3.98 crores; Education, Art and Culture—Rs. 60.15 crores; Health-Rs. 26.76 crores; Housing — Rs. 47 crores; Information and Publicity Rs. 60 Lakhs; Welfare of SC, ST and Backward classes-Rs. 15.50 crores; Labour and Employment — Rs. 3.99 crores; General Services, Stationery and Printing — Rs. 4.98 crores. The increased plan outlay, by the Planning Commission for Tamil Nadu was because of the State's satisfactory performance in 1985-86.

Agriculture is the main stay of Tamil Nadu's economy. Rice is being grown in 67 lakh acres every year. The yield is one of the highest in the Indian subcontinent amounting to 2240 kilos per hectares. Tamil Nadu Government is aiming at a goal of 5 metrictonnes per hectare and is seriously involved in achieving this but due to inclement conditions of the weather, the food production sometimes is affected adversely for instance, in 1986, samba crops were adversely affected in Thanjavur District as also in the districts of South Arcot and Chengalpattu. The Tamil Nadu Government is attempting to promote intensive cultivation of paddy in other areas and consequently a high productivity level was achieved during kuruvai season. The Government is hoping to achieve a production level of 50 lakhs metric tonnes.

At the end of the Sixth plan period, Tamil Nadu achieved a production level of 69.17 lakhs metric tonnes of rice and other cereals 3.42 lakhs metric tonnes of pulses, and 13.425 lakhs metric tonnes of oil seeds. For the Seventh plan period, the targeted production level is 105 lakhs metric tonnes of food grains, 6 lakhs metric tonnes of pulses and 18.98 lakhs metric tonnes of oil seeds. High technology is being imparted to achieve this impressive target.

Cotton is grown in 2.8 lakhs hectare and it is expected to yield 6 lakh bales There are 23 giant orchards where quality-grafts of fruit plants are prepared to be supplied to the farmers at cheaper rates. City Vegetable Development Scheme has been extended to Madras, Madurai, Tiruchirapalli and Vellore. Quality vegetable seeds in packets and vegetable and fruit seedlings are distributed for use in kitchen gardens. The Scheme for plantation crops improvement, Banana Development Scheme, Western Ghats Development Project are some of the productive schemes. About 30,150 farm families are so far benefited in the Nilgiris Hill Area Development. Project.

Because of the delayed arrival of the monsoon and the floods in January 1986 the production of pulses were expected to be first as usual. Now pulses will be grown in 18 lakh hectares and that may yield 20 lakh tonnes.

Despite the drought that stuck twice in 1984-85, efforts to increase production of pulses and vegetable oil seeds in Tamil Nadu proved a success. Against a target of 14.67 lakh hectares of cropped area for oil seeds, there was a 5 per cent increase and the production showed an increase of 12 per cent. During 1983-84, pulses were cultivated in an area of little over 8 lakh hectares which recorded a production of 2.5 lakh tonnes by registering a productivity of 340 Kg. per hectare. But during the year 1984-85 there was an increased yield of 50 per cent, and the area of cultivation was increased by 30 per cent. By producing 3.7 lakh tonnes over an extent of 10.4 lakh hectares, Tamil Nadu has broken the record.

Some Significant Projects

Tamil Nadu Industrial Development Corporation promoted a Rs. 23 crores industrial explosives manufacturing project. Named Tamil Nadu Industrial Explosives Ltd., this project is located at a 700-acres site in North Arcot District and has commenced commercial production. The unit is the third of its kind in the country at Rs. 22 crores detonator project and Rs. 23 crores ammonium nitrate and nitric acid project promoted by TIDCO are also coming up in the region.

The Myiladuthurai Cooperative Sugar Mill set up at a cost of Rs. 1777 lakhs commenced production from December 1986.

The Ariyalur Cement plant, a unit of the Tamil Nadu Cement Corporation, expanded its capacity. A letter of intent has been applied for setting up of a new cement plant in Palyam in Madurai District.

A project for the beneficiation of graphite at a cost of Rs. 1.50 crores was sanctioned at Sivaganga. Another project for cutting and polishing black granite at a cost of Rs. 3.85 crores is also underway with the Tamil Nadu Government's equity participation.

Tamil Nadu magnesite Limited implemented a project at a cost of Rs. 80 crores for the beneficiation of Magnesite. Another plant for chemically beneficiating the magnesite from mined one was started during 1987 at a cost of Rs. 26.5 crores. It is also proposed by the Government to start a special brick plant at an estimated cost of Rs. 45 crores to manufacture special refractory bricks in modern steel plants.

A project that was expected to save Rs. 40 crores annual in foreign exchange currency is the Tamil Nadu Newsprint and Papers Ltd. This plant uses sugarcane basgasse as its raw material for manufacturing newsprint for printing and writing paper.

The Government of India set up an Export Processing Zone at Madras to promote exports from the region. The Tamil Nadu Government has provided about 158 acres of land for the first stage of the project and has proposed to acquire about 300 acres of land for the second stage to set up 250 unit besides the 120 units under the first stage. The Government of India has cleared 74 applications to the Zone.

The Electronic Corporation of Tamil Nadu (EICOT) set up projects in the public sector such as the Aluminium Electrolytic Capacitor Manufacturing Unit at Hosur, Communication Systems Project at Madras and Digital Electronic Watch Project at Instronics Campus, Madras.

Tamil Nadu welcomed entrepreneurs and industrialists from India and abroad to set up industries in the State. The Government has constituted a high power committee with the Secretary to Government, Industries Department as Chairman to act as the "Single Window Agency" for medium and major industries in Tamil Nadu. The Committee meets once a month and clears all the formalities and infrastructural facilities needed in Tamil Nadu for setting up of industries. Tamil Nadu is one of leading industrialised States in India.

According to the annual survey of industries, the value added by factory sector in Tamil Nadu was Rs. 1266.42 crores in 1980-81. The share of Tamil Nadu to all India total is about 10 per cent. The annual rate of increase of value added in the factory sector between 1960-61 to 1978-79 in Tamil Nadu was 14.7 per cent compared to all India annual rate of 13.3 per cent.

The State's industrial growth during the past decades had been steady, the tempo of growth maintained with the number of favourable factors such as power availability, supply of crucial inputs, the turnover of the farm sectors and the labour situation besides the demand pattern as influenced by the general economic climate in the country between 1977 and 1987, the pace of growth from year to year ranged from 4 per cent to 15 per cent the annual average growth rate works out to an impressive 98 per cent. Compared with the national average of 5 per cent the State was notably better placed.

With about 1650 medium and large scale units and about 6400 small scale units, Tamil Nadu was ranked high among the States both in terms of industrial production and value added in manufacture. The State accounts for nearly one-fourth of India's spinning capacity, nearly one-fifth of cement, caustic soda and nitrogenous fertilizer and one-tenth of the nation's production of sugar, bicycles, and calcium carbide. It produces nearly 60 per cent of safety matches, 77 per cent of finished leather and it accounts for about 60 per cent of India's leather export.

Industrial progress, being Tamil Nadu's top priority, had created an ideal climate for the industries to prosper. The industrial sector accounts for about 26 per cent of the net domestic product of Tamil Nadu's economy. Abundant skilled manpower, a good transport system, better power situation and the State Government's encouragement have created vast scope of industrial activity.

In the Seventh plan allocations, the State had earmarked more than 30 per cent on power development amounting to Rs. 2000 crores. An additional installed capacity of 1.416 MW is to be commissioned during the plan period.

The increased pace of development had necessitated such increased allocation and the power shortage could not be completely wiped out. For example, the availability in the year 1984-85 was increased to 13,731 million units from 10,377 million units in 1983-84, but the demand is ever increasing.

Over a period of year 16,000 villages had been electrified till January 1988. It is worthwhile to note that at the beginning of the First Five Year plan (1951-56) only 2,430 villages were electrified. The fact that all but a handful of villages have been electrified is no mean achievement.

The Tamil Nadu Government had won the national award of Rs. 2.5 crores for its exemplary performance in the field of family planning during 1984-85.

Every year, Flag day was celebrated with utmost seriousness in Tamil Nadu. A committee called the Tamil Nadu Standing Flag day and Organisation Committee headed by the Governor of Tamil Nadu organises the 'Flag Day' and donations to the welfare of Ex-servicemen are collected. Towards the Flag day celebrations in 198,3, a sum of Rs. 30, 75, 066. 03 had been collected against the target of Rs. 23,35,000. For the year 1984, the committee had a target of Rs. 31,00,000 and as on November 18, 1985 a sum of Rs. 34,70,887 had been received at the Directorate.

The Flag collections were the source of income to the Tamil Nadu and Services 'personnel Benevolent Fund.' During the year 1984-85,3100 ex-servicemen and their dependants were given financial assistance amounting to Rs. 7,33,362 by way of various grants each as monthly pension, lumpsum grant, marriage grant, pocket money to TB and leprosy patients, immediate relief grant, funeral grant, fire and flood relief, scholarship to the children of Ex-servicemen, training to women dependants of Ex-servicemen and their dependants, etc.

Five tailoring units for training women dependants of deceased/retired/released service personnel were managed by the Tamil Nadu Ex-services Personnel Benevolent Fund. Jai Jawan stalls numbering 237 have been set up throughout the State for the rehabilitation of disabled Jawans (military personnels), war widows and deserving ex-servicemen under the self-employment scheme. Three typewritting and shorthand institutes are functioning at Madras, Thanjavur and Nagerkoil for the Ex-serviceman and their dependants. 12-bedded exclusive wards are kept for ex-servicemen in 14 taluk headquarters hospitals. An old age home for destitute military pensioners that can accommodate 58 persons has come up at Vellore, North Arcot District. A printing-cum-book binding training unit for training women dependants of ex-servicemen has been established at Chengalpattu. An ex-servicemen car park unit has been organised at Madras for engaging ex-servicemen to collect fees for parking fees. Ex-servicemen's aid is sought in the State for election bandobust duties.

Seven Jawans Bhavan (shopping complexes) had been constructed at Tiruchirapalli, Vellore, Salem, Coimbatore, Thanjavur, Madurai and Sivakasi at a cost of Rs. 59 lakhs. These Bhavans earn sizeable revenue that are used for ex-servicemen's welfare.

On 1st July 1982 Tamil Nadu pioneered the Nutritious Meal programme that had been well acclaimed as welfare project, internationally. Tamil Nadu takes care of all the basic needs of children starting from nutritional support and health back up to the free provision of clothes and text-books. At present, 86-88 lakh children are being benefited under the Chief Minister's Nutritious meal programme and 58 10 lakh children are to be benefited by the free supply of uniform.

The Chief Minister's nutritious meal programme had created additional benefits to people at large. Within two months after the implementation of the scheme, lakhs of children in the age group of 6-11 years have additionally enrolled in the schools. Another benefit is the employment opportunity provided by the scheme to thousands of women making the nutritious meal programme as the single largest employment programme for women in India.

The nutritious meal programme had also been extended to ex-servicemen, ex-servicemen's widows who draw old age pension. About 63,000 persons are served by the scheme.

One of the singular achievements of the Tamil Nadu Government was the creation of the Department of Institutional Finance in July, 1983 for monitoring the preparation and the implementation of long term and annual credit plans for the district and for the State. This department is also mobilising bank loans for assisting the weaker sections of society.

In 1983-84 and 1984-85 a number of programmes were implemented to extend loans. In 1983-84, about 5 lakh persons received loans and in 1984-85, more than 6 lakh persons received loans. A target of 8 lakh persons to be reached was being implemented for the year 1985-86.

The Cooperative Societies in Tamil Nadu had been playing a significant role in supporting the farmer, the worker, the artisan and the consumer. Particularly, they offer a countervailing force against the exploitative propensities that develop the economy and thus project and promote the interest of the weaker sections.

On account of drought and floods that prevailed in the State during 1982-83 and 1983-84 short-term loans to an extent of Rs. 30.81 crores were converted into medium-term loan repayable over the succeeding three years and converted loans to the extent to Rs. 2.20 crores were rephased repayable over the succeeding four years. 1.89 lakhs borrowers have thus become eligible to obtain fresh cultivation loans for further seasonal operations. Long-term loan instalments of the extent of Rs. 13.03 crores have also been postponed. The State Government bear 15 per cent of the burden of conversion of short-term loans into medium-term loans.

With a view to reducing the debt burden of agriculturists, Government had given financial assistance to the extent of Rs. 99 crores since 1979-80 upto 1983-84 by way of waiver/ refund of interest to the extent of Rs. 42 crores and write-off of converted/ rephased loans outstanding against small farmers to the extent of Rs. 57 crores. During 1984-85, Government had refunded the amount of interest on overdue instalments and penal interest collected during 1983-84 to the tune of Rs. 82 lakhs to 48,476 borrowers of primary land development banks, who had fully repaid their entire overdues in the year 1983-84. The Government also waived recovery of interest on overdue instalments and penal interest from borrowers of primary land development banks who repaid their entire overdues as on 30th June 1984 before 31st March 1985. More than 45,000 borrowers availed themselves of this interest concession to the extent of Rs. 2.75 crores.

As an incentive for prompt repayment of dues by the borrowers of agricultural service cooperative societies, the Government were providing since 1981-82, a rebate of two per cent in the interest to small farmers, who repay their short-term loans and medium-term loan instalments promptly.

The net work of consumer cooperatives consisted of 3,839 Primary cooperative stores (including 3,013 stores for college and high school students, 302 stores for industrial and plantation workers and 15 strores for women) with 449 branches, 29 cooperative wholesale stores with 1,134 branches and the State Consumers Cooperative Federation. The value of retail sales effected by the consumer cooperatives increased from Rs. 228 crores during 1982-83 to Rs. 268 crores during 1983-84 and to about Rs. 285 crores during the year 1984-85. This was further increased to Rs. 300 crores during 1985-86.

In order to enable the cardholders to draw the essential commodities from the fair price shops quickly, it was decided no fair price shop should have more than 1,000 cards attached to it. Accordingly, shops having more than 1000 cards each were identified and bifurcated with Government assistance. Consequently, 2,850 additional shops have been opened by Cooperatives, 1437 in rural areas and the rest in urban areas.

At present, the Tamil Nadu Milk Producer's Cooperatives Federation was procuring about 6,41,611 litres per day as against 3.65 lakhs litres per day in 1982 through 4,010 Milk producer's Societies covering 6,55,547 animals and benefiting 5,67,399 farmer members. An average of Rs. 18.60 lakhs were paid towards the procurement of milk per day in 1985 as against Rs. 7.80 lakhs in 1982.

The per capita availability of milk had been increased from 68 gms in 1970 to 108 gms. The milk procurement has been increased from 1325 lakh litres per annum to 2343 lakh litres per annum.

The amount paid to the farmers had been increased from Rs. 2847 lakhs per annum to Rs. 6789 lakhs per annum between. 1981-82 to 1984-85.

The Milk powder production had been increased from 984 tonnes per year in 1981 to 3460 tones in year 1984.

Tamil Nadu is committed to attaining the goal of 'Health for all by 2000 AD' through the universal provision of Comprehensive Health Care Services, which laid considerable stress on the preventive, promotive and rehabilitative aspects of delivery, especially, among the rural masses, at their doorstep and in which various health care parameters were to be achieved. In order to achieve the above objective it is proposed to establish one sub-centre per 5,000 population, one primary Health Centre for every 6 sub-centre (30,000 population) and one Community Health Centre for 1,00,000 population.

The Rural Health care facilities were provided by maintaining the primary Health Centres already functioning and by establishing additional primary Health Centres, organising Mobile Health Teams, Mini Health Centres and establishing of upgraded primary Health Centres to offer specialist's services. In Tamil Nadu, 434 primary Health Centres were functioning as on 31st December, 1984, out of 436 primary Health Centres sanctioned.

Out of 434 primary Health Centres, now functioning, 383 primary Health Centres deliver preventive, promotive, curative and Family Welfare Services, while the 51 additional primary Health Centres established under curative and Family Welfare Services. The 30 primary Health Centres which were upgraded into Community Health Centres provide specialists, services with the employment of 2 post-Graduate qualified doctors, one with M. S. qualification and the other with D.G.O. qualification, together with operation facility, X-ray facility, biological and pathological laboratory facilities and facility to admit 30 patients.

Each of the above upgraded primary Health Centres will serve as a referral centre for every four surrounding primary Health Centres. Additional buildings for the 23 Community Health Centres (upgraded primary Health Centres) are nearing completion. During the first year of the 7th Five-year plan period (i.e. 1985-86) it has been proposed to establish 2 Community Health Centres (upgraded primary Health Centres). A total number of 1,315 posts of Assistant surgeons is sanctioned and posted to all the 434 primary Health Centres. Siddha wings are also attached to selected primary Health Centres and they are functioning.

Tamil Nadu, the cradle of Dravidian culture has a variety that is unique to offer to the world. Apart from the marvellous temples, it is the Bharata Natyam and the Karnatic music that makes Tamil Nadu a living civilization.

Tamil Nadu through its 'Iyai Isal Nataka Mandram' encourages and supports artists. Apart from numerous awards, financial aid is given to indigent artists. Film artists are appreciated through the annual Film Awards function. Films especially on Family planning are aided by heavy subsidies.

Handicrafts and handlooms play an important role in the life of Tamil Nadu, where 13,206 craftmen living below poverty line are given assistance and training at a cost of Rs. 137 lakhs. *Khadi* and Village Industries Board provides employment to 6.13 lakhs people.

Almost 18 lakh weavers in Tamil Nadu were included in the Tamil Nadu Governments' insurance plan for agricultural labourers, goldsmiths and craftsmen. It provides a payment of Rs. 10,000 upon death to the next of kin, on a monthly premium of Rs. 10.

There was a retirement plan for weavers that will provide them a minimum gratuity of Rs. 25,000 and a maximum gratuity of Rs. 30,000. The cooperatives could assist the members in paying a monthly premium of Rs. 10 or the members themselves can pay.

Welfare of Women and Children

Being a man of vision M.G. Ramachandran was a great patriot who always stood for India's unity and integrity. He has left a clear stamp of integrity and uprightness in public life. He was an ardent advocate of social reforms.

Child welfare was the infrastructure of a nation's progress and prosperity. It is more so in the case of all developing countries. All sociologists agree that the future of a country depends upon the care and priority accorded to children and their development, physical and mental as well. What the child needs is a package of inputs for fuller and richer development of its personality. The package includes clean environ, nutrition, health care and education. As per the 1981 census, there are 1.21 crore children in the age group of 2 years to 10 years in Tamil Nadu. They form

25 per cent of the total population. Of them, nearly 63 lakhs are estimated to live below poverty line. Article 47 under the Directive Principles of the Constitution of India lays down that "the State shall regard the raising of the level of nutrition, standard of living, the improvement of public health as one of its primary duties".

It was true that ceaseless efforts have been made by the Government of India, State Governments and Nutrition experts to fight malnutrition and under-nutrition by implementing schemes like applied nutrition programme, etc. However, these programmes have touched only a fringe of the problem of malnutrition among children. They deal only with nutritional disorders and not with the wholesome development of the child in its formative stage. The child mortality and morbidity are high in Tamil Nadu. Malnutrition and undernutrition have a grip over this vulnerable group. Calorie—protein malnutrition has been identified as a crucial problem among the children.

Nutrition experts asserted after their researches that at least 60 per cent of the children in the age group of 1 to 6 suffer from nutrition anaemia and calorie protein malnutrition in one form or the other.

True to its tradition of being the path finder in rural rejuvenation work and social uplift, Tamil Nadu launched another new programme called "Chief Minister's Nutritious Noon Meal Scheme" for the benefit of the rural poor children in the age group of 2- 10. This programme is a multi-pronged attack on undernutrition, poverty and illiteracy. It is a catalyst bringing about a transformation in rural areas where it makes a dent in the life of the poverty stricken weaker section and also strikes a blow at the obsolete outlook of tradition bound society.

This programme was born out of the deep love of M.G.R., Tamil Nadu Chief Minister, for the children whom he considered as builders of the society of tomorrow. The pangs of hunger and poverty that he suffered during his childhood were evergreen in his mind. The emaciated physique, the sunken eyes and races of abysmal poverty which describe thousands of poor children in rural areas had moved the Chief Minister and, as a result of his deep study of the chronic poverty of the budding children, he had come out with pragmatic plan to feed the poor children of Tamil Nadu.

A new chapter in the educational history was opened on July 1, 1982, when the noon-meal scheme was inaugurated at Pappakudi village in Tiruchirapalli District. Inaugurating the scheme, Chief Minister MGR said "I request you to forget politics. Look at the sunken stomachs of the 60 lakhs of children and think of their future". He added that the scheme would wipe out the tears of millions of mothers who, toiling below poverty line, were unable to provide even one full meal a day to their children.

The Social Welfare and the Education Departments were engaged in this massive programme. The former looks after the children in the age group of 2 to 4 while the children on the age group of 5 to 9 and 10 to 14 are under the care of Education Department.

The scheme had brought about a phenomenal increase in the school enrolment by 1.60 lakh children. It has stemmed the tide of dropouts. Over 39 lakh children are fed with nutritious noon meal at 32,470 school feeding centres. They are in the age group of 5 to 9. Another facet of the programme is that the Kuzhanthaigal Kappagams (Child Welfare Centres) provide nutritious food to the age group of 2 to 4 *Balasevikas* trained in the art of child-care supervise cooking and feeding. The scheme has now been extended to urban areas also.

The nutritious noon meal scheme had, for the first time, generated stable assured paid employment for nearly 1,65,482 rural women. They are employed as *Balasevikas*, cooks, and helper in 61, 984 child welfare centres. While selecting candidates preference is being given to widows had destitute women. The noon meal scheme has given employment to 42.457 widows and destitutes and 30,000 scheduled caste women work in different capacities. Schemes of this category, spread over the State, involving a number of Government agencies, may naturally have some Saws and loopholes. To plug such loopholes and to ensure; strict supervision, the Government have given training and guidelines to the concerned persons. A high-power committee headed by the Chief Minister and consisting of senior officials and leading public men monitor the programme regularly.

An official-level committee with the Chief Secretary as Chairman advised and assisted field functionaries in charge of implementation of the programme. The Director of school Education and Director of Social Welfare keep a close watch and try to resolve day-to-day problems and also improve the daily functioning pattern. District level committees have also been constituted to ensure the smooth working of the programme.

No one can deny that late Congress leader Kamaraj whom the people of Tamil Nadu affectionately call Perunthalaivar (Great Leader) fathered the Mid-day Meal Programme in Tamil Nadu and thereby made a break through in shattering the dens of illiteracy and in bringing a considerable segment of poor children under educational cover. The Chief Minister's Nutritious Noon Meal Scheme goes a step further and covers all children upto 14 years and the free meal is available throughout the year. The cost of food and its caloric content are increased. Teachers are no longer burdened with the task of collection of funds for the programme or by cooking the food.

Philanthropists, industrialists and other organisations contribute to this laudable cause. The food supplied is not only balanced and nutritious but tasty as well and geared towards the study of physical and mental growth of the children. Rice, Daal, Oil, and locally available vegetables constitute the meal.

Overall Development

If continuity is the hallmark of political success, few will deny the Government of Tamil Nadu its claim to glory. Only west Bengal's Left Front could match the record of the AIADMK which began its 11th year in office in June 1987. On the face of it, M.G. Ramachandran's Government could certainly boast of some achievements, agricultural productivity was higher than in neighbouring States, the irrigation potential had been fully tapped, there had been a marked increase in rural power consumption. But it was by no means certain that Tamil Nadu's progress sustained the momentum that was generated in the 1960s when Kamaraj was Chief Minister. Though regional income increased by an average of 3.8 per cent in the 1977-87 decade it was still well below the all India average of 5.25 per cent. What was more significant, however, was that after a decade in power Government appeared to have gained much of its initial zest and dynamism.

While it might be difficult for Dravida loyalists, reared on iconoclasm and anti-Brahminism, to stomach a Brahmin successor to Annadurai's heir, MGR could at least had the comfort of knowing that the Centre and the Congress would back him, even if erstwhile supporters decided to make their peace with the DMK and Karunanidhi. In fact, Tamil Nadu presented an opportunity for the Congress which might otherwise despair of its future in States that were ruled by Opposition parties. The inevitable realignment that was expected, once the succession was settled, might witness the return of two-party politics which faded out in 1971 when Indira Gandhi in effect abandoned the State to the DMK.

In the words of MGR, "Tamil Nadu occupies a prestigious position in the Industrial map of India. It has a large reservoir of natural resources, and skilled labour. But the growth was hitherto lopsided, for industries developed around major cities alone, leaving the vast rural area industrially barren. This has led to the regional imbalance many areas remaining backward. The AIADMK Government took stock of the situation and started re-drawing the industrial map of Tamil Nadu. With a view to ensure uniform growth, the Government encouraged establishment of small scale industrial units in backward areas, tapping the locally available manpower and generating employment for the rural poor. Though the accent is on developing small industrial units in rural areas, the Government is equally anxious in encouraging the setting up of large and medium industries also in backward areas to ensure harmonious growth in public, private and joint sectors. A number of corporations are engaged in developing necessary infrastructure and providing financial, technical and marketing assistance required for the orderly growth of the private sector. The Tamil Nadu Industrial Development Corporation has set up some large and medium industries in public sector and also promotes industrial units in joint sector in collaboration with private entrepreneurs.

The State Industries Promotion Corporation of Tamil Nadu is engaged in promoting large and medium industries in the private sector hastening the industrial dispersal to the backward areas in the State. The Corporation implements a package of incentives and provides financial assistance to industries under the refinancing scheme of the Industrial Development Bank of India. The incentives offered by SIPCOT include Central subsidy and interest free Sales tax loan of the Stats Government which has been recently increased from Rs. 50 lakhs to Rs. one crore. This institution has so far rendered financial assistance to the tune of Rs. 6,136.65 lakhs generating direct employment for over 46,000 persons. Out of the total assistance, Rs. 5,328 lakhs were sanctioned for projects in backward areas.

The Tamil Nadu Industrial Investment Corporation Ltd. functions as the State's Financial Corporation, assisting establishment of new units and expansion and modernisation of existing units by providing medium term loans, guaranteeing deferred payments for acquisition of machinery and underwriting equity and preference shares, implementing special schemes like financial assistance to technocrats, rural medical practitioners, transport operators and hotels, loan assistance under soft loan schemes and Technician-Entrepreneur schemes, etc.

Upto the end of 1981 3799 units had benefited by the financial assistance extended by this Corporation, which was to the tune of Rs. 3118.4 lakhs, of which Rs. 2515.91 lakhs were sanctioned to small scale industry. In backward areas, 2,045 units were benefited by financial assistance of this Corporation which was of the order of Rs. 1640.42 lakhs. The long coastline of Tamil Nadu is the second largest producer of salt. We have taken up the development of two large salt projects. The recently formed salt Corporation has been entrusted with this work. It will also take up new areas for the purpose and extend financial and marketing facilities to small salt cultivators. It will also establish projects for manufacture of marine chemicals.

Sugar industry being an agro-based industry, occupies an important Place in the rural economy. After the announcement of policy by the Government that in addition to cooperative sector and public sector, private sector is also welcomed, we have had good response. A large number of sugar factories are being planned now. The major break through towards fuller utilisation of bagasse is sought to be done by setting up of a plant for the production of newsprint and writing paper. This project is being implemented with World Bank aid. The project is estimated to cost about 190 crores. The Electronic Corporation of Tamil Nadu has been formed to stimulate the growth of electronic industries in the State by setting up modern electronic units in the public sector and joint sector. The Tamil Nadu Handicrafts Development Corporation provides employment to the unemployed rural artisans and in order to use the local resources available, the Corporation has opened training centres. The labour policy of the Government of Tamil Nadu in securing a fair deal to the labour by various new legislations and amendments to the existing labour laws has been responsible, in large measure for promoting a healthy relationship and understanding between the management and labour, conducive to industrial peace and industrial progress."

Tamil Nadu cultivates variety of crops like rice, millets, pulses, oilseeds, fibres, narcotics, plantation crops and other horticulture products. It is making a steady progress in the field of food production inspite of adverse conditions due to scanty monsoon, untimely rains and floods at times. In the case of rice, Tamil Nadu had excelled in its productivity during the year 1985-86, reaching an all- time high of 2,507 kgs. of rice per hectare. The total production of rice in the State was 56 lakh M.T. during 1985-86, though the coverage was only 22.33 lakh hectares against the normal coverage of 26.5 lakh hectares.

For the year 1986-87 the tempo 'in productivity was to be maintained to reach a target production of 64 lakh M.T. The Agriculture Department under the Chief Ministership of MGR launched a five-step approach with specific production goal at the grassroot level, and it was aiming to increase the Samba production by 750 kgs. of paddy (500 kgs. of rice). This made a breakthrough in production in the State as 80 per cent of the paddy area came under Samba and Thaladi. The Agriculture Department was able to translate the strategy of five tonnes/hectare with a specific target for different cultivating seasons. During the year 1985-86, the Department programmed to reach the five Tonnes/Hectare in 60 per cent of area of Kar and 40 per cent of Samba to have an overall achievement in 50 per cent of the area.

But actually the five Tonnes/Hectare coverage had exceeded the 50 per cent target, and this had reflected in the high production attained that year. Similarly for the year 1986-87 the target of five T/Ha, was fixed at 80 per cent for first crop, i.e., Kar and 50 per cent for the Samba to have a coverage of 65 per cent of the rice area. The five-step approach to increase production of rice will be complimentary to make the five M.T. strategy a successful one over the large area. Under the five-step approach the production technology is to be demonstrated by the subject matter specialist at the sub-division level as a nucleus for the demonstrations to be conducted by the assistant agricultural officers (village extension workers) in their groups.

Accordingly, there would be 32,000 demonstrations on crop production. Pest and disease management is to be monitored through similar technology development and demonstration centres by the subject matter specialists. The IBM concept is emphasised and field adoption has become a reality in the State. To manage the pest and diseases, roving survey and surveillance over 7,116 centres in the State is being initiated in collaboration with the Tamil Nadu Agricultural University in different agro-climatic conditions.

New varieties are introduced in the State through Minikit and demonstrations. In the case of rice one lakh of Minikit are to be distributed to popularise new varieties. In the case of millets, 30,800 Minikits are to be distributed. During this year more than 8,000 Minikits of minor millets are to be distributed. About 3.5 lakh hectares land is cultivated under minor millet in this State and this programme will go a long way in helping dryland farmers. The State is planning to reach a production of 24 lakh tonnes under millets. The major and minor millets are normally cultivated over 18 lakh Ha. The present productivity of millets is around one Megatonn/Hectare and it is to be stepped up to 1.5 Megatonn/ Hectare during this year.

In the case of pulses production an all-time record has been set with 3.67 lakh tonnes from out of 9.67 lakh hectares. New technologies are made use of in the case of pulses like high-yielding varieties, seed treatment, rhizobial culture and spraying of D.A.P. Productivity of pulses has gone up from 270 kgs./ hectare to 386 kgs./hectare. In the case of sugarcane, Tamil Nadu always stands first in its productivity with 100 tonnes/hectare and above. During 1985-86, the area of sugarcane had reached

2.05 lakh hectares with a productivity of 108 Megatonn of cane per hectare. The department is programming to reach still higher productivity in the coming year. In the case of cotton, the all-time high production of six lakh bales reached during the year 1985-86, with a productivity of 358 kgs. per hectare. The offtake of fertilizer has doubled in the past years. During 1976-77, the fertilizer consumption was in the order of 2.9 Megatonn, which showed an increase to 6.68 tonnes during the year 1985-86 and the per acre consumption of fertilizer had reached 100 kgs./hectare.

The Agriculture Department is popularising bio-fertilizers, integrated post-management, integrated nutrient management with systematic planning to create new dimension in the field of agriculture to extend full benefit to the farmers. Among the bio-fertilizers, blue-green algae for rice, azozpirillum for millets, ryzobium for pulses are popularised and the department is taking all steps to meet the increased demand of this low cost technology. The department is forging ahead in bringing the impact of technology in the field of adoption to boost the production in farmlands, with the aid of proven extension approaches under the training and visit scheme.

MGR had stated: "Our efforts for industrial development after Independence have resulted in creation of a sound infrastructure and a number of industrial growth centres. India has emerged as a leading industrialised country. Our products in their quality and performance, stand comparison with the highly industrialised regions. Tamil Nadu has not lagged behind in joining the march of industrial progress in the country. Our performance in areas like textiles, sugar cement and automobiles has given the economy a new fillip and a further leap forward in other areas of industrial development. Tamil Nadu accounts for one-fourth of the spindlages and twenty per cent of cement production in the country. The Industrial climate in Tamil Nadu is conducive for capital investment not only by industrialists in this State, but also by industrialists from other States and non-resident Indians.

The institutional financial facilities available through different sources and promotional activity of District Industries Centres have triggered off development at the village level. The State has done very well in the implementation of the programme for self employment of the educated unemployed.

Increase in employment opportunities was the main objective of the industrial policy pursued by the Government of Tamil Nadu. While steps are being taken to increase agricultural production with a view to increase income and employment generated in this sector, further progress in generating more income and employment in the economy can be made more by broadening and deepening the industrial base in the State.

In the context of the planned development, large, medium and small scale sectors had been assigned roles in such a way that they function in a complementary manner and help in activising and catalysing the forces of growth in the States' economy.

This had been the policy formulated and followed for a decade by the Government of Tamil Nadu under the leadership of dynamic and popular Chief Minister M.G. Ramachandran.

The State Government laid utmost emphasis on encouraging the private entrepreneurial talents in the State and would enter directly only those areas of production which needed Government intervention from angles of social justice, innovation of technology or to correct any imbalances.

Some of the major areas of growth in addition to the textile industry which had existed even earlier, had been in such diverse fields as commercial vehicles, motor cycles, earth moving equipment, casting and forging, heavy electrical equipment, cement, paper and fertilizers to mention only a few. The growth had not been confined to any one sector, but operated over a wide canvas. While a number of important public sector units like Neyveli Complex and the Integral Coach Factory had come up earlier, a large number of new units had also been established in the organised sector.

A few indicators of progress deserved mention. The State accounted for nearly one-fourth of the Country's spinning capacity, nearly one-fourth of commercial vehicles, nearly one-fifth of cement, caustic soda and nitrogenous fertilizers and one-tenth of the Nation's production of sugar, bicycles and calcium carbide. It produces nearly 60 per cent of the Safety Matches, 77 per cent of the Finished leather and accounts for about 60 per cent of the country's leather exports. With its broad-based and well balanced industrial development policy of MGR, Tamil Nadu occupied an important place in the Industrial map of India.

The growth and dispersal of the Industries all over the State was largely due to the infrastructure and other incentives -including financing and training facilities offered by the State. A noteworthy point was that above one third of the Industrial Licences issued between 1977-81 in the State have been given to units in 'backward areas'.

According to the IDBI study of the Statewise distribution of assistance between July 1980 and June 1981, Tamil Nadu held the first place in the sanctions and second position in the disbursement among the States of the country. This indicates significant progress made inspite of various difficulties.

To give a powerful thrust to the dispersal of Industries in backward areas, several incentives had been provided by the Government to enable entrepreneurs to establish industries undertakings in backward areas. This included, in addition to concessional finance extended by the All India Term Lending Institutions, outright subsidy on fixed capital investment, Interest Free Sales Tax Loan, etc.

Another unique scheme introduced by the State Government was regarding the development of Electronics, Drugs and Pharmaceuticals and Automobile Ancillary Industries. Considering the large employment potential of these industries, subsidy to the extent of 10 per cent of the fixed assets or at the rate of Rs. 20,000 for every regularly employed worker of Rs. 10 lakhs, whichever was lower, available to these industries located anywhere in Tamil Nadu.

Originally, 33 talukas in Tamil Nadu were made eligible for 15 per cent Central Subsidy. The detailed analysis of the blocks in which the Central Investment Subsidy was in force (i.e. in 33 talukas in this State consisting of 90 blocks) revealed that, thanks to the Central Subsidy Scheme of the Government of India, there had been rapid growth of industries in a large number of blocks. Nevertheless, the analysis also revealed that in as many as 41 blocks out of 90 blocks there was no major or medium industry. Hence, following the spirit of the policy decision of the Government of India, these Blocks would need assistance to grow.

TIDCO had promoted a large number of units in the joint sector in association with private entrepreneurs, and it has also started a number of large and medium industries which are in the public sector. Some of the areas in which this Corporation has ventured are in the field of Steel Casting, Cement industrial explosives, Nitric acid, Ammonium nitrate, Magnesium metal, Petrochemicals, Tobacco, Television,. Leather, Pharmaceuticals, Fertilizers, etc.

The task of promoting and developing major and medium units in the private sector and of hastening the process of industrialisation in underdeveloped areas had been entrusted with the State Industries Promotion Corporation of Tamil Nadu (SIPCOT) which implements a Package of incentives are: subsidy for conducting feasibility studies, routing of interest free sales tax loan, sanction and disbursals of Central and State subsidies, direct financial assistance, etc.

The development of potential growth centres in the backward districts of State and provision of developed industrial plots, provision of ancillary services to entrepreneurs are among the other services rendered by this organisation. SIPCOT which presently administers two Industrial Complexes in Hosur and Ranipet is setting up five more such complexes at Tuticorin, Manamadurai, Cuddalore, Gummidipoondi and Pudikottai. The units coming up in these new complexes will be eligible for the Central/State Capital investment subsidy, Interest free Sales Tax Loan and exemption from power cuts for an initial period of five years from the date of the commencement of the unit.

To encourage investment in industries in Tamil Nadu by non-resident Indians, a special International Cell had been set up in SIPCOT. The non-resident who wishes to set up an industry in the State can entrust all the preliminary work with SIPCOT which will arrange for obtaining clearances and the entrepreneur is required to come in only at the final stage.

The Tamil Nadu Industrial Investment Corporation Limited (TIIC) functions as the State Financial Corporation of Tamil Nadu.

It assisted in the establishment of new units and the expansion and modernisation of existing units by providing medium term loans guaranteeing deferred payments for acquisition of machinery and underwriting of equity and preference shares.

The TIIC was also implementing special schemes like financial assistance to technocrats, rural practitioners, transport operators and hotels, loan assistance under soft loan schemes, Technocrat-entrepreneur schemes, etc. With a view to promote larger employment opportunities, especially in the small scale sector, this Corporation disburses loans of the order of Rs. 50 crores per annum.

To promote and accelerate the industrial growth of small scale and tiny sector industries Small Industries Development Corporation (SIDCO) had been formed for the following functions:

(i) Provision of infrastructural facilities (ii) procurement and distribution of key raw materials (iii) Marketing products of SSI units (iv) implementation of a package of incentives, viz. Central Investment Subsidy, State's Capital Subsidy, Margin Money Assistance under sick industries, Rehabilitation scheme, Seed Money Assistance, Interest Free Sales Tax Loan Assistance and I.T. Power Subsidy, etc.

Spectacular growth had been witnessed in the small scale sector where there has been more than 100 per cent increase in the number of permanent registration certificates issued by the State Directorate of Industries (such certificates being given for units which are either actually in production or are in readiness to do so).

The number of such units had gone up to 47, 735 at the end of February, 1983 as against 18, 789 at the end of March, 1978. This sector accounted for an impressive range of goods including the sophisticated and high technology-oriented items. A vibrant ancillary had emerged to meet the diverse needs of the large public and private sector units.

As the development in the small scale sector was left largely to private initiative, the State Government has been using the Industrial Cooperative Sector as an instrument for generating development in employment-oriented industries like Matches,

Tea, Coir, etc., particularly in rural areas of the State and with Government's assistance and support the number of such societies has increased from 297 in March, 1978 to 898 at the end of March, 1983.

One of the major assets of the State was the highly trained and disciplined manpower which the State possesses in abundance. This force can truly provide the base for a technocrat entrepreneurship with progressive improvement in technology. This would clearly indicate that the direction of future growth is in high value added, high technology products. Among the areas which come to mind in this context are high precision engineering, electronics, basic and fine chemicals and sophisticated machinery.

The Electronic Corporation of Tamil Nadu (ELCOT) which had been set up by the State Government for the development of electronics industries in the State and has already implemented various projects for manufacture of components and it has also taken up production of digital Electronic watches and welcomes entrepreneurs for establishing joint sector projects.

Tamil Nadu sought to be a pioneer in the use of non-conventional sources of raw materials for the manufacture of newsprint and writing paper. The public sector, Tamil Nadu newsprint and Writing Paper. Limited is implementing a Rs. 190 crores project for the manufacture of newsprint and writing paper based on bagasse from sugar mills.

A novel arrangement had been entered into with the sugar factories under which Tamil Nadu Newsprint and Writing Paper Ltd., has undertaken to supply steam for the process and power needs of the sugar factories in exchange for bagasse. The World Bank is extending as 100 million assistance for this project. Considering the large availability of bagasse in the country, the successful completion of this project is likely to lead to many more such units coming up in the country.

As a result of the concerted efforts taken by the Government of Tamil Nadu, the Government of India had now sanctioned the formation of the third Free Trade Zone in Tamil Nadu.

A site very near to the Meenakkam Air port at Madras comprising 500 acres had been selected and speedy steps are being taken to provide infrastructural facilities, more than hundred applications have been received for allotment of land for locating their industries. The applicants who have applied are mostly from sectors like Electrical and Electronics; Textiles and ready-made Garments, Leather and Leather products, Engineering and Building materials and automobile ancillaries, etc. The opportunity for setting up of Industrial units in Tamil Nadu is open to entrepreneurs all over India.

In the words of MGR: "Tamil Nadu has been waging a valiant fight to bring about a big change in the rural landscape. All economists agree that the vast rural masses have yet to reap the fruits of our planned endeavour. The nine-point rural self-sufficiency programme which we have launched has been designed with a view to providing better amenities to rural community. Tamil Nadu has industrial culture. Our skilled manpower are manning the shop-floors in many major undertakings all over the country. The institutional finance and the Industrial infrastructure that the various industrial corporations of the Government provide serve as a fillip for further growth and development of industries in the state."

According to MGR: "Massive increase in employment through promotion of industries, particularly in the small scale and cottage industries sectors continues to be the basic objective of the State Government. An environment conducive to progress has been created with bids fair to bring about a faster and a more balanced growth in the coming years. While there will be increasing emphasis on the growth of small industries and rural industrialisation, the Government of Tamil Nadu is also taking necessary steps to promote large and medium industries in a harmonious manner to strengthen the industrial infrastructure and to generate additional employment. It has been the constant policy of this Government to instil confidence in the minds of entrepreneurs and create favourable conditions for growth and development of industries. The tempo of industrialisation in the State could be gauged from the fact that the number of registered factories increased from 8,506 in 1977 to 9, 139 in 1979. The major instrument for development in the large and medium-scale sector is the Tamil Nadu Industrial Development Corporation. At present it is implementing 58 projects in public and joint sectors. I would like to mention that one of the powerful agencies of the Industries Department for employments generation for weaker sections and the rural population has been the industrial cooperative. During 1979-80 the number of cooperative societies registered was 559 as against 297 in 1977-78. The role of the State Industries Promotian Corporation of Tamil Nadu Limited (SIPCOT) is to plan, promote and develop medium and major industries. SIPCOT has been playing an effective role in fulfilment of its task. This Government is determined to banish poverty, hunger, disease and unemployment from the State. In the name of our leader, Anna, I dedicate myself to the service of the people. The Government of Tamil Nadu is making a determined effort to work for the establishment of an egalitarian social order envisaged by Arignar Anna (late C.N. Annadurai)."

Not Controversial

As a Non-Congress Chief Minister M.G. Ramachandran built a rapport with the Congress ruling Centre without being controversial.

Congress Working Committee on December 26, 1987 expressed a deep sense of grief at the demise of M.G. Ramachandran.

In a resolution adopted at a meeting, presided over by the party President Rajiv Gandhi, it paid glowing tributes to the founder and leader of the AIADMK.

The resolution said that the passing away of Ramachandran had deprived the country of the services of a leader who not only served Tamil Nadu but always kept the interests of the country at heart.

The Congress would keep itself away from the process of AIADMK electing a successor to Ramachandran.

"We will keep mum in this matter. It is their internal affair to elect a new leader. Why should we interfere?"

Congress general secretary in charge of Tamil Nadu said in New Delhi.

At the Helm for a Long Time

Except for a brief spell of some months in 1980, Ramachandran had been at the helm of affairs in Tamil Nadu since 1977. His attitude towards the Centre was conciliatory and not confrontationist. In this he has been different from another actor-turned-Chief Minister of Andhra Pradesh, N.T. Rama Rao late, Ramachandran's constructive and positive ideas had been of help to the Centre in handling the emotive Sri Lankan issue. It was only a few days before his death that Prime Minister, Rajiv Gandhi, spent some hours with Ramachandran in Tamil Nadu. Indicative of the close relationship between the Centre and Ramachandran was the decision of the President, the Vice-President and the Prime Minister to visit Madras (Now, Chennai) immediately after the news of his demise reached New Delhi.

On the cold night of December 17 1987, MGR was waiting in New Delhi for return of the Prime Minister to the capital and demanding a near- midnight meeting. MGR was said to be greatly disturbed over certain Congress faction's campaign against him in Tamil Nadu and wanted to complain to Rajiv Gandhi about the attempt to project Union Minister P. Chidambaram, of Harvard fame, as the next Chief Minister. He had his own angle about Sri Lanka affairs. He was also demanding inclusion of atleast one AIADMK nominee to Union Cabinet. Because of MGR's furious insistence, Prime Minister's office had to grant the late hour interview and MGR returned to Madras next morning; that was his last air journey. He wanted to strengthen his position vis-a-vis factional politics of Tamil Nadu Congress by ensuring himself of the visit of President Venkataraman. In Tamil Nadu politics, Chidambaram was Resident AICCI General Secretary. Shri G.K. Moopanar's choice and MGR presumably wanted Rashtrapti to restrain Gandhi family's favourite General secretary. Now, after MGR's death, it will not he surprising if the Congress formally appeals to AIADMK to merge itself with the ruling: party.

Rapport with Centre

MGR had managed not only to establish an excellent working relationship with the Centre but also maintained some balance in the relationship between the ruling party and the Congress because such a strategy suited him to keep the DMK at bay. With his exit from the political scene and with the second rank AIADMK leadership enjoying a diminished Stature in relation to Karunanidhi, it should not be surprising if a sea change were to take place in Tamil Nadu politics. However, the one issue which will engage some attention in Delhi is the level of support which can be expected from the AIADMK for India's Sri Lankan policy in the immediate future.

MGR himself was not always in agreement with Delhi's policies and approach towards the Sri Lankan Tamil problem but he nonetheless acted as a strong buffer between Delhi and the intense and emotional public opinion in the State on the Sri Lankan question. MGR did not conceal his partiality for the militant Liberation Tigers of Tamil Eelam (LTTE) leadership, particularly V. Prabhakaran, whom he used to help in many ways without Delhi's knowledge and consent. The grant of Rs. 4 crore out of the State's contingency funds to the LTTE announced publicly by MGR had taken Delhi by surprise. At that time Indo-Sri Lankan relations were considerably strained, and MGR's gesture was interpreted as a factor which would exacerbate feelings in Sri Lanka. The July 29, 1987 agreement between Rajiv Gandhi and the Sri Lankan President Jayewardene received only a lukewarm endorsement from MGR.

He appeared to have been disappointed with the turn of events in Jaffna after the agreement began to be implemented. Available reports suggest that he was bitter at the way IPKF was put in the situation of fighting and killing cadres of the LTTE, and he had expressed himself strongly in a letter to Rajiv Gandhi from Baltimore, where he was convalescing. The Prime Minister had to send a special emissary from Vancouver to Baltimore to explain the Government's stand and also persuade MGR to be more emphatic in his support for the agreement. Delhi was initially opposed to MGR's suggestion for a limited ceasefire in Jaffna to enable the LTTE leadership to fall in line.

However, it subsequently realised that MGR was serious, and in the belief that he could play a major role in persuading the LTTE leadership to lay down arms, it declared a 48-hour truce.

The LTTE leadership did not adhere to the truce, and the IPKF resumed operations. However, there was little evidence to support the theory advanced in New Delhi that MGR was disenchanted with the LTTE over its response to the limited truce. If anything, available evidence suggests that MGR not only made another substantial financial grant to the LTTE leadership on condition that its cadres would remain disciplined while in Tamil Nadu but also renewed his request to Mr. Gandhi to resume negotiations with V. Prabhakaran with a view to ending a political settlement. Even now after five months of the IPKF operations in Jaffna, the Centre has no clear assessment of the range of public opinion in Tamil Nadu over the happenings in Sri Lanka's northern and eastern provinces. It has been merely content to rely on the political clout and influence of MGR to curb adverse public opinion in the State and continue his role as a buffer, notwithstanding the popular feelings of MGR's death, therefore, comes at a time when Delhi had set much store by his support for its policies in Sri Lanka.

Only one Minister in MGR's Cabinet- S. Ramachandran (Food and Civil Supplies) — had been closely involved in shaping the State's policy in respect of the Tamil militants who had taken shelter in Tamil Nadu during the past four years. He also invariably accompanied MGR to the Capital for talks with the Prime Minister on the Sri Lankan issue. He was also present in Colombo on July 29, 1987, at the time of the signing of the agreement. In effect, Ramachandran acted as MGR's spoken and interpreter during the latter's discussions in New Delhi.

MGR had remained physically incapacitated for the better part of the last two years since he suffered a stroke and had to be flown to New York for treatment. He had distanced himself considerably from day-to-day administrative chores. After his return from his recent trip to USA, his physical condition did not improve significantly. However, his mental faculties had not been affected, and knowledgeable sources here say that he was able to convey through his Minister S. Ramachandran, his strong views on the Sri Lankan situation and clearly indicate what he thought should be done.

By steering an even course under MGR, Tamil Nadu perhaps lost in the race for limelight as a Non-Congress State. Unlike the other non-Congress states, it did not raise shrill voices against the Centre and join in conclaves with the one-point objective of continuing a campaign against New Delhi. This kind of politics helps individual politicians too. It gives them an image of strong men, tilting at powers higher up. Taking on the highest authority lends to the opponent an aura all its own to MGR's great credit, he turned his back on this kind of politics. This, when it was specially highly fashionable to be part of the trade union of non-Congress Chief Ministers.

By doing so, in a way he opted out of the confrontationist role. Instead of being shrill, he went in for deep sobriety in public affairs even if it often seemed to put him in the wrong. The dark glasses and the fur cap became synonym with a constructive attitude to politics, particularly the Centre State politics. In the process, MGR has a lesson or two to teach in Indian politics. He showed that it was possible for a political leader to get the affection of his people even without taking strident postures, without having to resort to anger and invective. He proved that it was even possible to improve one's standing with the people without making confrontation the stock in one's trade, provided, of course, one followed the right policies. He also proved that it was possible for a Non-Congress State to cooperate with the Congress Government at the Centre. Tamil Nadu did not lose out in the long run nor did the Centre try to topple the non-Congress Government there. This is not an ordinary lesson. It has immense importance for the development of our federal structure.

End of Legend

With the demise of Chief Minister of Tamil Nadu M. G. Ramachandran ended the legend of a celluloid politician. But it might well mean a sharp twist in the politics of a volatile State which has defied the national pattern consistently since it rejected the Congress at the 1967 elections. One Dravidian party replaced another during the 20-year interregnum. The Dravida Munnetra Kazhagam, the result of a split in the Dravida Kazhagam (DK) shortly after independence, swept to a awesome victory riding a frenzied anti-Hindi wave which began in 1965 when Madras (Now, Channai) was on fire over the imposition of an official language. But after the death of the DMK's founder leader, C. N. Annadurai in 1969 the party was inevitably to split. The clash of interest was between the organisation man M. Karunanidhi and the matinee idol M. G. Ramachandran. Unlike Andhra Pradesh Chief Minister N. T. Rama Rao, another celluloid politician of the latter day, Ramachandran did not quit films to found a party. He combined his cinematic role with his politics. Karunanidhi peripherally belonged to filmdom as a successful script writer like his mentor Annadurai but his son was arising star in the Tamil film firmament and was sought to be built up with Karunanidhi's clout as the Chief Minister and the party leader invoking of course the "Dravidian" (synonymous with Tamil) ethos. The result was Ramachandran's Anna Dravida Munetra Kazhagam flater to give itself a misleading prefix "All-India" but despite its spectacular debut at a by-election, the new party had to wait till 1977 to win power which it has held without break.

The Congress relationship with the AI-ADMK represented a co-option model. Where one cannot regain a state, come to terms with the regional party. The DMK's secessionism of the 1950s had been subdued into Tamil nationalism by the early 1960s. A degree of special federal accommodation was called for and it did materialise. But Tamilnadu and Ramachandran became a pivotal factor in India's Sri Lanka policy. India's involvement in Sri Lanka had two compulsions. One was domestic because of the cultural identity of Sri Lanka's ethnic Tamils (not only the immigrant Tamils of the plantations) and the empathy of fifty million Indian Tamils for the smaller number of their linear descendants across the Palk Straits. This was the basic domestic compulsion behind India's support to the aspirations in Jaffna. Ramachandran's own support for the Liberation Tigers of Tamil Eelam in particular exerted pressure on New Delhi's policy options here. The ethnic Tamils of Sri Lanka owe much to him.

Sea of Mourners

Never in the history of the world have so many people mourned so intensely the death of a leader as that of Tamil Nadu Chief Minister, M.G. Ramachandran. More than 15 lakh people followed MGR's body to the burial place. More than 15 persons embraced death to escort him to the other world. Men, women and children cried in such frenzy as if one of their own blood brothers had died. No wonder MGR addressed them as "my blood-brothers and sisters" when he spoke to his people. India has seen the death of great leaders, Mahatma Gandhi, Jawaharlal Nehru, Indira Gandhi People were seen shedding tears at their funeral. But such sorrow is seldom witnessed. Lakhs of men and women crying aloud, tearing their hair and beating their breasts in maddening grief. What is that unseen cord that tied MGR with his people? To say that it is the film image of a saviour-hero, will be too simple. No doubt, the Tamils are a sentimental people and often forget the line dividing fantasy with reality.

The saviour-hero, whose part MGR played in film after film, stuck to the actor. When he was inducted to politics by the late C.N. Annadurai, MGR entered the public scene as a political saviour of Tamil masses. But other equally capable actors too had entered the Tamil Nadu politics without reaching anywhere near MGR. Shivaji Ganesan, the Congress Member of Parliament had such a hero image, but is a political zero in the State. MGR had the knack of making his misfortunes serve him. The villain in his films, M. R. Radha, once shot him in real life and injured his neck. This got him much public sympathy. And whenever his image was getting a bit tarnished, he was blessed with some "mishap" in the shape of serious illness, so that public attention was diverted.

His arch-rival, DMK leader M. Karunanidhi, had tried all the weapons in his armoury against MGR. What could be more damaging to a Tamil leader than to be proved that he was no Tamil? In fact, MGR's family was from Kerala, his father Marudur Gopala Menon was an official in the service of the Ceylon Government in Kandy. The DMK partymen tried to paint MGR as a Malayali, so that he might be alienated from Tamils. But people did not care. It was Karunanidhi's statue they broke into pieces on the day MGR died. MGR's AIADMK and Karunanidhi's DMK are all offshoots of the original Dravida Kazhagam of E.V. Ramaswami Naicker, the atheist-iconoclast who still remains the philosopher patron of Tamils. It is an irony that the followers of the great atheist made gods of men. And the iconoclast's disciples installed own statues while they were still alive.

Surprisingly MGR kept a low profile during the war of words between his party functionaries. His announcement at the last Cabinet meeting offering his resignation from the Chief Ministership stopped abruptly the infighting. Everyone trooped to him with his resignation letter. One party activist, Ganapathy, could not bear it any more. He attempted self-immolation in front of the Secretariat. It was clear that without MGR they were nobody. Their own political career was inextricably linked to the charismatic leader. When reporters asked, later, whether the storm in the party was over, M. G. R. said with a smile: "There has not been even a breeze."

A Critical Review

Raise a star to catch a star: having failed to make any dent in the politics of the State after 1967, the Congress (I) then seemed to be in mood to put its future in the hands of a filmstar in Tamil Nadu. The last Congress Chief Minister in the State was Bhaktavatsalam who was wiped out by C.N. Annadurai's Dravida Munnetra Kazhagam in 1967; in fact, it would be accurate to say that the last popular Congress Chief Minister in the State was Kamaraj Nadar and after him came the deluge. Since 1967, the DMK movement has split, with M.G. Ramachandran splitting the party and then winning the polls to be elected and then re-elected as Chief Minister but even after the split, the Congress (I) could not become the second most important force in the State with the two DMK parties, and it had not always chosen the winning side.

While its alliance with Karunanidhi's DMK worked in the parliamentary election of 1980, suffered a defeat in the subsequent elections to the State Assembly when MGR was able to get the better of the formidable alliance against him. Now that election were scheduled for 1984, the time had come to search for the correct partner. This time it seemed likely that Indira Gandhi would opt for Ramachandran. Karunanidhi himself seemed to have realised that in 1983 he was being coy about the opposition conclaves held in Vijayawada and Srinagar but during the year 1984 he had already come to Calcutta, and, more than that, announced that his party would live to host the next conclave in Madras in April.

But before Indira Gandhi entered the expected alliance with Ramachandran, she was doing what she could to beef up her party's support in the State and the man given the job seemed to be the Congress star Shivaji Ganesan.

There was a demand then that Ganesan be made the President of the Tamil Nadu Pradesh Congress (I) Committee so that he could formally lead the troops into battle rather than M. Palanianoi who could hardly claim to send the masses swooning in the fashion that Ganesan might manage. Ganesan had given us a preview of political histrionics when he "broke down" and cried beside the body of a fan who died accidentally on the way to his rally and he could be expected to use his fan clubs and repeat his emotional appeals for a "Congress revival" all over the State. Ganesan had begun claiming the mantle of Kamaraj Nadar, though it was not known whether this was being done with the permission of his "Amma" Indira Gandhi since Kamaraj had no love lost for Indira Gandhi after she broke the Congress in 1969. However, this might be the least of Indira Gandhi's problems vis-a-vis Ganesan. What she and Ramachandran should be more worried about were Ganesan's transparent aspirations to become the Chief Minister. MGR might be willing to hand over Lok Sabha seats to Indira Gandhi, but he surely was in no mood to give up his chair, was he? In fact, this was why he wanted the State Assembly elections and the Lok Sabha elections to be held simultaneously in his State, so that the chances of a knife in the back after the elections were eliminated. Ramachandran was a wise man.

What gave MGR popularity? It began with his career as an actor, unsurpassed in appeal since cinema began in Tamil Nadu. This appeal was based both the positive and the negative aspects of the specific kind of social movement which got embodied in the Dravida Kazhagam to begin with. It was an appeal that conveyed the sense of oppression of those among the down-trodden who had arrived and found there was no place to go. Their frustration enabled them to appreciate, mobilise and utilise the grievances of those still more down-trodden but it kept the latter in a state of semi-stupor by focusing on anti-Brahminism and so-called Dravidianism. This illusion of awakening was not just illusion. It produced results of a certain measure of movement upward and coming up from anonymity. It was both illusion and reality. Nothing could have created a better atmosphere for a superstar to emerge. MGR filled that role with his inimitable verve and skill.

There is no reason to call it a Tamil renaissance. It was not Bharati who strode forward inspite of all the official respect paid to him and to the eminent figures of Tamil's tremendous past. It was its degradation and cheapening in the name of popularisation. There was the spread of vulgarity and corruption on a massive scale and a lumpenisation all-round. This was possible because while the Congress failed to appreciate the need for taking the lead to initiate radical socio-economic reforms, the Communists underestimated the need to spread revolutionary anti-imperialism and to take up the weapon of culture.

Both these national formation compromised with the Dravida Kazhagham (DK), Dravida Munentra Kazhagham (DMK) and All India Anna Dravida Munnetra Kazhagham (AIADMK) at different times and in different ways. Nevertheless, MGR did not simply continue the movement which had created him, he began to try to give it a somewhat different orientation. He had the quality which above all, distinguished all those who had stayed in the hearts of the poor and the deprived-compassion. He felt for them and the charity he bestowed was not false, though there were political considerations behind the distribution of vests, plastic rain coats and then, the midday meal for school-going children. This was mainly non-productive populism but the mid-day meal was a help, of much needed nutrition supply on a mass scale.

But it conveyed a sense of genuine caring helping both he who cared and those he cared for. In addition in the last period there was a turn towards understanding Tamil Nadu's place in India and as a part of it. In this he was helped and even guided by Prime Minister Indira Gandhi (whom people in Tamil Nadu called "Amma", the mother) who represented par excellence the capacity of Indian culture and civilization of absorption by enlargement, enriching itself by bringing in the new and not by obliterating what it encountered. He was also greatly assisted by the Communist leaders Baladendayutham and Kalyansundaram. These two leaders were outstanding in their capacity to combine anti-imperialist nationalism with directly class tasks. They were Indians but rooted among the working people and the oppressed of Tamil Nadu. The result was the greatest contribution that MGR made to history—the indispensable support that he gave to the central Government in its efforts to help solve the ethnic problem in Sri Lanka. In this process there have been errors of judgement. The main thing, however, is that the Indira-MGR united front and that of Rajiv Gandhi MGR illustrated that Tamils needed India even when not a part of it, what to speak of within India.

It also illustrated that the whole of Indira is affected by the problems of Tamils even when they are citizens of Sri Lanka. What to speak when they are part of ourselves but the weakness inherent in the great popularity of MGR remained and was constantly fed by that popularity and required by it and that was hero-worship. The hero needed the masses to remain always as worshippers. He did not realise that this in fact, lessened him. Perhaps he could not do more and, therefore, could not take his place among the Himalayan peaks where Mahatma Gandhi, Nehru and Indira stand.

This is one of the reasons why MGR would be critically assessed when the Gramscian test is applied—the stature of your successors. Mahatma Gandhi and Jawaharlal Nehru passed this test admirably. Indira Gandhi is still being tested in this respect, among Rajiv Gandhi's many responsibilities this is most important. MGR, however, never thought or even reacted the very thought of there being somebody who could be his successor. After all, the successor could also be an usurper. A superstar has only rivals, because there is no person to succeed it does not mean that there could have been one. The AIADMK is, in fact, a contradiction in terms. It can neither be all-India nor can it be the DMK. It can be either. It cannot be both. It is here that there is reason for hope.

The bitterest enemy of the man was the DMK leader Karunanidhi. It was no accident that the crowds mourning MGR tried to destroy the Statue of Karunanidhi. Indeed, if Tamil Nadu is to fully find itself and play its fully role as part of India it must rid itself of the DMK. It owes this to India, to itself and to MGR. This would not happen spontaneously. It cannot be accomplished by the AIADMK more so when MGR is not there. It cannot be done by the Congress (I) which lacks the organisation, the personalities and the requisite mass support. Indeed its greatest asset is that Prime Minister Rajiv Gandhi is recognised by the Tamil masses as Indira Gandhi's worthy son. It cannot be done by both these parties together. The left is required to give the anti-DMK alliance, the perspective and the radical cutting edge that is needed.

MGR and Rajiv Gandhi

Prime Minister Rajiv Gandhi said in Madras (Chennai) on December 24, 1987, that M.G. Ramachandran would be remembered not only by the people of India but also of Sri Lanka.

In a condolence message released at the Rajaji Hall, where Ramachandran's body had been kept for public homage, the Prime Minister said: Ramachandran was unswerving in the struggle to ensure honour and respect for the Tamils of Sri Lanka, their safety, security and full participation as equal citizens in the country.

M.G. Ramachandran, he said, was equally unswerving in his insistence that violence was no answer to the problems. He had stressed that "not through mindless killings and maiming of innocents will the legitimate rights of Tamils be secured, but through the path shown by Mahatma Gandhi".

In his message, Prime Minister Rajiv Gandhi said, "the nation mourns the passing away of one of the great sons, MGR was above all, a patriot imbued with deep feeling for his country. He had a profound pride in her glorious heritage and love for all her people. To him, unity of India was sacrosanct and the preservation of her integrity a sacred duty.

He sought unity of India as rooted in the hearts of every Indian stretching back thousands of years of history. His mind soared above all narrow divisions and petty loyalties. To him the service of the people of Tamil Nadu was the service of the people of India.

Ramachandran's life's work exemplified with the ethical and moral values which have kept our nation united through all deeds for centuries.

Earlier Prime Minister Rajiv Gandhi said in Pudukottai, (Tamil Nadu) on December 21, 1987, that the late Tamil leader Satyamurthi made a lasting contribution to the principles and ideologies of the Congress and truly laid the foundation on which modern India was being built today.

After unveiling a statue of the late leader at the public office buildings complex, the Prime Minister drove in an open jeep to the Rajah College ground where he addressed a rally.

Describing his visit to Pudukottai as a "pilgrimage to the hallowed spot in our freedom movement", the Prime Minister recalled how 50 years ago, in 1937 Jawaharlal Nehru and Satyamurthi motored to Pudukottai. The then British regime banned their entry into the town but undaunted the two made a padayatra (walking by feet). It was Satyamurthi who was instrumental in organising the first tour of Mahatma Gandhi in Tamil Nadu.

Describing him as an orator par excellence and one who wielded a powerful pen, Rajiv Gandhi said, Satyamurthi through his cogent arguments aroused the people of Madras Presidency to follow Gandhiji and come into the Congress fold.

Satyamurthi was also a mentor and guide, and Rajaji and Kamaraj came under his inspired leadership. His political diplomacy in making Kamaraj the President of the Tamil Nadu Congress Committee (TNCC) himself opting to work as the General Secretary of the party demonstrated his "dignity and humility".

Sacrificing his lucrative practice as a lawyer, he joined politics at a time when there seemed little prospect for freedom and what he faced was only struggle, imprisonment, lathis, exile and even the hangman's noose.

Rajiv Gandhi said he was a brave man like Satyamurthi and Subramanya Bharathi who were attracted to the freedom struggle in those tough days. In Bharathi, Satyamurthi found a patriot on whose tongue the goddess of patriotism danced. Though Satyamurthi did not live to see the country free, "he is certainly one of the builders of modern India".

Rajiv Gandhi emphasised that through these four decades, "we have followed the ideals and principles of the founding fathers of freedom".

Pointing out that more than statistical and material development what was important was the development of the human beings, Rajiv Gandhi said, "We have to uplift the poorest in this country." Contending that there was no point in merely repeating the slogans of the past, Rajiv Gandhi declared, "We have to follow the path of Mahatma Gandhi and Jawaharlal Nehru and simultaneously apply the ideas and advances of the modern world to uplift the poor materially and spiritually".

Rajiv Gandhi adorned Madam Lakshmi Krishnamurthy, daughter of Satyamurthi with a *ponnadai* (a piece of cloth in honour) and also presented a silk saree to her on behalf of the Tamil Nadu Government. Before leaving the dais, Rajiv Gandhi spent a few minutes with Madam Lakshmi Krishnamurthy exchanging pleasantries.

R.M. Veerappan, Tamil Nadu Minister for Local Administration, who presided over the function organised by the Tamil Nadu Government said, Satyamurthi was not only an eminent parliamentarian and an orator but also a great leader and disciplinarian who nourished the Congress organisation.

V.V. Swaminathan, Tamil Nadu Information Minister said, Prime Minister Rajiv Gandhi hailing from a patriotic family which has made great sacrifices is the most appropriate person to unveil the statue of Satyamurthi.

S. Thirunavukkarasu, Housing Minister, Tamil Nadu said, the people of the State would always remember with gratitude Indira Gandhi and Rajiv Gandhi for all the consideration shown by them in the well being of the Chief Minister M.G. Ramachandran.

Prime Minister Rajiv Gandhi on December 21, 1987 (in Madras) called for inculcating in every mind scientific temper and attitude which would give the nation the strength and ability to cope with the challenges of technology and science of the decades to come.

Rajiv Gandhi recalled how seven decades ago Jawaharlal Nehru earnestly looked for an India there where would be a scientific temper in all the people which would overcome superstitions and be morally and mentally ready to face the difficulties and challenges that lay ahead.

Rajiv Gandhi while unveiling a 10-feet bronze statue of Jawaharlal Nehru at the Kathipara Junction, the southern entrance to the city, "Let us today pledge anew to Jawaharlal Nehru's ideals of independence, unity and integrity, democracy, socialism, secularism and non-alignment," he said amidst cheers from the audience.

Presiding over the function, M.G. Ramachandran said, the people of Tamil Nadu wanted to have in Madras a statue of the architect of modern India, Jawaharlal Nehru. "Their long cherished desire is being fulfilled today."

Ramachandran said, successive generations of the Nehru family had been playing a crucial role in the development and progress of India. On the foundation laid by Nehru, his daughter, Indira Gandhi, had built up his grandson, Prime Minister Rajiv Gandhi who is taking India to new heights and creating history to the marvel of even the developed countries.

In his 30- minute speech, Prime Minister Rajiv Gandhi, touched upon the unique civilization and culture of India which was 5,000 years old and had flourished in diversity. For centuries, India was a nation that was sought from every corner of the globe. "Although we succumbed politically, sometimes, economically, spiritually India was always India, no matter whatever influence came upon it". Too often today, he said, in the race for development and progress [the people's attention is diverted only towards economical or material development. "This is against the ethos and spirit of India; India needs total development of the human being, material with spiritual, and that is what our attention must go to today," he said.

Since Independence, Premier Rajiv Gandhi said, whenever the country had come to cross-roads, where decisions had to be taken, "We have looked for direction to Jawaharlal Nehru; he has always shown us the right direction and it is symbolic that you have placed his statue at this important intersection in Madras.

Referring to the secular outlook of his grandfather, Prime Minister Rajiv Gandhi said that Jawaharlal Nehru knew the dangers of fundamentalism and communalism and what they had cost the country at the time of partition. He had known the dangers of the caste system and divisions based on castes and wanted all communities to live together in peace and harmony.

Nehru had a deep appreciation of the contribution of the South to the culture of India and more than that to the culture of the whole region. "During his long years of imprisonment he read about wrote, it about it, thought and reflected about it". He had frequently referred to Tamil literature in his writings and speeches. He had made a listing of Tamil literary achievements. For Nehru, language was a binding force, a force for the unification of culture and not something to be used to divide people or for parochialism and chauvinism to be built upon. For true development of all languages and cultures there was need for crossfertilization between languages and cultures and interaction between them; translations helped people to know about languages, he said.

Jawaharlal Nehru had stressed the point that Tamil heritage belonged to all of India and India's heritage was strengthened by it. "In the same way today, Madras city, Tamil Nadu, has honoured Panditji (i.e. Jawaharlal Nehru) with this statue", Rajiv Gandhi said, and thanked M.G. Ramachandran for having it installed.

Madras, Prime Minister Rajiv Gandhi said, was associated with two momentous events in Jawaharlal Nehru's life. In December 1927, at the Madras session (of the Indian National Congress) Jawaharlal Nehru who had just returned from his long tour of Europe and the Soviet Union, had demanded complete Independence on a socialistic platform on which Mahatma Gandhi was taken aback and Motilal Nehru was stupified. It was a full two years later that he again called for "Poorna Swaraj" at Lahore on the banks of Ravi, and the whole nation stood behind him. Almost two decades later, 'in 1955, in Madras (Avadi) he set out the blueprint for a socialistic pattern of society, the goal for Independent India.

"It is, therefore, entirely appropriate that the city that was involved in two such momentous events, has his statue", Rajiv Gandhi said.

Prime Minister Rajiv Gandhi had more or less perfected the official act of sorrow-sharing into a line art. His air-dash to Madras in the first week of November 1985 to survey the flood-hit areas had re-emphasised this point. His visit to Madras had also some long-range political overtones. The charm and self assurance with which he shared the people's sorrow with their local political leaders were quite authentic.

Parts of Tamil Nadu and Pondicherry were still reeling under the impact of torrential rains and the consequent floods that took a heavy toll of life and food crops over the past several days. After making an aerial survey of the worst-affected areas including several city districts in Madras, Rajiv Gandhi announced an initial relief of Rs. 5 lakhs for Pondicherry. By any account, this sum was a pittance, compared to the Tamil Nadu Government's preliminary request for an overall flood relief of Rs. 91 Crores. Yet, the Prime Minister not only emphasised that the initial payment was purely in the nature of first -aid from out of the Prime Minister's Relief Fund; but he also gave impression that he would consider Tamil Nadu's case sympathetically.

Also, by his own admission, he could not zero in his attention on small pockets of intense distress, because he had undertaken an aerial survey which would help define only a broad outline of the problem.

Nonetheless, Prime Minister Rajiv Gandhi's primary purpose in opting for a hurried aerial survey was to let the people of Tamil Nadu know that he would be on their side in their hours of crisis. He passed on this message to them by taking the first opportunity to discuss their flood-induced distress with their Chief Minister MGR.

Significantly, on a previous occasion, when MGR was struggling for his very survival in a hospital in New York, Rajiv Gandhi chose to visit flood-hit parts of Madras city by car and on foot.

On that occasion in November 1984, Rajiv Gandhi who had only a few weeks earlier found himself pitchforked to the post of Prime Minister on the assassination of his mother, did not undertake an aerial survey that would have precluded face-to-face encounters with the suffering people.

There were two reasons for his choice of face-to-face encounters on that occasion. First, he was still a stranger to the people of India. Secondly, he had by then more or less made up his mind about an electoral alliance with MGR's AIADMK party. The Lok Sabha and State Assembly elections were then round the corner.

With MGR also absent from the scene, Rajiv Gandhi had then set out to comfort the people of Tamil Nadu in an hour of distress and make his political presence felt in the State.

Rajiv Gandhi had then come a long way from those debutante days. He was quite a political celebrity in his own right and was pretty well known in Tamil Nadu. The result: he could now make did with an aerial survey of the flood-hit areas !

But his long-range political objective was quite clear. By continuing to cultivate the friendship of the people of Tamil Nadu, through such sorrow-sharing exercises and to her measures as well, Rajiv Gandhi seemed to have set out to inherit at least a significant part of MGR's phenomenal vote-bank.

Some of Rajiv Gandhi's remarks during his visit to Madras in July 1985, when he participated in the local Congress centenary celebrations, also gave rise to such political speculations.

Rajiv Gandhi had then quite openly proclaimed his Platonic political love for MGR and till this moment, he had not publicly dropped any hint about calling off, if at all, his political honeymoon with MGR.

The late MGR had kept on his bedroom table a framed letter sent by Rajiv Gandhi in 1985. When Rajiv Gandhi went to the house of MGR on hearing about his death, he was emotionally upset to see his own letter being kept there by the late Chief Minister. In 1985 Rajiv Gandhi wrote to the ailing MGR that his health was very valuable to him. MGR frame this letter and kept near his bedside. One of Premier's aide said that Rajiv Gandhi was visibly moved by the gesture of the late MGR.

M.G. Ramachandran was the most dependable political partner for Prime Minister Rajiv Gandhi, and in the last three years (1985-87) played a politically important role which transcends that of even any Congress (I) Chief Minister. He was instrumental in many initiatives which eventually culminated in the Indo-Sri Lanka Agreement. Rajiv Gandhi himself acknowledged that the accord would not have been possible without MGR. This made him perhaps the only Chief Minister to have decisively intervened on a crucial aspect of foreign policy, so much so, that without him even what little survives of the Indo-Sri Lanka accord will be further jeopardised. He was the last link between the Union Government and the Sri Lankan Tamil militants, prodding the former and restraining the latter to arrive at a conciliatory mean.

As much, as the multitudes of Tamil Nadu, the Sri Lankan Tamils are also bound to feel bereaved because Ramachandran was the only Governmental quarter that provided an umbrella of protection in India. Ramachandran, who was adored by women, had sustained in politics also his image of the do-gooder, crusader against alleged corruption and swashbuckling protector of women and the poor. This earned him the tremendous popularity as an actor and politician, which enabled him to run the AIADMK with an iron hand. He was noted for his passion for prohibition, though his policy in this regard was inconsistent, and the free noon meal scheme which benefits several lakh school children in Tamil Nadu.

Political alliances are certainly not Hindu marriages. Their blatant opportunism is well known and even accepted. MGR's death, although expected by everyone including his own partymen was nevertheless a shock. It left the people stupified; but, much more than that the event stunned AIADMK leaders who sobbed like little children. They knew that the party would be in total disarray because MGR was more than just a founder-leader of the party. His was a father figure and everyone in the party, from the humblest village level worker to the top luminaries, looked upon him personally for help guidance and supervision. His sudden exit has left the organisation rudderless. At such a juncture, what they had expected from the senior partner in their alliance, the Congress, was sympathy, understanding and active help to hold together and look to the future with a modicum of confidence and hope. In sharp contrast to the expectation, what upset AIADMK men, was the moves of Congress leaders to pressurise and armtwist them into accepting unquestioningly their suggestions.

The sudden descend of P.V. Narsimha Rao, Buta Singh and M.L. Fotedar on Madras ostensibly to represent the Centre at MGR's funeral had all the signs of a virtual ultimatum being delivered to the squabbling AIADMK leadership to accept their suggestion and elect one of "pro-Congress" leaders, successor to MGR. It was no secret that the majority of the AIADMK legislators (believed to be around 80 out of the 133) were backing Veerappan. At the most generous count, Jayalalitha and S. Ramachandran commanded the support of only about 40 members but the Congress made it a point to back either of them in the hope that if the AIADMK accepted their suggestion, the Congress would be safely entrenched for the backseat driving If the suggestion were to be rejected, it would have sworn the seeds of an imminent split in which case, the breakway group (which will be safe from attracting the anti-Defection law) could with the Congress support of 62, make a bold bid to take over as a coalition Government. Either of these developments would have suited the Congress and its designs. The only snag was that in either case, the AIADMK would be irretrievably weakened, if not split in the middle.

This was hardly the way to repay the debt the Congress owed to MGR for all that he had chosen to do in the last three or four years to stand by the party. MGR had staked everything in his politics when he decided to back steadfastly the Congress, especially in the last three years. He not only kept away from the innumerable opposition conclaves but had been a lone defender of Prime Minister Rajiv Gandhi and all his indefensible acts. He thus chose to become the odd-man-out among Non-Congress parties and Chief Ministers apart from many other things, this proved to be an unexpected bonanza to his arch rival, Karunanidhi. The DMK leader became the "much sought" after leader from Tamil Nadu in all opposition groupings. This unintended MGR gift to him by the same token, represented the heavy price which MGR paid by backing Rajiv Gandhi and the Congress.

MGR had to share all the discredit and criticism directed against Rajiv Gandhi's actions and decisions, the latest in the series being the Sri Lanka Pact, followed by the IPKF hunt of the Tamil Tigers. Had it not been for the continuing MGR charisma, he would have been mercilessly pilloried by the Tamils for his support to Rajiv Gandhi. He did, however, came down a peg or two because of his complicity in the Sri Lanka Pact. MGR again risked his unquestioned hold over his partymen, who had begun feeling chafed by their leader's silent approval of everything that the Centre did. If there had not been any sign of an open revolt in the party, part of the reason must be sought in the heroic struggle MGR was then waging against serious illness and the all round-sympathy and admiration that this had evoked.

None of these, however, deterred the Congress leadership from trying every trick available to encourage a vertical split in MGR's party. Ever since MGR fell ill seriously in 1984 the Congress had been acting more like a vulture anxiously awaiting its pickings from the corpse. Its entire strategy was hatched around Jayalalitha, a one-time screen heroine of MGR whom he had for some time been building up in the party hierarchy. Her membership of the Rajya Sabha gave her enough opportunities to move close to Indira Gandhi and later to Rajiv Gandhi. The Congress began entertaining visions of riding his party back to power in Tamil Nadu on the shoulders of the AIADMK led by Jayalalitha.

In fact at one stage things had advanced to such an extent that Jayalalitha presented Rajiv Gandhi with a list of 42 partymen who stood by her and plans were prepared for their crossing over to the Congress *en masse* for a coalition Government to be installed in power in Madras. Jayalalitha's precipitous fall from MGR's grace came down when news about this strategy leaked out to MGR in his sick bed. Three years between February 1984 (when he left for New York for a medical check up) saw the Congress exerting relentless pressure on the stricken ally. At first it was to compel MGR to nominate a Deputy Chief Minister who will take over all the functions of the Chief Minister. The reason given out was that MGR should be free from the responsibilities of running the Government so that he could recoup his health fast. But, the secret plan was to strike a bargain with, whosoever was designated as the Deputy Chief Minister which will ultimately pave the way for the return of the Congress to power. Persistent attempts were made both by Rajiv Gandhi himself and through his trusted emissaries to stampede MGR to nominating either Jayalalitha or Panroti S. Ramachandran as the Deputy Chief Minister. Both of them had been identified as willing to walk into the Congress parlour....

MGR had to use all his undoubted endowments of public relations to head off these pressures. He used to fend them by pointing out that the acceptance of the suggestion would lead the party to an imminent split, because neither Jayalalitha nor S. Ramachandran had majority backing in the AIADMK. What was the use of a divided party to the Congress, ha repeatedly asked. Instead, he even went to the extent of suggesting that at the appropriate time, he would himself lead the party into the Congress, lock stock and barrel. A third line of attack mounted just prior to MGR's last visit to the United States was the formation of a Congress-AIADMK coalition Government straightaway in Tamil Nadu. MGR could continue as Chief Minister.

MGR proved too wily to bite this bait. He wriggled out of it by saying that a majority of the legislators now were supporters of Veerappan because he was in charge of party nominations during the last elections. They would not therefore agree to any such arrangement, especially when the party has still an absolute majority. MGR therefore suggested that the Congress should accept his proposal for a mid-term poll which would give him an opportunity to replace Veerappan supporters.

The Congress did not walk into the trap so cleverly laid for it by MGR because it knew that there was just no chance of the Congress ever securing more than 60 members in any future election. Its strategists had insisted that the party should first share power in the State before it could hope for any increase in its strength. Even when Rajiv Gandhi met MGR in New York last, he again impressed on MGR stepping down in the interest of his health. MGR was cut up with this gratuitous advice. The first thing he did was to induct Veerappan back into the Cabinet, thereby sending signals to New Delhi that he was in no mood to oblige one Congress and commit harakari.

7

Farewell to the Leader

State Honour

The mortal remains of the late Chief Minister of Tamil Nadu M.G. Ramachandran, were interred with full State honour on December 25, 1987 evening on the sands of the Marina adjacent to Anna Samadhi. It was a sea of humanity that had turned on the shores of the Bay of Bengal to have a glimpse of their departed leader.

Three volleys of small arms were fired and buglers sounded the Last Post as the sandalwood coffin containing the body was lowered into the grave at 4.30 pm.

The body, draped in National Flag and placed on a flower-decked cortege was earlier brought in a procession from the Rajaji Hall where it was kept for public view after he breathed his last on December 24. Before the funeral procession started, the firing party presented arms with officers in uniform offering salute and then reversed arms. The cortege moved slowly with the bands and drums playing the dead march. Troops and police lined the 10 km long procession route.

The procession was stopped near the Triumph of Labour statue and the pallbearers carried the body to the side of the burial east of the Statue.

The body was transferred to the coffin made of sandalwood weighing 338 kg with a silken lining. Close relatives of late Ramachandran, principal mourners, dignitaries, Ministers, officials and party functionaries placed wreaths and paid their homage.

Eminent Mourners

Wreaths were placed on behalf of the President, the Vice-President and the Prime Minister. Prominent among those at the funeral ceremony were the former President N. Sanjiva Reddi, the Kerala Governor, P. Ramachandran, Tamil Nadu Governor S.L. Khurana and the Chief Ministers of Andhra Pradesh and Jammu and Kashmir, N. T. Rama Rao and Dr. Farooq Abdullah. The Union Ministers P.V. Narsimha Rao, Buta Singh, M.L. Fotedar, P. Chidambaram, R. Prabhu and M. Arunachalam, and Vyjayanthimala Bali and Madam Maragatham Chandrashekar, members of Parliament were among the strong contingent of the ruling party at the Centre that attended the function.

The acting Chief Minister V.R. Nedunchezhian, his Cabinet colleagues, AIADMK party leaders, the AICC I General Secretaries, G.K. Moopanar and K. N. Singh, Karanataka Minister K. Raghupathi and the Lok Sabha Deputy Speaker Thambi Dorai also offered their last respects.

As the coffin was lowered, Central and State Ministers stood around the grave and placed sandalwood sticks. Polished granite slabs were then placed over the grave and sealed.

Chief Secretary A. Padmanabhan said that a full armed guard would be posted to protect the grave till a permanent arrangement was made.

The police had made elaborate arrangements and the PWD and the Corporation of Madras worked overnight and built the grave, laid a gravel road, and erected barricades to hold the crowd at a safe distance. But the whole arrangements went awry minutes before the cortege reached Kamaraj Salai. Unmindful of the scorching sun, people had taken position and sat on the hot sands of the beach as early as 10 am. They stood up to have a glimpse of Ramachandran as the body was carried to the grave. But they could not. They became restive when the Chief mourners, Ministers and the VIPs crowded around the grave which prevented them from seeing even the manner in which the body was being laid to rest.

The military band struck the hymn '*Abide with me*' and buglers sounded the Last Post, while a three volley gun salute was given. An aircraft hovered over, showering flowers. The Sri Lanka Government was represented at the funeral by Minister S. Thondaman and High Commissioner in India Bernard Thilakaratne.

Mounted policemen tried to control the crowd, push it back and prevent it from surging forward and breaking the barricade. But the strength of thousands made the efforts ineffective and as they started throwing stones, chappals, sticks and sand, the mounted police retreated, both the policemen and their mounts sustaining injuries. The police fired buckshots and burst tear-gas shells. As even these were ineffective, they opened fire. The crowd then started melting away.

The funeral procession left the Rajaji Hall a little before 1.30 pm on December 25, 1987. Though it was announced that the body would lie in State only till 11 am the authorities decided to extend the deadline by an hour to enable the people who had poured in from all parts of the State and neighbouring States to pay their last respects. So till noon, it was kept for public view.

The Jammu and Kashmir Chief Minister, Dr. Farooq Abdullah placed a wreath. Shortly before the body was removed into the hall for religious rites. P.V. Narsimha Rao, Buta Singh and M.L. Fotedar arrived from Delhi and paid homage on behalf of the Union Government and the Prime Minister.

Leading lights of the film industry and Late Ramachandran's heroines of yesteryears were among the mourners to offer floral tributes. It took over two hours for the procession to pass through Anna Salai, Cathedral Road, Radhakrishnan Salai and Kamaraj Salai before reaching the Marina.

People lined up on both sides of the procession route to have a last glimpse of their 'Puratchi Thalaivar' and his young fans took vantage and even dangerous positions from roof tops, hoardings, lamp posts, tree tops, walls and the Anna fly over, they strained themselves to see their leader on his last journey.

An open lorry with people scattering flower petals for the gun carriage led the funeral procession. The Ministers travelled in two jeeps and the MLAS were huddled into an open chasis. A glider aircraft overflew the funeral procession and kept showering flower petals.

Lakhs of mourners paid homage to late Ramachandran till noon on Friday. After the initial confusion and rioting on Anna Salai soon after the official announcement about the sudden death of the Chief Minister, the police took control of the situation and thins worked to a plan, up to a point. Conveys of buses and lorries poured into the city till Friday morning bringing thousands of party workers and Ramachandran's fans and they were allowed up to Pallavan Salai via the beach.

For two days the service systems in Madras were under severe pressure and the mourners found it very difficult to come by some food. The Railway catering turned out to be a major source on both days and long queues were seen both at the Egmore and Central Railway stations, with the Railway Police Force regulating them. Some resourceful women in the slums managed to prepare and sell mixed rice. Fruits were sold for a premium on the pavements. Within minutes of the funeral the traffic returned to normal and vehicles were allowed to ply. The PTC buses were off the roads for two days and were back to operation on December 26, 1987.

Special Trains

The Southern Railway operated special trains on the broad guage and metre guage sections. A little delay came in the way of embalming the body of Ramachandran. Just as the body of the Soviet leader Lenin was preserved, the AIADMK leaders wanted the body of the *'Puratchi Thalaivar'* also to be embalmed.

They sought the help of Prime Minister Rajiv Gandhi, in this respect and Moscow was approached. The AIADMK leaders were told that much time had been lost and it was too late to embalm the body.

An unseemly controversy just before the funeral procession of Ramachandran commenced from the Rajaji Hall marred an otherwise solemn and ceremonial occasion on December 25.

After performing religious rites inside the Rajaji Hall, family handed over Ramachandran's body to the police and the Army for the final honours. The body was placed on the army gun carriage.

The AIADMK Propaganda Secretary Jayalalitha, got into the carriage, placed a wreath on the body and was about to take a seat beside it, creating a flutter. But she was soon seen climbing down from the carriage with the assistance of military personnel.

It appeared as if she was going to sit in the truck cabin, when a ruling party MLA from the vehicle behind the gun carriage signalled to Madam Janaki Ramachandran's nephew and made for the truck Deepan, nephew of Madam Ramachandran and an actor himself, pushed her down.

Red in the face Jayalalitha walked off, with a police cordon round her. Some Ministers standing in a vehicle behind the cortege offered her a place, but she left declaring "I won't come".

The showdown appeared inevitable as the constant presence of Jayalalitha beside Ramachandran's body, as soon as it was brought to the Rajaji Hall on December 24 morning, was creating an "emotional upheaval" in the family. All through Thursday she stood at the head of the body wearing a black saree and at 4 am on Friday, she returned to take her place, this time in a white saree. She stood through till the end and was seen going towards the hall where the family members performed the religious rites.

The whole of Thursday Madam Janaki Ramachandran was in very bad shape, vomiting blood, and a panel of eight doctors was attending on her. She wanted to be fit atleast to be with the body on Friday and came to the Rajaji Hall in the morning.

Jayalalitha's Statement

The AIADMK Propaganda Secretary Jayalalitha, Member of Parliament had, in the course of a Statement to the press, said: "I was inexpressibly shocked and pained by the ill treatment out to me by some of my own party functionaries before the start of the funeral procession of my beloved leader yesterday afternoon (Friday 25th December). Despite innumerable sights, unbearable humiliations and insults heaped on me during the last two days (24th & 25th Dec.), I was determined to remain cool and dignified in the face of the gravest provocation which was a calculated, methodically worked out strategy by a section of my partymen, deliberately planned to drive me away from the Rajaji Hall and prevent me from attending the funeral. The body of my leader was taken inside the Rajaji Hall for performing family rites on Friday afternoon but I was not permitted to participate in the last rituals and was not allowed inside. "I attempted to place a wreath when the army pall bearers placed the body on the gun carriage at the Rajaji Hall. The security forces personnel were kind enough to assist me in performing my last duty to my departed leader.

"Since there was no facility to climb up, they helped me to climb up on to the gun carriage.

"At the instance "I was doing that, I heard violent shouts behind me. My party colleague Dr. K. P. Ramalingam was seen moving menacinlgly towards me".

"Actor Deepan jumped on to the gun carriage and pushed me out. The armed forces personnel attempted to help me back on top of the carriage. Again I was pushed, beaten and thrown out." The body of Ramachandran was buried in Madras on December 25, 1987 with his characteristic white fur cap and dark glasses still in place perpetuating his fans image of him as an evergreen dashing hero.

Cap and Dark Glasses

The fur cap and dark glasses have been identified with Ramachandran making him easily recognisable. Ramachandran once travelled in a car with a senior Congress (I) functionary during an election campaign. When he removed his cap and glasses, none recognised him or waved out. Ramachandran told the Congressman: "all the respect and adulation seems to be for the cap and the glasses."

With his invincible record in electoral battles, his partymen would say: "MGR need not come and campaign for us. It would suffice he sends his fur cap and dark glasses."

In many a home the hearths did not burn as entire families kept weeping for their 'anna' (brother). The roads were adorned with MGR portraits, garlanded and decorated.

Small photos of M.G. Ramachandran and garlands fetched high prices, a garland selling for Rs. 30 and a picture costing as high as Rs. 180. The shops were shuttered and bus services which had began as usual, were quickly called off as lungiclad young followers of the 'Puratchi Thalaivar' (the revolutionary hero) went berserk, trying to rush to Rajaji Hall. The inevitable clash with the police took place at several points on the arterial Mount Road, Madras.

Distance, no Meaning

Distance from home made little difference to MGR fans. The Tamils in the north felt no less miserable and distraught than did their near and dear ones in the south on the death of their hero.

This was patently so in Chandigarh which next to Delhi has the largest Tamil concentration in the north. At least 10,000 Tamils earn their living in Chandigarh through construction activity and odd jobs.

In Bapu Dham Colony, which has an exclusive south Indian concentration of labourers, dozens of them got their heads shaven in grief. Eight labour leaders left for Madras immediately on hearing the news in the morning bulletin of All India Radio.

Every house hold in the colony, which is situated close to the railway station, wore a family mourning atmosphere. No meals were cooked for two days. Even the children and the ailing observed fast. Women were seen wailing. "Oh our father took excellent care of us for 17 long years". Daily wage earners abstained from work for two days.

A labour leader, Selvaraj, said "MGR was my elder brother. That's why I have got my head shaven for his *Kriya Karma* (Death). Several mourning processions moved in the city's labour colonies. A joint 'funeral' procession of all the colonies wended its way to the cremation ground in Sector-25 on December 25. A life-size cutout of MGR carried by the processionists was consigned to the flames at the same time as the mortal remains of MGR were laid to rest on the Marina beach in Madras.

Tamil Nadu politics is a little difficult to understand. Even the burial/cremation of a leader has its symbolism. So when MGR was buried on Marina beach the question that intrigued many people was why he was not cremated. When asked AIADMK leaders, they all gave what would seem like a standard answer- "because Anna was buried". Well, MGR was actually not cremated because the all-time great of Tamil Nadu politics, Annadurai, was buried. The reason —the unwritten law, is that the mortal remains of Dravidian leaders must never be consigned to flames.

The eruption of violence that marred the mourning in Madras on the death of Ramachandran may be dismissed as a temporary emotional outburst which will subside after the people regain their equilibrium. Many, however, feel that this outburst of violence in which many, were killed and which resulted in the smashing of the massive bronze statue of the opposition DMK leader Karunanidhi has deeper political overtones. These overtones provoke people to wonder whether their State politics is at the crossroads. For ten years Ramachandran had kept the State on an even keel giving it political stability and taking it along the path of progress with many imaginative steps initiated for popular welfare.

Several persons had immolated themselves when M.G. Ramachandran lay critically ill in an American hospital in 1984. Reports of self-immolation by some of his fans in overwhelming grief over his death have been reported. The acts of lawlessness and disorder in some parts of Madras on December 24, 1987 could be another expression of important anger over his sudden death. The secret of commanding such fierce loyalty and adoration was known to the departed leader MGR alone, and he seems to have made use of this secret in politics also.

Overwhelmed, a 40 years-old man of Chidambaram and a 25 years-old youth of Tindivanam died due to shock. One person of Ulundurpet Taluk committed suicide by consuming poison. Four people at Cuddalore, Valavur, Chinnasalem and Kudumbuliyur areas attempted to commit self-immolation.

Twenty-five Tamil men of Dharavi in northeast Bombay got their heads shaved clean, while different groups of people hailing from Tamil Nadu took out silent processions in Bombay to pay homage to Ramachandran.

Portraits of the late leader were garlanded by hundreds of weeping women at street corners in areas with a large Tamil population.

It is both sad and distressing to note that even as the body of MGR was lying in State and leaders from all over India were pouring into Madras city to pay their last respects to the departed soul, armed vandals should have let loose a reign of terror compelling the authorities to issue shoot-at-sight orders. While self-immolation under intense emotional stress is to an extent understandable, violence marring the solemnity of the occasion deserves to be condemned in the strongest terms.

Mad Fans

Why should people stop buses and trains just because MGR died? why stone shops and break windows of buildings? Why all this rioting and arson? These are some of the questions that people are asking, on seeing the trail of destruction in the wake of the death of people's leader MGR.

Psychiatrists have a simple answer: these were the manifestation of the acute sense of grief among the people. Hardened criminals took advantage of the violence to loot shops.

Dr. N. Gopalakrishnan, consultant psychiatrist at the Apollo Hospital, Madras, said many people hero-worshipped MGR. The image tended to get internalised in their minds and they saw MGR as an ideal son, brother, uncle or as a fatherly figure. The demise of the role modelled to an acute sense of loss in the minds of the hero-worshippers and operated as a severe stress.

Dr. Gopalakrishnan said, people react in different ways to the stress, depending on their socioeconomic characteristics. Some exhibit intra-punitive behaviour (punishing oneself) in the form of suicidal attempts such as self-immolation. Others show extra punitive behaviour (punishing others) in the form of anger, aggression, violence and destruction of public property. Mob violence could be acute catastrophic reaction manifesting as goal—less destruction of public property, clearly anti-social behaviour that is goal-oriented; self-seeking in the form of looting and violent behaviour starting off as impulsive acting—out of one's frustration, which develops into anti-social behaviour fanned by forces of mob psychology.

Dr. O. Somasundaram, former Superintendent of the Institute of the Mental Health, Madras, said, people who are grief-stricken often do not know what they are doing as all their emotions are paralysed. Some of them imgine that the dead person is in front of them or is talking to them.

Dr. Peter Fernandez, Deputy Superintendent of the Institute of Mental Health, said, a certain percentage of the population consisted of people harbouring criminal tendencies. During mob violence, they were also able to act out their feelings. Often, hardened criminals took advantage of confusion to loot shops and indulge in violence.

However, the cult of violence has, of late, come to stay in India. At the slightest provocation and at times even without any reason-people resort to vandalism of the worst type causing extensive damage to life and property. Should even grief be expressed in this fashion ?

An answer to this question calls for some introspection by the people themselves. The politician has a vital role to play in its evolution. But looking at the way in which he himself, behaves even within the precincts of the legislature, at is highly doubtful if he will take up this challenge.

8

The Tributes

President R. Venkataraman, Vice-President Shankar Dayal Sharma and Prime Minister Rajiv Gandhi led the nation in mourning the death of Tamil Nadu Chief Minister M.G. Ramachandran.

The curtain of time had fallen on one of the most remarkable personalities of modern India. M.G. Ramachandran thought and felt with the masses and for the masses.

R. Venkatraman

"Ramachandran's passing away is a national loss and my sorrow at his demise merges with the people of Tamil Nadu," the President said. President Venkataraman said adding that he was a charismatic leader whose life pulsated with the common people.

S.D. Sharma

Dr. S.D. Sharma described Ramachandran as a great leader of the people who had the quality of fathoming the true interests of the people even in a very complex situation.

"The death of Ramachandran is an event of great magnitude in the history of the country," Dr. Sharma said.

M.N. Chandurkar

Chief Justice M.N. Chandurkar, in his reference, said, Ramachandran had carved out a special place in the hearts of millions of people by his benevolence and generosity.

'Mr. Ramachandran strode on the political scene in Tamil Nadu like a colossus for a decade and achieved eminence as a statesman and administrator', the Chief Justice added.

He said, MGR believed in the unity and integrity of the country and had tremendous faith in the judiciary.

It said: Ramachandran had given lustre and glory to the post of the Chief Minister and made several achievements for the progress of Tamil Nadu during his tenure.

Tamil Nadu Governor S.L. Khurana said, he was deeply shocked at the death of M.G. Ramachandran who was a source of strength to the Government, party and the State.

T.N. Cabinet

The Tamil Nadu Cabinet, which met under the chairmanship of Interim Chief Minister V.R. Nedunchazhiyan expressed deep sorrow and anguish over the death of 'the darling of the masses'.

DMK

Opposition Dravida Munnetra Kazhagam (DMK) President M. Karunanidhi said, despite several differences he had with Ramachandran, he was shocked by the sudden death of Ramachandran.

Karunanidhi said that their forty years of friendship continued despite several hurdles and tests. He had built a party and captured the rule in a short time which showed his capacity and drive the Government.

Governors

In Trivandrum, the Kerala Governor P. Ramachandran, condoled the passing away of M.G. Ramachandran, and described him as "a great leader of national eminence". In a message to the bereaved family, the Governor said: the immense mass appeal and popular influence MGR wielded, marked him out as a phenomenon among contemporary political leaders of the country. "A towering personality of the World of Arts MGR made his presence felt in public life with equal vehemence and force for more than two decades," the Governor added.

Andhra Pradesh Governor Ms. Kumudben Joshi expressed shock at the sudden demise of M.G. Ramachandran.

In a condolence message, she said: "Ramachandran's death creates a void in our national life. Mass politics would never again be the same without this crowd puller of this century, and like Indiraji (Late Prime Minister Indira Gandhi) he had the rare quality of quiet courage and national outlook. He was one of the most outstanding leaders, who endeared himself not only to the people of Tamil Nadu but made his impact at the national and international levels".

Ramachandran possessed the pragmatism of the common man, the dynamism of a great leader, the charisma of a hero, the charity and love of humanism. His is the best example of a strong and healthy regional leadership that became universal in spirit and nationalistic in our look, a great lesson for lesser mortals. People saw a miracle in his medical recovery and continued national service.

Conveying her heartfelt condolences to Madam Janaki Ramachandran, the Governor said "the whole of Tamil Nadu was like MGR's family and convey her heartfelt condolence to all".

In Bangalore, Karnataka Governor A N. Beneraji, has conveyed his heartfelt condolences. "The nation in general and Tamil Nadu in particular has lost a great Statesman and seasoned administrator," he said.

Chief Ministers

In Bhubaneshwar, B.N. Pande, the Orissa Governor, expressing profound grief, described MGR, as a versatile public leader, who dominated the political scene for many years. As a leader of the People his popularity was matchless and he did his best to fulfil the hopes and aspirations of the people.

Orissa Chief Minister J.B. Patnaik also deeply mourned the death. He said, "MGR commanded tremendous love and respect among the people of Tamil Nadu as their leader and an able administrator for a long time".

In Patna, the Bihar Chief Minister Bindeshwari Dubey said, "MGR was an able administrator known for his progressive steps and popular schemes which were mostly for the poor and downtrodden, particularly women, children and other neglected sections of society".

In Guwahati, Assam Chief Minister P.K. Mahanta said, "the departed leader served the people by dint of his administrative dynamism".

In Agartala, Tripura Chief Minister Nripen Chakraborty paid homage describing him as an outstanding national leader. The Chief Minister said, "MGR was one of the builders of Tamil Nadu. In a condolence message Chakraborty said, 'though we differed in political ideology, I pay homage to the departed on behalf of the people of Tripura and share the grief of his family'.

Chief Minister N.T. Rama Rao said that it was an extremely unfortunate day (December 24, 1987).

"It is with deep anguish that I express my sincere condolences as a younger brother on the demise of beloved elder brother MGR," Rama Rao said in his condolence message.

Rama Rao who left for Madras on hearing the sad news said, 'I was the recipient of his all pervading affection, love and advise for the past nearly 40 years, going back to my days in filmdom'.

"In a highly personal tribute to Ramachandran, Rama Rao said, he always treated me with utmost affection as a younger brother. He was always very first to encourage me in blessing and affection".

"Ramachandran was always Anna (elder brother) to me in all matters". The Chief Minister said, "the loss sustained by Tamil Nadu members of the AIADMK party and millions of his devoted followers was irreparable".

The Jammu and Kashmir Government announced a day's closure of all State Government offices and educational institutions.

Chief Minister Dr. Farooq Abdullah described his death as a great loss not only to Tamil Nadu but to the entire country.

The Polit Bureau of the Communist Party of India (Marxist) said "in Ramachandran's death, Tamil Nadu had lost an eminent leader who was immensely popular with the Tamil people."

Gujarat Chief Minister Amarsingh Chaudhary said, Ramachandran's services would be long remembered by the people of the State.

Uttar Pradesh Chief Minister Veer Bahadur Singh said, Ramachandran was a great patriot who always stood for the country's unity and integrity.

West Bengal Chief Minister Jyoti Basu remarked, although ailing for some time, he was carrying on his responsibility with unabated zeal.

Haryana Chief Minister Devi Lal said: in the death of Ramachandran the country had lost a great statesman and a true patriot who had been on the political scene for two decades.

Sikkim Chief Minister Nar Bahadur Bhandari said, the country had lost a great patriot and charismatic leader.

In Imphal, Manipur Chief Minister Rishang Keishing said, the departed leader's life was devoted to the cause of peace, prosperity and progress. In a condolence message Keishing said "his demise would create a void not only in the public life of Tamil Nadu but also in the entire nation".

The Madhya Pradesh Government declared a day's mourning and ordered closure of its offices.

In a message, the Kanchipuram Mutt said, Ramachandran was an idol for millions and a parity among politicians. "May the goddess Mukambika guide the departed soul for its future peaceful birth', the Mutt said

Eelam Revolutionary Organisation of Students (EROS) spokesman Mahadevan expressed his deep shock over the death of Ramachandran, at a time when the Tamils of Sri Lanka had looked forward for his sincere help to resolve the ethnic issue.

Chitta Basu, Member of Parliament, and General Secretary All India Forward Bloc said: "Ramachandran had always been a friend to the downtrodden and sought to improve their lot. In his death, the people of Tamil Nadu have lost one of architects of modern Tamil Nadu. His loss is irreparable", Basu said in a statement.

Bharatiya Janata Party Chief L.K. Advani said, Ramachandran's death has created a void which is impossible to fill. He has left a clear stamp of integrity and uprightness in public life.

ASSOCHAM President M.K. Kumar, remembered him as a champion of the downtrodden, an ardent advocate of social reforms.

Karnataka Chief Minister Ramakrishan Hegde said, Ramachandran's rise from a stage artist to Chief Minister's post- symbolised the Struggle of the less privileged to attain the best and it had many lessons for future generations.

Lok Dal Vice-President K.V. Krishnaswamy said, Ramachandran was not only a political leader but he was the Lord of the Tamil people.

The South Indian Film Chamber of Commerce said, in Ramachandran's death the film industry in the South had suffered an irreparable loss.

FICCI President K.S.G. Haja Shareeff said, Ramachandran was a man of vision.

M.A. Latheef, Joint Secretary of Indian Union of Muslim League, said that the country had lost a noble son, a patriot and popular leader in his death.

Rashtriya Swaymsewak Sangh (RSS) Chief Balasaheb Deoras has expressed shock over the death of Ramachandran. Deoras in his condolence message said, 'MGR's death is a great loss to the country.

Information and Broadcasting Minister Ajit Kumar Panja in a condolence message said, MGR always kept the welfare of the people at his heart and 'took extra pains for their upliftment.'

The Punjab Government on December 24 closed all its offices and ordered a day's State mourning. Former Chief Minister S.S. Barnala also mourned the death of Ramachandran.

The Kerala Government too declared a closure of its offices. Chief Minister E.K. Nayanar expressed shock and grief over the death of Ramachandran.

Speaker Varkala Radhakrishnan described Ramachandran as the darling of the poor and the downtrodden. Opposition Leader K. Karunakaran and PCC(I) President A.K. Anthony said, Ramachandran stood loyally by the people through thick and thin.

All the courts in the city, including Madras High Court, remained closed on January 4, 1988 as a mark of respect to Late Tamil Nadu Chief Minister M.G. Ramachandran.

In the High Court, all the judges, advocates and staff observed silence for two minutes to condole the death of MGR.

The Polit Bureau of the Communist Party of India (Marxist) mourned the passing away of M.G. Ramachandran: "In his death, the State of Tamil Nadu has lost an eminent leader who was immensely popular with the Tamil people. He won their electoral support in successive elections and served for almost a decade as Chief Minister of the State. The Polit Bureau conveys its condolences to his wife, family members and his colleagues in the AIADMK."

Ajit Panja, Union Minister for Information and Broadcasting recalled his meetings with MGR fondly and said, whatever be the subject the late MGR discussed with him. MGR always did it with a smile of love. "Before the last elections in Pondicherry, my party had deputed me to negotiate with MGR the seat adjustment. I never saw him lose his cool. He used to take decisions with a smile and confidence, and had the knack of convincing others", Panja added.

G. Venkateswaran, President South India Film Chamber of Commerce has referred to MGR as 'Minimum Guarantee Ramachandran' in filmi parlance.

Rich tributes were paid to late M.G. Ramachandran, Tamil Nadu Chief Minister at an all-party meeting organised by the All India Freedom Fighters' Organisation and the Friends of Palestine in New Delhi on December 24. The meeting, which had been originally convened to denounce Zionist excesses on unarmed Palestinians, began with a minute's silence as a mark of condolence to the departed leader.

A resolution passed on the occasion described MGR as an illustrious son of the country who had stood for the unity and integrity of the nation. MGR was a great friend of the poor and his untimely death was a great national loss. Ramachandran was extolled for his rich contributions to the world of art and culture.

In Cuddalore for the first time in its history, the Patalees warar temple in Thirupapuliyur was closed on both on December 24 & 25 without days poojas as a mark of respect to the late Ramachandran. However, in a few other temples in the district, special prayers were held for the peace of the departed soul.

The Archbishop of Madras, Mylapore, Dr. Casimir Gnanidickam, said prayers and sprinkled holy water on the body of Ramachandran, at the Rajaji Hall, before the last journey began. A large number of nuns and sisters also prayed for the departed soul of Ramachandran.

After the public veneration was stopped around 1100 hrs., the body, which was kept atop the imposing steps of the Rajaji Hall in the Government estates, was taken inside the high domed hall. The huge doors were closed and prayers said:

Christmas in Tamil Nadu lacked the usual festive mood with the sudden death of its much loved son Ramachandran.

The lights and decorations at the churches were almost totally absent and the midnight masses, which usually see happy, and thronging crowds, had only thin attendance. The mourning mass appeared to have more worshippers.

With the street violence which marked the city's mourning went off without incident.

Special services and prayers were held in many churches for the "repose of Ramachandran's soul," when the departed leader's service to society and the downtrodden were recalled.

'Moksha Deepam' (prayers for the departed soul) for Ramachandran was lit on the four sides of each tier of the gopurams (towers) of the Kamakshi Temple and Ekambares-warar temple in Kancheepuram about 70 km from Madras on the Friday, December 25 evening.

The Kamaaskshi temple has five tiers and the other seven.

The lighting of the *deepam* was ordered by the three sankaracharyas of the Kanchi Kamakoti Mutt.

At the famous Meenakshi temple in Madurai the 'moksha deepam' was lit atop the southern tower.

Paying his floral tribute CPI General Secretary C. Rajeswara Rao said, "We are deeply grieved at sad demise of M.G. Ramachandran Tamil Nadu Chief Minister, a patriot and doyen of Tamil films and beloved of Tamil people. He was one of the famous film stars who effectively projected misery of downtrodden people and progressive social ideas through media of films. After he became Chief Minister he devoted his attention to implementing his ardent desire to uplift downtrodden people. In his passing away Tamil Nadu and the country have lost a defender of secularism and integrity of the country. While paying homage to his memory I convey heartfelt condolences to the member of the bereaved family".

The Music Academy, Madras on December 27, 1987 decided to create an endowment to perpetuate the memory of M.G. Ramachandran and award a prize to a young talented dancer, every year.

At a condolence meeting T.T. Vasu, Academy President, said that the late Chief Minister had learnt Karnatic vocal music and dance and found immense joy and relief in listening to leading artists. Hence the Academy particularly felt the grievous loss. Paying homage, Vasu said, MGR was a patron of arts and artists. Only two weeks ago, he was in the Academy witnessing the Russian folk dance, sitting for full two hours. MGR was intensely humane. His identification with the suffering people was spontaneous and anyone who approached him for help to get over some distressing situation, evoked his instant sympathy.

Ramachandran was also humble. When he inaugurated the 52nd Conference of the Music Academy, he mentioned that he had come just to participate along with other. "Do not make me a leader here I am one of you", he then said. He delivered a memorable lecture on various features of music, and the condition and problems of artists. He was one of the most unassuming Chief Ministers Tamil Nadu had produced. He was easily at home in any company and his fingers were always on the pulse of the people. MGR was a phenomenon.

Various Leaders

Home Minister Buta Singh, expressing his shock and grief, described Ramachandran as a great leader, who touched the heart of the masses.

Buta Singh said that Ramachandran was an able administrator, nationalist and true champion of the poor and the downtrodden. His demise has left a void in the State and National politics.

Indian National Trade Union Congress (INTUC) President G. Ramanujan said: Ramachandran was a true friend of the labourers, the poor and destitutes and had devoted himself to the masses, both as an actor and a Chief Minister.

Maharashtra Chief Minister S.B. Chavan said: "we have lost an eminent personality of our time". Defence Minister K.C. Pant said that in MGR's passing away, India has lost a great national leader. "Ramachandran was a towering personality in political life because of which he won the hearts and minds of the people in Tamil Nadu to an extent very few could achieve," he added.

Union Finance Minister Narayan Dutt Tiwari said: the country has lost a great patriot, able statesmen and charismatic leader of the masses. 'The void created by his death is difficult to fill', he added.

Lok Sabha Speaker Balram Jakhar said, the country has lost a dedicated patriot and of the poor, a great friend.

United States

The United States Government had also condoled the death of M.G. Ramachandran.

The passing away of MGR was noted in lengthy despatches in the US press.

A wire service obituary published in the Washington Post said. "Ramachandran was a central figure in efforts to end the guerrilla war by Tamil rebels in Sri Lanka".

"MGR has also made his mark in international war against poverty. The Tamil Nadu nutrition scheme launched by MGR is now the standard by which the World Bank measures similar anti-poverty schemes elsewhere," the despatch said.

9

The Life Partner

[V.N. Janaki Ramachandran]

A new Council of Ministers for Tamil Nadu, headed by Vaikkom Narayani Janaki Ramachandran, was sworn in at 9 am on January 7 at Raj Bhavan, Madras.

Janaki Ramachandran was called on by Governor S.L. Khurana at Raj Bhawan on January 5, 1988 and was with him for about half an hour.

Janaki at the Helm

Vaikkom N. Janaki Ramachandran's assumption of power in the State—a triumph for woman power—is inline with growing tradition in the south for heroes and heroines of the silver screen rising in politics. Her major handicap is that she has been far removed from the political centre-stage. However, with experienced politicians like Veerappan by her side, she could pick up the basic elements of political craft in course of time. Political power can sometimes work wonders.

With MGR's passing his charisma on which AIADMK was prone to depend on sustenance may well further rise in the motherly figure of Jankai. Without, however, doing any crystal gazing into the future, it is pertinent to note that 1987-88 seems to be the year of Women in the subcontinent. Jayalalitha and Janaki made news in Tamil Nadu while two other women Sheikh Hasina Wajed and Begum Khalida Zia hitted the headlines not only in India but abroad, with their doings in Bangladesh. General Mohammad Ershad is reeling under their body blows. He has gone to the length of offering a fresh Presidential election to demonstrate his hold on the people, but the two women are adamant on their stand that the President must step down first before any democratic process is tried.

It is true that Asia is no stranger to the presence of women at the commanding heights. Smt. Indira Gandhi became a legend in her lifetime and so did Srimao Bhandaranaike in Sri Lanka. In the Philippines, Aquino, widow of the murdered senator, Benigno Aquino, is riding the storm as President elected by a popular mandate. What is happening or is likely to happen in other Asian countries, can only be a matter of speculation but what is happening nearer home is a pointer to the increasing participation of women, manipulated or otherwise. In the affairs of the country, especially in the policy-making reaches of women at a critical time are in the country's history.

Considering the progress made by women in India, more especially in the political field, the number of women Chief Ministers has been small. There was Sucheta Kripalani in Uttar Pradesh, Nandini Satpathy in Orissa, Anwara Taimur in Assam and Shashikala Bandodkar in Goa.

Politics in a sense is in fact a part and parcel of human life. It should stimulate constructive nation-building activities. If she believes in power politics, it is the politics which must be free of personal bitterness and human conflicts. It must promote social justice and moral progress. And it should be punctuated with frugality, temperance and ethical considerations. This is her code, her creed.

Madam Janaki had been a pillar of strength to her husband while he was Chief Minister of Tamil Nadu. Ever since they were married, husband and wife had adjusted to staying in most difficult situations.

Born in 1923 in a family of musicians at Vaikkom in Kerala, Janaki who has•acted in about 15 films bid adieu to the tinsel world in 1950 after her marriage with her co-star of "Marathanattu Illavarasi", M.G. Ramachandran, who went on to become the charismatic "revolutionary leader" of the Tamil masses.

The heroine of the silver screen who played a minor role in *Manmathavijayam* (1939) her first film, has been propelled into the race for the leadership of the Government as a consequence of the events that followed her husband's demise.

Janaki shot into prominence in the film world for her role in the *Velaikarai* scripted by C.N. Annadurai. The film was considered a turning point in the film world.

Janaki who is proficient in Bharata Natyam joined the dance troupe of director K. Subramaniam before graduating into world. She has also paired with the legendary actor M.K. Thiagaraja Bhagavathnar in "Raja Mukti" in 1948. Her father Rajagopala Iyer was a renowed musician.

Adding spice and conjecture to the melodramaic tale that is unfolding in Tamil Nadu, apart from the *filmi* ingredients, is the little-known past of Janaki Ramachandran. MGR's third wife, she is said to have married him in 1952 after the deaths of both his wives. His first wife, Sadanandavati, was a Malayali. His second wife suffered from tuberculosis (TB) and wasted away over a period of ten years or more. The grapevine has it that Janaki who left her husband, Ganapati Bhat, a make-up artist, for MGR, lived with him during this time. Their marriage was registered some later time. The daughter of a musician, Rajagopala Iyer, Janaki was a Bharatnatayam dancer before poverty drove her into the film world. She acted in 15 films, playing the heroine opposite MGR in *Maruda Nattu Elavarasi, Naam* and *Jenovah.*

Bhat died a few years ago. Although she and MGR did not have any child, Janaki's son from her first marriage, Appu, was adopted by MGR, but did not measure up as worthy heir either in politics or cinema. ('Riff-raff' is the dismissive, one-word comment of a senior Madras journalist.) Today he has managed the party paper, *Anna*. It was the film *Maruda Nattu Elavarasi,* in which Janaki played the princess, that brought her and

MGR together. Despite MGR's statement they were married in a temple, persistent rumour in Madras is that they were never legally married. If the temple marriage occurred, it is one more similarity that Janaki ironically, shares with her rival, Jayalalitha who has also claimed that MGR married her in a temple. [The other similarity is that they are both *Brahmins* (Upper caste) in the avowedly anti-Brahmin political corridors of Tamil Nadu]. The two women in MGR's life are now standing MGR's legacy, which includes control of the party as well as a private fortune estimated, perhaps a bit wildly, at anywhere above Rs. 50 crores.

Whatever the nature of her association with MGR, Janaki is believed to have wielded considerable influence over him towards the end of his life and, as a result, over the men who surrounded him. Her important rolë in MGR's *Durbar* first became obvious when he suffered a stroke in 1984 and could not communicate with anybody. It was janaki who was by his side in the United States where he went for treatment, and who alone was privy to his every gesture and inarticulate command. Until then, says a journalist in Madras, many people in Tamil Nadu did not even know the name of the woman who was Janaki. What was known was that she was a stoic and behind-the-scenes wife, who handled her husband's long-term association with Jayalalitha with dignity and finesse, never making her feelings public.

Janki in MGR's Life

Among the many ironies of MGR's life is his transformation from a drama troupe actor playing feminine roles to the most machoman of the Tamil screen. By the time MGR burst into stardom with *Rajkumari* in 1947, the fair-skinned effeminate boy had vanished. And, in the next few years the metamorphosis was complete with MGR becoming a symbol of manhood and a darling of millions of cinema-going Tamil women. But the ultimate irony lay in the way MGR, who rose to be the most powerful figure of Tamil Nadu politics, succumbed to the two women in his life; Janaki and Jayalalitha. Who these two women were to MGR is, paradoxically, a little difficult to define. Janaki, who lived with MGR in his palatial Ramavaram Gardens residence, was considered by towns people to be his official wife.

The rural masses, on the other hand, accepted Jayalalitha as their superhero's wife and called her *Anni* (meaning elder brother's wife). Both women claim to be officially married to MGR, both are former actresses and both are Iyengar Brahmins. But all this apart, there is very little similarity between the two—the salient point of their relationship is an intense mutual hatred that dates back to more then two decades ago. And the last few years of MGR's life were increasingly conditioned by the conflict between the housewifely Janaki and the politically ambitious Jayalalitha.

As MGR's grip on life, politics and the Tamil Nadu administration faltered, following the stroke he suffered in 1984, the battle between his two women became pivotal in the State's conspiratorial politics. Information minister R.M. Veerappan shared Janaki's dislike for Jayalalitha and her unabashed ambitions. Fearing that he would ultimately be manoeuvred by Jayalalitha, who was busy building a mass base through her fan clubs and the AIADMK organisation with MGR's blessings, Veerappan colluded with Janaki to prepare a scheme for her downfall. When MGR went abroad for medical treatment, Janaki accompanied him. Veerappan, in the meanwhile, began putting up poster of MGR with Janaki.

It was the first time that Janaki was projected as MGR's wife. When MGR and Janaki returned to Madras, Veerappan began using Janaki in two ways. At one level, he persuaded her to intervene in administrative decisions, manipulating officials in his favour. MGR's unusual advertisement in the press in July, 1986, warning that his "relatives" should not interfere in Government functioning, appears to have been directed against the Janaki-Veerappan combine. At another level Janaki began influencing her husband, portraying Jayalalitha as a political upstart bent on ultimately upstaging her mentor. MGR's reluctance to help Jayalalitha after she had been stripped off the posts of deputy leader of the AIADMK Parliamentary party and party propaganda secretary is attributed to Janaki's influence.

But Jayalalitha, after seven long months got the better of MGR and was finally brought back as propaganda secretary. Janaki is believed to have intervened again when Veerappan was dropped from the State Cabinet and position as information minister. Janaki put pressure and waited to see him reinstated. Governor S.L. Khurana, who was indisposed at the time wanted the swearing-in to be postponed. At MGR's insistence, Khurana made Veerappan to take the formal oath in the gubernatorial bedroom. For the last three years of his life MGR see-sawed between the conflicting demands of his two ladies. And the ladies themselves constantly fuelled their mutual hostility. Why MGR tolerated their unconcealed machinations is difficult to explain.

Especially, since MGR was only too used to women fighting over him. More then in the film world, it was the women of Tamil Nadu who thirsted for their godlike hero. Canny MGR fan club organisers would prepare mattresses pasted with, life-size cutout of MGR and hire it out to village women for a rupee a night. Women hungered for every bit of him—at one time the remnants of the soda that MGR drank at public meetings would be sought out by women. A clever organiser decided to spread the good stuff around by pouring soda tasted by MGR into a large drum of water so that the village women could be distributed thimblefuls of this *Prasadam.*

His fans similarly marvelled at his capacity to attract the most beautiful of actresses. MGR began his long association with women by marrying actress Sathanandadevi in 1942. Both his first wife and his second wife, Amu, are lost to public memory; both having died shortly after their weddings. MGR's other women included the famed Saroja Devi, who initially acted only opposite MGR but ultimately drifted away and moved to Bangalore. His other and much shorter associations were with actresses Lata and Manjula. But among all the women, only two were destined to survive his affections. The first was Janaki, who came into his life in the late 1940's when she was working with Jupiter Films as a monthly rated artist and MGR was with Modern Theatres at Coimbatore. Their affair reached consummation in 1950 with MGR arranging to have her cast opposite him in the movie *Maruthananttu Illavarasi* (Princess of Marutha).

Janaki, who was at that time married to stageactor Ganapathy Bhat, deserted her husband and moved in with MGR. She gave up acting and became the perfect housewife. This arrangement was irrevocably shattered after Jayalalitha entered MGR's life, starring opposite him in her first film *Ayirathil Oruvan* (One Man in a Thousand) in 1985. MGR was so enamoured by this young beauty that he took her to life with him and Janaki moved out, taking up residence with MGR's elder brother Chakrapani.

For the next years, Jayalalitha luxuriated in Ramavaram Gardens —she ultimately went on to star opposite him in more than 25 films. But the tables turned in 1972 when MGR was persuaded by his brother to take back Janaki and push out Jayalalitha, who, on the rebound had a fling with Telugu actor Shoban Babu. The next upturn in Jayalalitha's fortunes came in 1977 when MGR reportedly married her in Mookambika Temple in Karnataka. Jayalalitha maintained a separate residence while Janaki ruled in Ramavaram Gardens. MGR had managed to retain both women but was destined to suffer their undying bitterness till the very end of his legendary life.

People of Vaikkom—this temple town—on January 7, 1988 received with joy the news that Janaki Ramachandran, who was born in a musician's family here 64 years ago, had been sworn in as Tamil Nadu's first woman Chief Minister.

Though she migrated to Tamil Nadu when she was 12, Janaki still owns a small house and a piece of land near the famous Shiva temple, where the first temple entry *satyagraha* was launched by Mahatma Gandhi.

The last time Janaki visited her birth place was in 1982 along with her husband to select a site for a memorial to the late E.V. Ramaswamy, founder-leader of the Dravida Kazhagam, who participated in the temple entry struggle.

Tamil Nadu Chief Minister, Janaki Ramachandran visited the Sankara Mutt at Kancheepuram on January 19, 1988 and had "darshan" of Paramcharya Sri Chandrasekharendra Saraswathi.

This is the first visit to the Mutt by Janaki Ramachandran after the became the Chief Minister. She was accompanied by Tamil writer Manian and his wife.

She sought the blessings of the Acharyas of the Mutt, where she spent about 30 minutes.

A scheme of providing free footwear to the poor children and women, announced by the late Chief Minister M.G. Ramachandran, was implemented by his wife and successor, V.N. Janaki.

At a Government function in Madras on January 19, 1988, 50 pairs of chappals to children in the age group of two and four years as a token implementation of the scheme.

Some seven million children and four million women would be benefited by the scheme, which would also provide regular employment to 6,000 cobblers in the State.

However, Janaki had a brief stint in politics and abandoned power.

10

Great Achievements

[M.G. Ramachandran's Career - a Critical Assessment, based on Various Accounts]

Cine Career

MGR starred in his first major film role "Raajakumari (1947)" and for a larger part of his film career spanning 30 years till "Madhurayai Meetta Sundarapaandiyan (1977)", he was the reigning superstar of the tamil filmdom. MGR's popularity as an actor was well pronounced and more readily seen after his own production and directorial venture "Naadodi Mannan (1958)" broke and set new box office records.

MGR's Potential

It was a complete underestimation of MGR's potentials on Kalaignar's part that brought MGR into the political arena of Tamilnadu. Once he was in, he never turned back and was outrageously successful. MGR was never a serious politician in his beginning years or till the death of C.N. Annadurai in 1969. Annadurai called MGR his "Idhayakkani" and he was **generally** used by the DMK to mobilise people for political rallies and meetings. Annadurai has once openly commented on the vote-garnering capability of MGR. Out of DMK in 1972, MGR starts his own political party AIADMK and won the state assembly in 1977. What are his political achievements ?. Lets have a look ...

Ten Year Rule

MGR's rule during 1977 to 1987 resulted in an apparently visible setback in terms of Industry and Commerce infrastructure and performance of Tamilnadu. The Economic indicators of the state were on a rampant back-foot during his governance. The development activities only slumped during his regime and this should be seen in light of the fact that MGR's party enjoyed a real continuous reign of the state, close to 11 years except for a brief period in 1980. Single party, Single administrator and hence uniform policies and governance should have only elevated the growth of the state, which sadly didn't happen during his period.

Popular Programmes

MGR was straight from the studio sets of "Madurayai Meetta Sundarapandiyan" to the Chief Minister office and hence his administrative capabilities were below par, at least during his first term. His government always concentrated on the populous schemes like the mid-day meal scheme, etc. (Which would keep his vote banks intact) rather than Infrastructure oriented schemes which should have put the state in a good shape in future.

MGR Style Politics

MGR is credited with setting up a faction-ridden AIADMK and factionist politics saw its peak during his regime. A large degree of misuse of powers and government funds was reported and this only deepened the economic disparities in the state. If it was DMK under M. Karunanidhi which introduced corruption into the state, ADMK under MGR institutionalised and mastered the course. His fans and devotees used to dismiss these facts with a simple explanation, "It is the people around MGR who do all these and that he isn't aware of things around him".

MGR's Glamour

MGR was very much aware of the saleability of his brand and was very consciously preserving his image. He was heavily made-up in all his public appearances. His fur cap and black glasses were only hiding his balding head and sunken eyes — signs of ageing. He never let people knew that he was ageing, for them he was still the same young man romancing with youthful ladies in cinema reels. MGR's brand of politics, the so-called "glamour politics" only set a bad example in the state that almost every actor in this state nurtures political ambitions just after delivering a box office hit. I completely admit that the filmstars are also part of this democratic system and hence own every right to contest elections and lead people. But "Right" doesn't provide an automatic implication of administrative efficiency, which many of them lack at the outset.

Phenomenon of MGR

His politics never projected AIADMK as a party, it's policies or its plans / manifesto for the state and MGR remained the sole cynosure for AIADMK and its political propagandas. Whenever questioned about the policies, agenda and manifesto of the AIADMK party, MGR never came up with a concrete or complete explanation. He used to blabber Annaism, democracy, socialism, "Naadodi Mannan", etc. Apparently, In AIADMK's political entry and succeeding electoral duels with DMK, the wholesome attention is paid to the MGR Phenomenon only. Interestingly, the then Tamilnadu Food Minister Tirunavukkarasu once said, "We all are zeros. We gain our value because of the number one before us. The number one is MGR". In all the 200+constituencies, people always believed that they were casting their vote for MGR as they punched their ballots on the two-leaves symbol.

Mid-day Meals Scheme

His Mid-day meals scheme has been analysed and applauded worldwide. In 1982, MGR started the noon-meal scheme for children below five years which was then expanded to include pre-schoolers, all primary school children, children up to 15 years of age in rural areas, old age pensioners, the destitute, widows and all pregnant women. The noon meal scheme has had a long run in Tamilnadu with a wider coverage and as a result various indicators of malnutrition showed a downward trend in Tamilnadu during the period.

MGR's Role in DMK

The relationship that MGR and DMK had before the formation of AIADMK was a symbiotic one. MGR required the party's light on him for a successful cinema career and also, it was the DMK's propaganda cinema and DMK's script writers who provided a kick-start for MGR's film career. DMK also took his services for adding glamour to the party and nobody can deny the importance of the sympathy wave (MGR was shot at the throat, 1967) that put DMK on the political saddle. Later MGR-MK fallout and the formation of AIADMK produced a wholesome shift in the state's politics.

Actor vs Director

Early 50s were a crucial period for tamil cinema as this period saw the emergence of a large number of films with social themes (transition from Mythology based movies). If not for the star system (MGR and Sivaji Ganesan) that developed during this period, the control of the cinema would have rested with the directors instead of the lead actors. MGR paid ample attention in moulding his on-screen persona and encouraged hero worship. In MGR's case, it is said that, he would interfere in each and every department of his film and that lead to the sidelining of the actual creator of the movie — the director, forever.

The Hero

MGR rewrote almost all the prevalent notions that defined a film's lead actor. In tamil popular culture where moustache is seen as a *macho-symbol*, MGR never acted with his original moustache. Also, when he made his way into the cinema, the lead actor should be in a position to lend his voice for the songs also. Playback singers weren't popular that time. MGR acted out what a film-hero should and shouldn't do on-screen. He was a definite milestone in tamil cinema's history and even today, actors like

Rajinikanth, Vijayakanth and Vijay just follow him. The image of Robin Hood that he left behind was picked up by later generations of actors.

Masala Cinema: There is a very common term that we use these days, Masala film. What is a masala film ?. The film won't have a great plot ... The story never stands on its own but on entertaining scene sequences, good songs and stunts. I think MGR institutionalised and popularised this concept ... Sword/Silambam fights, romantic songs with attractively dressed ladyleads were almost universal in his later movies. "Enga Veettu Pillai", "Ulagam Sutrum Vaalibhan", etc. offer grand examples of how a masala movie should be made.

Philosophical Songs: One good thing that formed a part of each and every MGR movie is his introductory / thathuvam / philosophical song. They really educated and inspired a generation of audience. Again, the credit for the song was never given to the lyric writer or the singer but to MGR. Even after the defect in his voice (M.R. Radha shot MGR at his throat, 1967), people discussed, "Vaathiyaar paatellam nalla dhan paaduraaru, dialogue pesum podhu dhan prachnai pola", which means, "MGR is able to sing the songs properly but only while delivering dialogues, he has the problem with his voice".

MGR never looked at cinema as an art. For him, it was sheer business. For producers, he was the most reliable brand available, MGR would stand for Maximum Guarantee of Returns for them. People never complained or expected *real performances* from him. They just wanted to watch him on-screen and whistle at his gimmicks for three hours. Interestingly, the MGR fanatics were referred to as "Whistleadichaankunjugal". MGR's films, in a way desensitised the film-going audiences in Tamilnadu and made them very mediocre. On the other side, if you speak of monotonous performances, even Chaplin did the same. Entertainment is what people looked at and they got it in him. That's how it went !!!

Last Phase

By the fag end of his political career, MGR was largely sick and was unable to deliver his duties effectively. The party was in dangers of disintegration and there was an apparent unrest among the partymen. As long as he was alive, he successfully kept the party intact but left behind a chaotic and leaderless AIADMK. Lots of turmoil followed before things fell into place under Jayalalitha. This is a more serious blunder on the part of the leader of a party. Literally, the second rung was absent in AIADMK during his premiership of the party and AIADMK still remains so under Jayalalitha. For all these party people who call themselves patrons of C.N.Annadurai, Anna was a magnanimous leader who encouraged a second rung leadership in DMK and fondly called them"*Thambigal*", meaning younger brothers.

That's a lot of criticism. So, What has his government given Tamilnadu. My father gave me the following information and when I asked him, "Is that all ?", he said, "That's it". He was of a firm opinion that, even if MGR would have lived more, his party would have been defeated in the next polls because of apparent administrative negligence on his part and corely corrupt-head politicians of his party.

- Housing scheme for Harijans or the untouchables.
- Good Transport network or town bus facilities to small towns.
- Immensely popular Chief Minister's mid-day nutritious meal scheme.

11

Great Life at a Glance

1917, Jan. 17: Dr. M.G. Ramachandran, endearingly known as *MGR*, was born on *17th January, 1917*, at Kandy, Sri Lanka, to Marudhar Gopalan and Satyabhama. After his father's death, *MGR* settled with his family at Kumbakonam in Tamilnadu. He could not pursue his studies beyond the primary stage and joined a drama troupe. Gaining considerable experience on stage, he entered the world of cinema, and gradually rose to enviable positions by persistent efforts and endurance.

1935: He made a debut in films.

1949: Birth of the Dravida Munnetra Kazhagam (DMK). Politics and cinema have intermingled in Tamil Nadu. But the only full-time film actor whom the Tamil electorate was prepared to accept as a full-fledged politician fit to lead the State was MG Ramachandran, popularly known as MGR. For he was the man who symbolised their travails, struggles and aspirations.

1953: He joined politics through DMK.

1956, Sept. 4: Thaaikkuppin Thaaram, a Tamil language film starring M.G. Ramachandran in the lead role was released. It is most notable for Ramachandran (MGR) using an older film as a flashback in the film.

1967: Jan. 12: An attempt was made on his life. But he survived.

1969: Author Mohandas met M.G. Ramachandran, the movie star for the first time. While he was the superintendent of police, Madurai, and when MGR was camping for his location shooting of the movie Mattukkara Velan. It was just a courtesy call by the author (in his position as a law enforcement officer) and lasted only a few minutes.

1972: The charismatic actor-turned-politician M.G. Ramachandran - popularly known as MGR broke away from DMK and formed AIADMK.

1976, May 14: Stronger ties were forged with political leaders in Tamil Nadu such as M. Karunanidhi.

1977, Jun. 10: The sixth legislative assembly election of Tamil Nadu was held. Anna Dravida Munnetra Kazhagam (ADMK) won the election defeating its rival Dravida Munnetra Kazhagam (DMK). M.G. Ramachandran (MGR) was sworn in as Chief Minister for the first time.

1981, Jan.: Eelaventhan attended the fifth World Tamil Conference at Madurai in Tamil Nadu, M.G. Ramachandran was the chief minister, Indira Gandhi had just been re-elected as Prime Minister. MGR who had backed the Janatha Party in the elections was anxious to get back into Indira's good books.

1982, Jul. 1: The noon meal programme was launched by M.G. Ramachandran, the chief minister of Tamil Nadu. The nutritious noon meal programme was started initially in the rural areas and was then extended to the urban areas. Covering all children upto 15 years as well as old age pensioners brought under this 'beneficiary net'. This programme came under Social Welfare Department.

1983, Jul. 31: Tamil Nadu chief minister, M.G. Ramachandran, led a delegation to meet Prime Minister Indira Gandhi in New Delhi and gave her a memorandum that said, "The grim and inhuman killings in Sri Lanka cannot be dismissed as the internal affairs of that country . .

1984, Apr.: Pirapaharan met for the first-time Tamil Nadu Chief Minister M.G. Ramachandran, idol of legions of Tamils.

1984, Dec. 24: The eighth legislative assembly election for Tamil Nadu was held. Anna Dravida Munnetra Kazhagam (ADMK) won the election and its leader, incumbent M.G. Ramachandran (MGR) was sworn in as Chief Minister, for the third time.

1986, Nov.: On the eve of the SAARC summit in Bangalore, the police under instructions from the Chief Minister M.G. Ramachandran, raided and seized arms and sophisticated communications gear from the assorted Elam groups operating out of Tamil Nadu. Prabhakaran went on a much publicised fast-unto death in Madras quoting Mahatma Gandhi, whom he said he was emulating in peaceful protest for the return of the equipment.

1987: Even after MGR`s ill health, the party won the state elections in alliance with the Congress. But the demise of M.G. Ramachandran, led MGR's wife Janaki Ramachandran to ascend to the party`s leadership and lead the government as the state`s first woman Chief Minister.

Dec. 24, 1987: On December 23, 1987, Tamil Nadu Chief Minister M.G. Ramachandran passed away.

Appendices

Appendix - 1

Mega Serial on MGR

Mega Serial on MGR in Television: There is a saying in Tamil "Elephant is worth for thousand Gold coins while living and even after its death. This description fits MGR very much.

Even after so many years after his, death, so many people are hearing his songs, with emotional bonding. The life history of that great actor is going to be made as serial in Television. Definitely this serial will attract many people. This serial is going to be a made based on the serious of articles about MGR in the name 'Ettavathu Vallal' (The Eighth Samaritan MGR) in a Tamil weekly. Pon. Manikkam had written the screenplay for this serial. V.C. Thennavan, is going to produce this serial on behalf of MGR Vision. The Lyricist Pulamai Piththan, who had written many lyrics for MGR's films, is going to write song for this serial.

Radha Krishnan is going to direct this Mega serial. The inaugural function of this Mega serial was held in yesterday evening at Nadigar Sangam Auditoriam. Manorma lightened the traditional Kuthuvilakku to mark the beginning. Poets, Pulamai Piththan, Ilandhevan and many other actors have participated in this function.

The script of the serial 'Ettavathu Vallal' was released by Pulamai Piththan and received by the actor Vivek. The Tenth print of the book 'Ettavadhu Vallal' was released by Pulamai Piththan and received by the actor Srikanth. After this, Vivek got on to the mike to speak and had humored the gathering by his usual style of speech. There is a saying in Tamil "Elephant is worth for thousand Gold coins while living and even after its death. This description fits MGR very much.

Filmography

As Actor

- Indru Pol Endrum Vazhga, 1977
- Maduraiyai Meeta Sundara Pandian, 1977
- Meenaya Nanban, 1977
- Navaratnam, 1977
- Needhikku Thalai Vanangu, 1976
- Oorukku Uzhaippavan, 1976
- Uzhaikum Karangal, 1976
- Idayakkani, 1975
- Nalai Namadhe, 1975
- Ninaithatai Mudippavan, 1975
- Pallandu Vazhga, 1975
- Netru Indru Nalai, 1974
- Siritu Vazha Vendum, 1974
- Urimai Kural, 1974
- Pattikattu Ponnayya, 1973
- Ulagam Sutrum Valiban, 1973
- Annamitta Kai, 1972
- Idaya Veenai, 1972
- Naan En Pirandein, 1972

- Nalla Neram, 1972
- Raman Thediya Seetai, 1972
- Sangey Muzhangu, 1972
- Kumari Kottam, 1971
- Neerum Neruppum, 1971
- Oru Thai Makkal, 1971
- Rickshawkaran, 1971
- En Annan, 1970
- Engal Thangam, 1970
- Koi Ghulam Nahin, 1970
- Thalaivan, 1970
- Thedi Vantha Mappillai, 1970
- Adimai Penn, 1969
- Mattukkara Velan, 1969
- Naam Naadu, 1969
- Kanavan, 1968
- Kannan En Kathalan, 1968
- Kathal Vaghanam, 1968
- Kudiruntha Koil, 1968
- Oli Vilakku, 1968
- Pudhiya Bhoomi, 1968
- Rahasiya Police 115, 1968
- There Thiruvizha, 1968
- Arasa Kattalai, 1967
- Kavalkaran, 1967
- Thaikku Thalaimagan, 1967
- Vivasayi, 1967
- Anbe Vaa, 1966

- Chandrodyam, 1966
- Mugarasi, 1966
- Naan Anaittal, 1966
- Nadodi, 1966
- Parakkum Pavai, 1966
- Petral Tan Pillaiah, 1966
- Thali Bhagyam, 1966
- Thanipiravi, 1966
- Ayirathil Oruvan, 1965
- Enga Veetu Pillai, 1965
- Kalankari Vilakkam, 1965
- Kannithai, 1965
- Panam Padaithavan, 1965
- Thazampoo, 1965
- Daivathai, 1964
- En Kadamai, 1964
- Padakotti, 1964
- Panakara Kudumbam, 1964
- Thayin Madiyil, 1964
- Tozhilali, 1964
- Vettaikaran, 1964
- Ananda Jyoti, 1963
- Dharmam Thalai Kakum, 1963
- Kalai Arasi, 1963
- Kanchi Thalaivan, 1963
- Koduthu Vaithaval, 1963
- Needhikkupin Pasam, 1963
- Panathottam, 1963

- Parisu, 1963
- Periya Idathu Penn, 1963
- Kudumba Thalaivan, 1962
- Madappura, 1962
- Meri Behen, 1962
- Pasam, 1962
- Rani Samyukta, 1962
- Thayai Katha Thanayan, 1962
- Vikramadithan, 1962
- Arasilankumari, 1961
- Baghdad, 1961
- Nallavan Vazhvan, 1961
- Shabash Mappillai, 1961
- Thayi Sollai Thatthathe, 1961
- Thirudathe, 1961
- Baghdad Thirudan, 1960
- Mannathi Mannan, 1960
- Raja Desingu, 1960
- Thayi Magalukku Kattiya Thali, 1959
- Nadodi Mannan, 1958
- Chakravarthi Thirumangal, 1957
- Maha Devi, 1957
- Pudhumai Pithan, 1957
- Alibabavum Narpatha Thirudargalum, 1956
- Madurai Veeran, 1956
- Thaikku Pinn Tharam, 1956
- Gul-E-Bakavali, 1955
- Kundukkili, 1954

- Malaikallan, 1954
- Genova, 1953
- Naam, 1953
- Panakkari, 1953
- Andaman Kaithi, 1952
- En Thangai, 1952
- Kumari, 1952
- Ek Tha Raja, 1951
- Marmayogi, 1951
- Sarvadhikari, 1951
- Manthri Kumari, 1950
- Maruthanattu Ilavarasi, 1950
- Ratnakumar, 1949
- Abhimanyu, 1948
- Mohini, 1948
- Raja Mukti, 1948
- Paithiakaran, 1947
- Rajakumari, 1947
- Shri Murugan, 1946
- Meera, 1945
- Salivahanan, 1944
- Harichandra, 1943
- Thamizhariyum Perumal, 1942
- Thasippen, 1942
- Ashok Kumar, 1941
- Vedavathi, 1941
- Maya Machhindra, 1939
- Prahlada, 1939

- Dakshayagnam, 1938
- Veer Jagdish, 1938
- Iru Sahodarargal, 1936
- Sati Leelavathi, 1936

As Director

- Maduraiyai Meeta Sundara Pandian, 1977
- Ulagam Sutrum Valiban, 1973
- Hamen Bhi Jeene Do, 1962
- Nadodi Mannan, 1958

Appendix – 2

Tamil Nadu: the Political Backdrop

The region of Tamil Nadu in modern India has been under continuous human habitation since pre-historic times, and the history of Tamil Nadu and the civilization of the Tamil people are among the oldest in the world. Throughout its history, spanning the early Paleolithic age to modern times, this region has coexisted with various external cultures. Except for relatively short periods in its history, the Tamil region has remained independent of external occupation.

The four ancient Tamil Empires of Chera, Chola, Pandya and Pallava were of ancient origins. Together they ruled over this land with a unique culture and language, contributing to the growth of some of the oldest extant literature in the world. They had extensive maritime trade contacts with the Roman Empire. These three dynasties were in constant struggle with each other vying for hegemony over the land. Invasion by the Kalabhras' during the 3rd century disturbed the traditional order of the land by displacing the three ruling kingdoms.

These occupiers were overthrown by the resurgence of the Pandyas and the Pallavas, who restored the traditional kingdoms. The Cholas, who re-emerged from obscurity in the 9th century by defeating the Pallavas and the Pandyas, rose to become a great power and extended their Empire over the entire southern peninsula. At its height the Chola Empire spanned almost 3,600,000 km^2 (1,389,968 sq mi) straddling the Bay of Bengal. The Chola navy held sway over the Sri Vijaya kingdom in South East Asia.

Rapid changes in the political situation of the rest of India due to incursions of Muslim armies from the northwest marked a turning point in the history of Tamil Nadu. With the decline of the three ancient dynasties during the 14th century, the Tamil country became part of the Vijayanagara Empire. Under this Empire the Telugu speaking Nayak governors ruled the Tamil land. The brief appearance of the Marathas gave way to the European trading companies, who began to appear during the 17th century and eventually assumed greater sway over the indigenous rulers of the land. The Madras Presidency, comprising most of southern India, was created in the 18th century and was ruled directly by the British East India Company. After the independence of India, the state of Tamil Nadu was created based on linguistic boundaries.

British Rule

In 1858 the British Crown assumed direct rule in India. During the early years the government was autocratic in many ways. The opinion of Indians in their own affairs was not considered by Britain as important. However, in due course the British Raj began to allow Indians participation in local government. Viceroy Ripon passed a resolution in 1882, which gave a greater and more real share in local government to the people. Further legislation such as the 1892 Indian councils Act and the 1909 "Minto-Morley Reforms" eventually led to the establishment of the Madras Legislative Council. The non-cooperation movement started under Mahatma Gandhi's leadership led the British government to pass the Government of India Act (also known as Montagu-Chelmsford Reforms) of 1919. First elections were held for the local assemblies in 1921.

Failure of the summer monsoons and administrative shortcomings of the *Ryotwari* system resulted in a severe famine in the Madras Presidency during 1876–1877. The government and several charitable institutions organised relief work in the city and the suburbs. Funds were also raised from Europeans in India and overseas for the famine relief. Humanitarians such as William Digby wrote angrily about the woeful failure of the British administration to act promptly and adequately in response to the wholesale suffering caused by the famine. When the famine finally ended with the return of the monsoon in 1878, between three and five million people had perished. In response to the devastating effects of the famine, the government organised a Famine Commission in 1880 to define the principles of disaster relief. The government also instituted a famine insurance grant, setting aside 1.5 million Rupees. Other civic works such as canal building and improvements in roads and railway were also undertaken to minimise effects of any future famines.

Struggle for Independence

The growing desire for independence began to gradually gather pace in the country and its influence in Tamil Nadu generated a number of volunteers to the fight against the British colonial power in the struggle for Independence. Notable amongst these are Tiruppur Kumaran, who was born in 1904 in a small village near Erode. Kumaran lost his life during a protest march against the British. The location of the French colony of Pondicherry (now Puducherry), offered a place of refuge for the fugitives freedom fighters trying to flee the British Police. Aurobindo was one such living in Pondicherry in 1910. The poet Subramanya Bharathi was a contemporary of Aurobindo. Bharathi wrote numerous poems in Tamil extolling the revolutionary cause. He also published the journal *India* from Pondicherry. Both Aurobindo and Bharathi were associated with other Tamil revolutionaries such as V.V.S. Aiyar and V. O. Chidambaram Pillai. Tamils formed a significant percentage of the members of the Indian National Army (INA), founded by Netaji to fight the British occupation in India. Lakshmi Sahgal from Tamil Nadu was a prominent leader in the INA.

In 1916 Dr. T.M. Nair and Rao Bahadur Thygaraya Chetty released the *Non-Brahmin Manifesto* sowing the seeds for the Dravidian movements. During the 1920s, two movements focused mainly on regional politics began in Tamil Nadu. One was the Justice Party, which won the local legislative elections held in 1921. The Justice Party was not focused on the Indian independence movement, rather on the local issues such as affirmative action for socially backward groups. The other main movement was the anti-religious, anti-Brahmin reformist movement led by E.V. Ramasami Naicker. Further steps towards eventual self-rule were taken in 1935 when the British Government passed the All-India Federation Act of 1935. Fresh local elections were held and in Tamil Nadu the Congress party captured power defeating the Justice party. In 1938, Ramasami Naicker with C. N. Annadurai launched an agitation against the Congress ministry's decision to introduce the teaching of Hindi in schools.

Post-independence Period

The trauma of the partition did not impact Tamil Nadu when India was granted Independence in 1947. There was no sectarian violence against various religions. There had always been an atmosphere of mutual respect and peaceful co-existence between all religions in Tamil Nadu. Congress formed the first ministry in the Madras Presidency. C. Rajagopalachari (Rajaji) was the first Chief Minister. Madras Presidency was eventually reconstituted as Madras State. Following agitations for a separate Andhra state comprising the Telugu speaking regions of the Madras (Now, Chennai) state by Potti Sriramalu, the Indian Government decided to partition the Madras state. In 1953 Rayalseema and the coastal Andhra regions became the new state of Andhra Pradesh and the Bellary district became part of the Mysore state. In 1956 south Kanara district was transferred to Mysore, the Malabar coastal districts became part of the new state of Kerala, and the Madras state assumed its present shape. The Madras state was named Tamil Nadu (the land of the Tamils) in 1968.

Ethnic conflict in Sri Lanka during the 1970s and the 80s saw large numbers of Sri Lankan Tamils fleeing to Tamil Nadu. The plight of Tamil refugees caused a surge of support from most of the Tamil political parties. They exerted pressure on the Indian government to intercede with the Sri Lankan government on behalf of the Sri Lankan Tamilians. However, LTTE lost much of its support from Tamil Nadu following the assassination of Rajiv Gandhi on 21 May 1991 by an operative from Sri Lanka for the former Prime Minister's role in sending Indian peace-keepers to Sri Lanka to disarm the LTTE.

The east coast of Tamil Nadu was one of the areas affected by the Indian Ocean earthquake of 2004, during which almost 8000 people died in the disaster. The sixth most populous state in the Indian Union, Tamil Nadu was the seventh largest economy in 2005 among the states of India. The growing demands for skilled labour has caused increased number of educational institutions in Tamil Nadu. The widespread application of caste based affirmative action caused the state to have 69 per cent of all educational and employment vacancies to be reserved to the backward castes. Such caste-based reservations have huge public support in Tamil Nadu, with no popular protests organised against its implementation.

Evolution of Regional Politics

The politics of Tamil Nadu have gone through three distinct phases since independence. The domination of the Congress Party after 1947 gave way to the Dravidian populist mobilisation in the 1960s. This phase lasted until towards the end of the 1990s. The most recent phase saw the fragmentation of the Dravidian political parties and led to the advent of political alliances and coalition governments.

Annadurai formed the Dravida Munnetra Kazhagam (DMK) in 1949 after splitting from Dravidar Kazhagam. DMK also decided to oppose the 'expansion of the Hindi culture' in Tamil Nadu and started the demand for a separate homeland for the Dravidians in the South. The demand was for an Independent state called *Dravida Nadu* (country of Dravidians) comprising Tamil Nadu and parts of Andhra, Karnataka and Kerala. The increased involvement of the Indian National Congress party in Madras during the late 1950s and the strong pan-Indian emotions whipped up by the Chinese invasion of India in 1962 led to the demand for *Dravida Nadu* losing some of its immediacy. Consequently in 1963, when the Sixteenth Amendment to the Constitution of India, precluded secessionist parties from contesting elections, the DMK chose to formally drop its demand for an independent Dravidistan, focusing instead on securing greater functional autonomy within the framework of the Indian Constitution.

The Congress party, riding on the wave of public support stemming from the independence struggle, formed the first post-independence government in Tamil Nadu and continued to govern until 1967. In 1965 and 1968, DMK led widespread anti-Hindi agitations in the state against the plans of the Union Government to introduce Hindi in the state schools. Affirmative action in employment and educational institutions were pioneered in Tamil Nadu based on the demands of the Dravidian movement. The leadership of the Dravidian movement had very capable authors and literati in Annadurai and Karunanidhi, who assiduously utilised the popular media of stage plays and movies to spread its political messages. M.G. Ramachandran (MGR) who later became the Chief Minister of Tamil Nadu, was one such stage and movie actor.

In 1967 DMK won the state election. DMK split into two in 1971, with MGR forming the splinter All India Anna Dravida Munnetra Kazhagam (AIADMK). Since then these two parties have dominated the politics of Tamil Nadu. AIADMK, under MGR retained control of the State Government over three consecutive assembly elections in 1977, 1980 and 1984. After MGR's death AIADMK was split over the succession between various contenders. Eventually J. Jayalalitha took over the leadership of AIADMK.

Several changes to the political balance in Tamil Nadu took place during the later half of the 1990s, eventually leading to the end of the duopoly of DMK and AIADMK in the politics of Tamil Nadu. In 1996, a split in the Congress party in Tamil Nadu eventuated in the formation of Tamil Maanila Congress (TMC). TMC aligned with the DMK, while another party Marumalarchi Dravida Munnetra Kazhagam (MDMK), which split from DMK aligned with the AIADMK. These and several smaller political parties began to gain popular support. The first instance of a 'grand alliance' was during the 1996 elections for the National Parliament, during which the AIADMK formed a large coalition of a number smaller parties to counter the electoral threat posed by the alliance between the DMK and TMC. Since then the formation of alliances of large number of political parties has become an electoral practice in Tamil Nadu. The electoral decline of Congress party at the national level, which started during the early 1990, forced the Congress to seek coalition partners from various states including Tamil Nadu. This paved the way for the Dravidian parties to be part of the Central Government.

Dravidian parties have dominated state politics since 1967. One of the earliest regional parties was the South Indian Welfare Association, which was founded in 1916. It came to be known as the Justice Party after the name of its English-language daily, Justice. E.V. Ramasami, popularly known as "Periyar", renamed the party Dravidar Kazhagam in 1944. DK was a non-political party which demanded the establishment of an independent state called Dravida Nadu. However, due to the differences between its two leaders Periyar and C.N. Annadurai, the party was split. Annadurai left the party to form the Dravida Munnetra Kazhagam (DMK). The DMK decided to enter into politics in 1956.

In the 19th century, Western scholars proposed that Dravidian languages that dominates the south of India formed a different linguistic group to that of Indo-Aryan languages that are predominant in the north of the country. They also classified Indians into distinct Aryan and Dravidian races, it was supposed that the generally darker-skinned Dravidians constituted a distinct race.

This concept has affected thinking in India about racial and regional differences and had an impact on aspects of Tamil nationalism, which has appropriated the claim that Dravidians are the earliest inhabitants of India, and the Aryan population were oppressive interlopers from whom Dravidians should liberate themselves. History has shown that Dravidian linguistic family predates Indo-aryan linguistic family in India, however both language groups have been influenced by the other during the course of three millennia.

Re-organisation of Indian states according to linguistic and ethnic basis has moderated Tamil nationalism, especially the demand for separation from the Indian Union. The anti-Hindi agitations in mid-1960s made the DMK more popular and more powerful political force in the state. The DMK routed the Indian National Congress party in the 1967 elections and took control of the state government, ending Congress's stronghold in Tamil Nadu. C.N. Annadurai became the DMK's first Chief Minister, and Muthuvel Karunanidhi took over as Chief Minister and party leader after Annadurai's death in 1969. Karunanidhi's leadership was soon challenged by M.G. Ramachandran, popularly known as MGR. In 1972, he split from DMK and formed the All India Anna Dravida Munnetra Kazhagam (AIADMK). He was the Chief Minister of the state from 1977 until his death in 1987.

After the death of MGR, the party split again into two factions, one led by Janaki Ramachandran, wife of MGR, and the other led by J. Jayalalitha. After the defeat of AIADMK in 1989 assembly polls, both factions were merged and Jayalalitha took control of the party. She was elected as the General Secretary of the unified AIADMK. There have been splits in both the DMK and the AIADMK, but since 1967 one of those two parties has held power in the state.

In the State elections after M.G. Ramachandran's death, neither of the two parties could come back to power in consecutive assembly elections. Governments were formed by: DMK in 1989, AIADMK in 1991, DMK alliance in 1996, AIADMK alliance in 2001 and DMK alliance in 2006.

DMK has slowly moved from espousing backward classes to economic oriented politics. Its members wear branded clothes, mingle with business heads and talk about development growth. Now-a-days, DMK vote is mainly derived from urban areas.

Starting from 1990s, caste based politics is on the rise in Tamil Nadu. Pattali Makkal Kachi (PMK) party deriving strength from vanniars, Viduthalai Chiruthaigal Katch (VCK) party based on Dalit votes and Puthiya Thamilagam based on another sect of Dalits have been gaining prominence in Tamil Nadu.

These parties have been gaining modest electoral success and slowly eating into traditional vote banks of DMK and AIADMK. Recently an outfit supporting Kongu Vellala Gounders also joined this list, a caste decides electoral victories in West Tamil Nadu, with the launch of their own political party Kongunadu Munnetra Peravai (KMP) in February 2009.

Election History

DMK's worst poll performance ever in this state was registered in 1991 and its peak in 1971.

Madras State

Year	*General Election*	*Votes Polled*	*Seats Won*
1962	3rd Assembly	3,435,633	50
1962	3rd Lok Sabha	2,315,610	7
1967	4th Assembly	6,230,552	137
1967	4th Lok Sabha	5,524,514	25

Tamil Nadu

Year	*Election*	*Votes Polled*	*Seats Won*	*Alliance(s)*
1971	5th Assembly	7,654,935	184	INC(I)/CPI/AIFB/PSP/IUML
1977	6th Assembly	4,258,771	48	None
1980	7th Assembly	4,164,389	37	INC(I)
1984	8th Assembly	6,362,770	24	CPI/CPM]/JP
1989	9th Assembly	8,001,222	150	None
1991	10th Assembly	5,535,668	2	TMK/CPI/CPM]/JD
1996	11th Assembly	11,423,380	173	TMC
2001	12th Assembly	8,669,864	31	NDA
2006	13th Assembly	8,728,716	96	DPA (UPA, LF)
2011	14th Assembly	TBA	TBA	INC/PMK/VCK/IUML/KMK

Year	*General Election*	*Votes Polled*	*Seats Won*	*Alliance(s)*
1971	5th Lok Sabha	5,622,758	23	INC(I)
1977	6th Lok Sabha	3,323,320	2	JP
1980	7th Lok Sabha	4,236,537	16	INC(I)
1984	8th Lok Sabha	5,597,507	2	CPI/CPM]/JP/TNC
1989	9th Lok Sabha	7,038,849	0	CPI/CPM]/JD
1991	10th Lok Sabha	5,601,597	0	NF
1996	11th Lok Sabha	6,967,679	17	UF
1998	12th Lok Sabha	5,140,266	5	UF
1999	13th Lok Sabha	6,298,832	12	NDA
2004	14th Lok Sabha	7,064,393	16	DPA (UPA, LF)
2009	15th Lok Sabha	7,625,397	18	UPA

Puducherry

Year	*Election*	*Votes Polled*	*Seats Won*
1974	3rd Assembly	47,823	2
1977	4th Assembly	30,441	3
1980	5th Assembly	68,030	14
1985	6th Assembly	87,754	5
1990	7th Assembly	101,127	9
1991	8th Assembly	96,607	4
1996	9th Assembly	105,392	7
2001	10th Assembly	83,679	7
2006	11th Assembly		7

Year	*General Election*	*Votes Polled*	*Seats Won*
1984	8th Lok Sabha	97,672	0
1989	9th Lok Sabha	157,250	0
1991	10th Lok Sabha	140,313	0
1996	11th Lok Sabha	183,702	0
1998	12th Lok Sabha	168,122	1

Appendix – 3

Dravidian Politics

Dravidian parties include an array of regional political parties in the state of Tamil Nadu, India, which trace their origins and ideologies either directly or indirectly to the Dravidian movement of Periyar E. V. Ramasamy. The Dravidian movement was based on the linguistic divide in India, where most of the Northern Indian, Eastern Indian and Western Indian languages are classified as Indo-Aryan, whereas the South Indian languages are classified as Dravidian. Dravidian politics has developed by associating itself to the Dravidian community.

The original goal of Dravidian politics was to achieve social equality, but it later championed the cause of ending the domination of North India on the politics and economy of the South Indian state of Tamil Nadu. Thus Dravidian politics incorporates elements of Tamil Nationalism and has found support only in Tamil Nadu.

Most Dravidian parties are offshoots of Dravidar Kazhagam (DK). There are also a few other parties in Tamil Nadu that did not arise from DK directly. Nevertheless, both the former and the latter are considered as Dravidian parties because of the similarities of their ideals and goals. Dravida Munnetra Kazhagam (DMK) and its political rival All India Anna Dravida Munnetra Kazhagam (AIADMK) have been the major players among the Dravidian parties since the mid-1960s. Since the 1967 legislative assembly elections, only the DMK and the AIADMK have formed governments in Tamil Nadu. These two parties are political rivals.

Barring political alliances with the DMK or AIADMK, since the 1990s no other political party has won more than a few seats in the Indian Parliament or state legislative assembly of Tamil Nadu. Since 1996, members of the DMK and AIADMK have held portfolios in the Cabinet of the central Indian government. Other major Dravidian party is Marumalarchi Dravida Munnetra Kazhagam. Political media is pervasive in Dravidian politics, with five of the seven chief ministers from these parties being directly involved in Tamil cinema, either as script writers or actors. Recently television channels owned by these parties have been used for political propaganda purposes.

Dravidian Movement

The Dravidian movement was founded in 1925 by Periyar E. V. Ramasamy (popularly known as Periyar). The movement aimed to achieve a society where backward castes have equal human rights, and encouraging them to have self-respect in the context of a caste-based society that considered them to be at the lower end of the social hierarchy. In Tamil Nadu an array of regional parties, termed Dravidian parties, owe their origin either directly or indirectly to the Dravidian movement. Dravida Munnetra Kazhagam (DMK) and its political rival All India Anna Dravida Munnetra Kazhagam (AIADMK) have been the major Dravidian parties. One of the major platforms of the Dravidian movement was to achieve political change by means of awareness within the society in everyday life. Thus Dravidian politicians viewed film media as an apt vehicle to promote such a revolution.

Rise of Dravidian Parties

Most of the Indian population are classified as Aryans or Dravidians. Although genetic research has put in doubt the racial aspect of this classification, the classification is valid on the basis of language families. Most northern Indian languages are classified as Aryan, whereas most southern Indian languages are Dravidian languages. Sanskrit, a classical language of the Aryan group, was considered to be a sacred language, whereas in the former British Indian state of Madras Presidency, it was a commonly held opinion in that the Dravidian tongues were inferior. The linguistic divide was even more pronounced given the political dominance of

Brahmins in South India. The Brahmins, who occupied the higher strata in the Indian caste system, accounted for 3 per cent of the population in Madras Presidency, but held 60 to 79 per cent of the positions in major government departments in the early 20th century. It was observed by some leaders from the south that Brahmins were Aryans, and hence non-natives, who had taken positions in the government that should rightfully be filled by people indigenous to the area. The antipathy towards Sanskrit compounded with the animosity against the Brahmins paved the way for the rise of Dravidian politics in Madras Presidency.

Early Dravidian Period

An early pioneer in Dravidian politics was Iyothee Thass in the late 19th century. His efforts brought together the lower caste Dravidians with the establishment of the *Dravida Mahajana Sabha* organisation in 1891. A major leap in Dravidian politics was the formation of the *Madras United League* by non-Brahmin intellectuals, who considered the dominance of Brahmins in civil administration a threat to the non-Brahmin majority. The League was initially started as a workgroup that helped non-Brahmin students in Madras with accommodation. It later grew into a political party under the efforts of leaders like Sir Pitti Theagaroya Chetty and Dr. T. M. Nair. The party was christened *South Indian Liberal Federation (S. I. L. F.)* - popularly known as the Justice party.

Justice Party Era

A limited form of self governance was introduced in British India after World War I. While the Justice Party saw this as an opportunity to displace Brahmin dominance, the British government considered it favourable, since the Indian National Congress spearheading the Indian independence movement was dominated by Brahmins. The Justice party emerged as a winner in the 1920 general elections and brought about the reforms it had campaigned for, including establishing communal reservation through affirmative action for the first time in the country, and brought temples under state control. Soon after their electoral success the animosity between Tamil and Telugu members deepened, thus weakening the party. Nevertheless, the Justice Party electorally dominated the presidency for 17 years until it was defeated by the Indian National Congress party in 1937. Although out of power, the Justice Party was involved in demonstrations across the Province against the introduction of Hindi as a compulsory subject of study in schools by a Congress-led government, which led to the detainment of scores of Tamil scholars, academics and Justice Party leaders. This and other struggles for social justice helped create the social base of what emerged as the Dravidian Movement.

Dravidar Kazhagam

The next few years saw a decline in the Justice Party's popularity. In 1938, by then badly weakened party sought the leadership of Periyar E. V. Ramasamy, a leader of the Dravidian Movement, who became its president. In 1944, Periyar changed the name of the party to Dravidar Kazhagam (Dravidian organisation in English). This move was opposed by some members of the Party who continued contesting elections as the Justice Party under the leadership of P. T. Rajan until 1957. Periyar as the president of Dravidiar Kazhagam considered that contesting in elections would lead to compromises in principles and withdrew Dravida Kazhagam from parliamentary politics.

Dravida Munnetra Kazhagam

In 1947, when India attained independence, Periyar called for members of the Dravidar Kazhagam to boycott the celebrations. According to him, the Indian National Congress was dominated by Brahmins. He predicted that an independent India would bring South Indians, especially Tamils, under the dominance of Brahmins and North Indians. In other words, according to Periyar, independence would lead to the replacement of British dominance with Brahmin and North Indian dominance. He felt an independent nation called Dravida Nadu for the South Indians would be the best solution. Periyar declared 15 August 1947, the day of Indian independence, as a day of mourning.

This move was opposed by other leaders within the party, including C. N. Annadurai. Annadurai viewed independence as an achievement for all of India rather than solely of the Aryan North. On July 9, 1948 Periyar married woman 40 years his junior, leading to a split in the party. The leaders of the splitting faction eventually formed a new party, Dravida Munnetra Kazhagam or DMK (Progressive Dravidian Organisation in English), in 1949. Although initially both DK and DMK sought an independent Dravida Nadu, DK later moved on to work on bringing social changes whereas DMK leaders such as C. N. Annadurai and E. V. K. Sampath endeavoured to achieve their goals through parliamentary election processes. Sampath, who had earlier forfeited his seniority with Periyar's party to join DMK, saw the call for an independent *Dravida Nadu* was turning out to be an unrealistic goal. Sampath expressed concerns over using film stars to increase the popularity of the party.

His views led him to cross swords with the major leaders of the party and eventually caused the first split in DMK. Sampath left DMK to begin his own party called the Tamil National Party. Although leaders like Annadurai were firm in their separatist stance, the reorganisation of states in India on a linguistic basis removed Kannada, Telugu and Malayalam speaking regions from Madras Presidency, leaving behind a predominantly Tamil Madras State. Giving in to political realities, Annadurai and his DMK changed their call for an independent *Dravida Nadu for Dravidians* to an independent *Tamil Nadu for Tamils.*

Annadurai saw that remaining in the Indian Union meant accepting linguistic domination and economic backwardness. However, the Sino-Indian war brought about changes in the Indian Constitution. The Sixteenth Amendment (also known as the *Anti-Secessionist Amendment*) banned any party with sectarian principles from contesting elections. Consequently DMK preferred to keep the issue of Dravida Nadu on the backburner. From then on DMK's main focus targeted the dominance of North Indians in the Union Government of India.

Karunanidhi's Presidency

M.G. Ramachandran (MGR) who was a popular actor and the then party treasurer had played a vital part in popularising the party's ideologies. The political feud between MGR and the party president Karunanidhi emerged as an aftermath of the latter calling himself "Mujib of Tamil Nadu". In 1972, MGR called for a boycott of the party's General Council. With the crisis falling into call for corruption probe by MGR, he was eventually suspended from the General Council. Thus emerged a new party All India Anna Dravida Munnetra Kazhagam (AIADMK).

DMK Government

After dropping the demand for an independent Dravida Nadu, DMK changed its focus to the problems arising out of the disparity between North and South India. The DMK considered that the south was neglected by delays in sanctioning development projects and allotment of funds. Thus the Congress-led Central government became its major target for calls for reform. Immediately after Indian independence the Congress Party was popular throughout India and thus formed the government in many states including Madras Presidency. Even so, the Congress Party failed to obtain an absolute majority in the presidency in the state's first election. By the 1960s the popularity of the Congress party was in a steady decline.

DMK leaders also perceived that the attempts to declare Hindi as the sole national language of India was an attempt impose an Aryan language unwilling people in the South. According to the terms of the Indian Constitution dated January 26, 1965, English as an official language of India would come to an end and Hindi would become the sole official language. However, the Madras anti-Hindi agitation in 1965 compelled the Central Government in India change its language policy, allowing English to continue as an official language. Although DMK was not directly involved in the violence that marred the agitation, the protest itself catapulted DMK to political power in the State in the 1967 legislative elections. The electoral victory in 1967 led to an electoral fusion among the Non-Congress parties to avoid a split in the Opposition votes. Rajagopalachari, a former senior leader of the Congress Party, had by then left the Congress and launched the right-wing Swatantra Party. He played a vital role in bringing about the electoral fusion amongst the opposition parties to align against the Congress.

MGR's Entry

In 1953, actor M. G. Ramachandran (MGR) joined the DMK, popularised the party flag and symbol which at that time stood for secession from India by showing it in his movies. MGR was a member of the DMK, and he was seen as an icon of the DMK and spread its message through films like *Anbe Vaa*. DMK entered the electoral fray rather unsuccessfully in 1957 with even senior leader V. R. Nedunchezhiyan losing from Salem although M Karunanidhi won after initially having opposed all-Indian government and later supporting only those parties which promised to help its secession from India cause.

1960s: Annadurai wanted a separate Dravida Nadu but the DMK changed its stance with the Chinese invasion in 1962 and suspended its demand for the length of the war and supported India raising funds for the war. When the war ended, nationalistic feelings were so strong that DMK gave up the separate Dravida nation idea.

The anti-Hindi agitations of 1965 forced the central government to abandon its efforts to impose Hindi as the only official language of the country; still Hindi imposition continued as Indian government employees are asked to write as much as 65 per cent of the letters and memoranda in Hindi.

In 1967, DMK came to power in Madras province 18 years after its formation and 10 years after it had first entered electoral politics. This began the Dravidian era in Madras province which later became Tamil Nadu.

In 1969, party general secretary and founder, C.N. Annadurai died. After his death, there came the power tussle between M Karunanidhi and V. R. Nedunchezhiyan. Most of the elected MLAs of DMK, including leaders like Mathialagan, Nanjil Manoharan and the celluloid hero MGR favoured Karunanidhi as CM in preference to Nedunchezhiyan, the Senior leader after Anna. To pacify V. R. Nedunchezhiyan a new post called party president was created for M Karunanidhi and V. R. Nedunchezhiyan was the post of general secretary . MGR was appointed as the Treasurer of the Party.

During the Indian President election, there was divided opinion between the leaders of Indian National Congress. Though the party nominated Dr. Sanjiva Reddy as the Official Candidate, the then Prime Minister, Mrs. Indira Gandhi had suddenly switched her allegiance to Dr. V.V. Giri, the Opposition-sponsored Candidate. She had also advised all party elected members to vote according to their conscience. Dr. V.V. Giri was elected as the President of India with the support of Mrs. Indira Gandhi. This has resulted in the split of Congress Party and in October 1969.

Senior Leaders like Morarji Desai, Athulya Ghosh, Kamarajar, S. K. Patil and Nijalingappa on the one side as Congress (Organisation) and Indira Gandhi, Shankar Dayal Sharma, Jagjivan Ram, C. Subramaniam on the Other Side as Congress (Indira). The DMK, led by Mr. Karunanidhi took a stance to support Mrs. Indira Gandhi in certain reforms like abolition of privy purse, nationalisation of Banks.

In 1971 election, the DMK fought in alliance with Congress (Indira) and the Opposition alliance which consisted of the two Senior National Leaders, Rajaji and Kamarajar was termed as a strong alliance and was widely supported by Media to re-capture power in Tamil Nadu. However, the DMK emerged victorious with a vast majority of 183 seats out of 234. The Opposition Grand alliance could capture only 25 seats.

Split in DMK and Birth of AIADMK

M.G. Ramachandran, popularly known as MGR, was an actor in Tamil cinema and a well known propagator of Dravidian ideologies in his movies since 1953. In the 1970s as the then treasurer of DMK, he played a vital part in popularising the party, bringing many of his fans as supporters. A political feud between MGR and the party's president M. Karunanidhi had been ongoing since the death of Annadurai in 1969. It arose from Karunanidhi calling himself the "Mujib of Tamil Nadu". Soon after the electoral victory of DMK in 1971, some of senior members expressed concern that MGR's popularity was growing strong within the party cadres. Karunanidhi made several attempts to weaken MGR's position within the party.

MGR retaliated with corruption charges and a call for a boycott of the party's General Council. DMK's General Council suspended MGR from the party stating that he had involved himself in "anti party activities". Although MGR had lost support from top ranking leaders within the DMK, the strong public reaction following his suspension demonstrated his popular support within the party's volunteers. Inspired by this support from the party's lower cadres and his fans, MGR launched his own party, All India Anna Dravida Munnetra Kazhagam, AIADMK (named after Annadurai: Anna was his nickname).

AIADMK Government

MGR presented his new party to Indira Gandhi as the regional equivalent of her Congress (I) Party. Indira Gandhi was the head of her party, which she split from the Indian National Congress with the support of lower cadres and opposition from senior party leaders. Thus AIADMK could show itself as an equally strong alternative to that of DMK with which Congress (I) could ally. From then on, the Congress (I) Party fought elections in the State in alliance with one of the two parties. Ever since then the Dravidian parties have helped the Congress (I) sustain itself in the State, but with limited ambitions.

In 1977, the DMK government, led by Karunanidhi, was dismissed under corruption charges by the Central government of India, led by Congress (I), which had by then allied with AIADMK.

Further Divisions

Sivaji Ganesan, a veteran actor of Tamil Cinema, was a founding member of DMK party. The actor himself was christened Shivaji by Periyar E. V. Ramasami after his role portraying the Maratha King. Nevertheless, differences between the party leadership and the actor widened since he perceived that M. G. Ramachandran, his acting contemporary, was given more prominence than himself. Furthermore, he started distancing himself from the party's atheistic stance to satisfy his religious fans. Hence when E. V. K. Sampath launched his own splinter from DMK (in the name of Tamil National Party), Sivaji left DMK and joined Sampath.

However, Tamil National Party itself was short-lived and was merged into Congress. Sivaji, although a member of Congress party, maintained distance from the party activities and concentrated more on his film career. After the death of M. G. Ramachandran in 1987, Sivaji re-launched his political career with his own party Thamizhaga Munnetra Munnani (Tamil Nadu Development Front in English). The party lost every single seat it contested for in the 1989 elections. Sivaji dissolved the party, asked his party cadres to join the Janata Dal and openly regretted his decision to have ever launched his own party.

The Marumalarchi Dravida Munnetra Kazhagam (Progressive Dravidian Renaissance Organisation in English) or MDMK is yet another offshoot of the DMK. It was formed in May 1994, after V. Gopalswamy (popularly known as Vaiko), a senior leader and Member of Parliament from DMK, was expelled from the party. Barring, perhaps, their more radical support for an independent Tamil Eelam in the Sri Lankan crisis, the MDMK do not have major ideological differences with the other Dravidian parties. MDMK shares its goals with the DMK and AIADMK in respect to State autonomy, constitutional protection for the reservation formula and making Tamil an official language of the Indian Union. In 2004, Tamil film director and actor T. Rajendar who was earlier expelled from DMK launched the All India Latchiya Dravida Munnetra Kazhagam (All India Principled Dravida Munnetra Kazhagam in English).

Offshoots of AIADMK

Soon after MGR's death in 1987, his wife Janaki Ramachandran took over as Chief Minister of Tamil Nadu. This appointment was opposed by former actress and politician J. Jayalalitha. The resistance from Jayalalitha eventually led to the dismissal of the AIADMK government, the shortest lived government in the history of Tamil Nadu, by the Central Government of India then led by Rajiv Gandhi. The antagonism built up and the AIADMK split into two fragments.

The Election Commission of India refused to accept either of them as the successor of the original party and separate electoral symbols were allocated. The faction led by MGR's widow chose to use *two doves*, with a large dove holding leafy branch in its beak, as if feeding the smaller dove. Jayalalitha's faction was represented by a *crowing cock.*

Although both factions lost the 1989 state elections, Jayalalitha's AIADMK won 27 seats when compared to just one won by Janaki's.

Following the election defeat, Janaki retired from active politics and the two party factions rejoined into one party.

Other breakaways in AIADMK were witnessed in 1990s, when R. M. Veerappan and S. Tirunavukkarasu, due to personal differences with Jayalalitha, formed MGR Kazhagam (MGR's Organisation) and MGR ADMK (MGR's and Anna's DMK) respectively.

Dravidian Parties in Central Government

Although the DMK and the AIADMK started playing a minimal role in the decision-making process in the Central government in the late 1960s, their actual participation in coalition governments came only in 1979, when two AIADMK Members of Parliament, Satyavani Muthu and Aravinda Bala Pajanor, joined the short-lived Charan Singh Ministry, which followed the Morarji Desai-led Janata Party government (1977–79). The DMK's Murasoli Maran joined the V.P. Singh Ministry in 1989.

The DMK shared power with the subsequent United Front governments led by H.D. Deve Gowda and I.K. Gujral. In the Atal Bihari Vajpayee Ministry (1998–99), three parties from Tamil Nadu, the AIADMK, the Marumalarchi Dravida Munnetra Kazhagam (MDMK) and the Pattali Makkal Kachi (PMK) were represented. In the BJP-led National Democratic Alliance (NDA) Ministry, headed by Vajpayee (1999–2004), the DMK, the MDMK and the PMK all had representatives. In fact, it was in this Ministry that Tamil Nadu had the largest representation. At one stage there were 10 Ministers from Tamil Nadu, seven of them from the Dravidian parties. In the Vajpayee Ministry (1998–99), the AIADMK's presence lasted only a few months. The current central government led by Manmohan Singh includes Cabinet members from DMK.

Dravidianism and Tamilism

The principal ideals and goals of Dravidian parties at their incipience, which were borrowed from Dravidar Kazhagam, were social reforms such as ending religious superstitions, ending caste distinction, empowerment of women, ending Brahmin dominance in Tamil Nadu educational institutions and government, ending northern domination of the politics and economy of Tamil Nadu, opposition to Hindi as India's official language, and independence for Dravida Nadu from India. The call for Dravida Nadu in the initial days during the British Raj meant a "Dravidian state under the British Raj".

Although Annadurai defended his party's demand for Dravida Nadu in his maiden speech in the Rajya Sabha in 1962 and recorded his protest against a ban on demanding separation, a year later the demand had to be abandoned following the Sino-Indian War. This paradigm shift is often attributed to the *Sixteenth Amendment to the Indian Constitution* or *Anti-sectionist* amendment, as it is usually called.

In the 1960s, the formation of Tamil Nadu as a Tamil language state carved out of the erstwhile Madras Presidency fulfilled the goal of an encompassing Dravidian state. Since then, state autonomy and social justice through reservation for the underprivileged in education and employment have been the main political planks of the DMK. The Dravidian political ideology has evolved through the years and is now varied between parties.

Starting from an initial atheistic inclination with the strict anti-Brahmin outlook of the DK, the DMK moved on to a strong ethnic identity - initially that of "the Dravidian" and later of "the Tamilian" or "the common Tamil man". In fact it is considered that Dravidian politics developed into an inclusive Tamil nationalism since it associated the Dravidian community with the non-Sanskritic Tamil language and cultural tradition. With the rise of AIADMK in 1977, Tamil Nadu witnessed two Chief Ministers (MGR and Jayalalitha) who were not Tamils themselves.

Leftist Inclination

The Self-respect movement, which is at the root of Dravidian politics, was initially forged in the mid-1920s in emulation and in critique of the Gandhian Congress Party, but by the 1930s it was heavily influenced by Leninist socialism, atheism and Bertrand Russell's inspired rationalism. Former Chief Minister of Tamil Nadu and the first to hold that post in the Dravidian parties, C. N. Annadurai, declared that the DMK (and hence its offshoots) are "genuinely communist by principle".

Party Symbol

The party's election symbol is the sun arising from between two mountains, called the *Rising Sun*.

Status of *AIADMK*

All India Anna Dravida Munnetra Kazhagam (AIADMK) is a state political party in the states of Tamil Nadu and Puducherry, India. The party was founded by M. G. Ramachandran and is now headed by J. Jayalalitha. The party headquarters is in Royapettah, Chennai, and was gifted to the party in 1986 by its former leader Janaki Ramachandran, wife of M. G. Ramachandran.

MGR Era

The party was founded in 1972 by M. G. Ramachandran (popularly known as MGR), a veteran star of the Tamil film industry and a popular politician, as a breakaway from the Dravida Munnetra Kazhagam (DMK) led by M. Karunanidhi, the then chief minister of Tamil Nadu, owing to differences between the two. Relations between the two parties have been marked by mutual contempt.

Till the time MGR, also known as *Puratchi Thalaivar* (Revolutionary Leader), was alive, the AIADMK continued to be dominated by one man, despite the presence of formidable leaders like V. R. Nedunchezhiyan, R. M. Veerappan, K. V. Kandaswamy, S. Thirunavukkarasu, and J. Jayalalitha.

The government led by the DMK, was dismissed by a Central promulgation after MGR filed a petition seeking enquiry into corruption charges. The Central Government was held by the Congress Party, an ally of the AIADMK. The party came to power in 1977 after trouncing DMK in the next elections to the legislative assembly in the state and MGR was named the Chief Minister. He was sworn in as chief minister of the state on June 30, 1977. In 1979, AIADMK became the first Dravidian and non-congress party to be part of the Union Cabinet, when two AIADMK Members of Parliament, Satyavani Muthu and Aravinda Bala Pajanor, joined the short-lived Charan Singh Ministry which followed the Morarji Desai-led Janata Party government of 1977-79.

Relations between the Congress party and the AIADMK slowly became strained and the DMK got closer to the Congress Party. In the mid-term parliamentary elections of January 1980, the Congress Party aligned with the DMK and the alliance won 37 out of 39 parliamentary seats in the state; the AIADMK had just two seats.

After returning to power, the Prime Minister of India, Indira Gandhi's government dismissed a number of state governments belonging to the opposition parties, including Dr. M. G. Ramachandran's government. Elections to the state legislature were held in late May 1980. Reversing the trend of Lok Sabha elections, the AIADMK won a comfortable majority in the state assembly by winning 129 seats out of 234. MGR was sworn in as chief minister for the second time on June 9, 1980.

In 1984, even with MGR's failing health and subsequent hospitalisation abroad, the party managed to win the state elections in alliance with the Congress party that had improved relations with the AIADMK. Many political historians consider MGR's persona and charisma at this point of time as "infallible", and a logical continuation of his on-screen "good lad" image, strengthened by his mythical status in the minds of the masses. The victory of the AIADMK-Congress combine in the assembly elections seemed so certain that the DMK supremo M. Karunanidhi refrained from contesting the assembly elections of 1984. MGR continued to enjoy popular support in his third tenure, which ended with his demise on December 24, 1987.

Succession Crisis

MGR's wife Janaki Ramachandran subsequently rose to the party's leadership and led the government as the state's first woman chief minister until the state assembly was suspended and President's rule imposed. The party, in the absence of a personality of MGR's calibre, began to crumble, with infighting, and broke into two factions, one under Janaki Ramachandran and the other under J. Jayalalitha, a former film star and associate of MGR. The state elections in 1989 saw DMK regaining power with Karunanidhi at the helm. The factions led by Jayalalitha and Janaki merged in 1988 under the former's leadership. The DMK government was dismissed in 1990 by the central government led by Prime Minister Chandra Shekhar Singh, an ally of the AIADMK at that time, with accusations that the constitutional machinery in the state had broken down.

Post-MGR Period

In April 1974, the DMK government brought in a resolution in the House urging the Centre to accept the Rajamannar Committee recommendations on state autonomy and amend the Constitution of India to pave the way for a true federal system.

After MGR's death in December 1987, AIADMK split into two factions between Janaki (MGR's wife) and Jayalalitha. DMK returned to power in 1989 State assembly elections. Karunanidhi took over as chief minister in January 1989. Subsequent to this, the LTTE "sent personal emissaries to Karunanidhi for seeking his active support in their battle against the IPKF".

Then in 1991 elections are arranged to be held for both State and Central government. In 21 May 1991 Rajiv Gandhi was assassinated in Sri Perumbudur, near Chennai in an election campaign meeting. It was later found the he has been killed by suicide bomber from LTTE, citing IPKF atrocities in Sri Lanka as a reason.

This led to sympathy wave favour of AIADMK – Congress alliance and DMK is deprived of any seats in the Parliament. This brings the rise of political rival J. Jayalalitha to the DMK.

In 1996 election DMK came to power and M Karunanidhi form the government in the State. In 2004 parliamentary elections, DMK formed an alliance with Congress – Pattali Makkal Kachi (PMK) and swept a grand Victory, the alliance won all 40 seats including Puducherry. This enable.7 ministerial post in the Central government and influential power to DMK.

Two years later 2006 same alliance won in the state assembly election and DMK formed the government in the state. Mr. M Karunanidhi become fifth time the Chief Minister of the State.

J. Jayalalitha on Scene

The AIADMK swept to power in the elections of 1991. Many political observers have ascribed the landslide victory to the anti-incumbent wave arising out of the assassination of Prime Minister Rajiv Gandhi by suspected Tamil separatists fighting for a homeland in neighbouring Sri Lanka. The ensuing government was accused of large-scale corruption, but Jayalalitha managed to hold on to power for a full term of five years, after which she lost the next election to the DMK, in 1996.

The DMK held power till 2001, when Jayalalithaa won the next election to become chief minister once again. She has been very vocal in opposing the Liberation Tigers of Tamil Eelam (LTTE, or Tamil Tigers) since then and has had a wishy-washy political association with Subramaniam Swamy. Some AIADMK cadres were accused of being behind the acid-attack on Subramaniam Swamy's acquaintance, Chandralekha, an IAS officer.

In her second term as chief minister, Ms. Jayalalitha avoided the blunders she committed during the first term. However, she was plagued by corruption cases related to her earlier rule and had to sit out of the government for some time. After having been cleared by the courts she became chief minister again. She undertook economic reforms and took many popular decisions such as banning of lottery tickets, restricting the liquor and sand quarrying business to government agencies and banning tobacco product sales near schools and colleges. She also took action against gangsters, trouble makers, and striking government employees, and improved law and order in the state.

She sent a special task force to the Satyamangalam forests in October 2004 to hunt down notorious sandalwood smuggler Veerappan. The operation was successful as Veerappan was finally killed by the task force on 18 October 2004.

However, in the Parliamentary elections of 2004, the party lost all their seats to the opposition coalition comprising all major opposition parties in the state.

In the assembly elections of 2006, in spite of media speculations of a hung assembly, the AIADMK was pushed out of power owing to big sweep by the DMK led by M Karunanidhi. It managed to hold on to only 61 assembly seats.

AIADMK has spread out and has following in the states of Kerala, Karnataka and Andhra Pradesh with official units. The party under the leadership of Dr. Jayalalitha had floated 54 candidates across the state of Kerala in the Assembly elections of 2006 and had contested on its own.

Initially AIADMK had made an alliance with Democratic Indira Congress (Karunakaran) led by the former Kerala Chief Minister K. Karunakaran, but decided to go on its own when the latter went with the Congress led "United Democratic Front" at the last moment, as a result of the mediation talks from the constituents of the UDF. In Karnataka the party had members in the state Assembly. AIADMK has its following in various other places like Mumbai and Delhi. There are also units in various countries where the Tamil population is spread out.

Jayalalitha is intelligent and efficient, but her authoritarian style left with no visible second level leadership or youth faces in her party. In this era of development oriented politics, her party lacks well-known figures.

Recently she made an effort to attract youths, by forming "Ilaignar Pasarai", which gained momentum, but her effort was demolished in one stroke, when she asked youths to be patient in a marriage function. Various press articles reported that youth in her party was disappointed by her remarks. She has attacked the DMK over its role in the government's neglect of the economy, ignoring the rising cost of living and further ignoring the increase in political extremism.

Marumalarchi Dravida Munnetra Kazhagam

Marumalarchi Dravida Munnetra Kazhagam is a political party in the Indian state of Tamil Nadu formed in 1994 by Mr. V. Gopalswamy (also known as Vaiko), a member of Rajya Sabha and a party activitist of DMK. Mr. V. Gopalsamy grew in the party from his student days. He actively participated in the party agitations and courted imprisonment several times.

He was detained under MISA during emergency with other party leaders and workers. His style of speaking is his own, quoting world events and history, he attracted a lot of support. Particularly the youths of DMK had a liking for him. This created antagonism towards him by the leaders and was forced out of the

Parent body on false charges. His sympathy for the cause of the Liberation Tigers of Tamil Eelam is widely known. With the looming possibility of a vote of confidence in Parliament against the UPA, Two party MP's, L Ganesan and Genjee N. Ramachandran, claimed that they enjoy the support of the majority of party cadre, decided to pledge support to the UPA government.

They later withdrew their claim and joined DMK when it was found that they had forged letters of support of Party executives.

Tamil Cinema and Dravidian Movement

Tamil cinema has played a vital role in Dravidian politics in the South Indian state of Tamil Nadu. Films have been influential in Indian politics since the days of the British Raj, when movies were used for anti-British propaganda. Nevertheless, the leaders of the Indian National Congress viewed movie media with contempt. It was the Dravida Munnetra Kazhagam (DMK), a Dravidian party, that made extensive use of this media for propaganda purposes.

Adversaries of Dravidian parties despised the use of films and screen popularity for political gain, and Congress leaders like K. Kamaraj questioned the possibility of movie stars forming governments.

C. N. Annadurai, the first Chief Minister of Tamil Nadu from a Dravidian party, was the forerunner in introducing Dravidian ideologies into movie scripts.

Of the movies made by Dravidian politicians *Parasakthi* (1952) was a turning point, as it was a huge box office hit and made radical comments against the social hierarchy set by the caste system and glorified the Dravidian movement. M. Karunanidhi, who currently is serving a fifth term as Chief Minister, scripted the screen play for *Parasakthi*, in which Sivaji Ganesan and S. S. Rajendran, two founding members of the DMK, made their screen debuts.

Movies produced by the DMK Party received severe censorship from the then ruling Congress government. According to Murasoli Maran, a former Union Minister from DMK, the censors would remove parts of the movies, so that the coherence of the screen play was lost, making the movies a box office failure. The script writers used equivocating phrases and words to evade the censorship.

Five out of seven chief ministers from Dravidian parties were actively involved in Tamil cinema either as writers or as actors. M. G. Ramachandran was the most successful.

He launched his own Dravidian party after personal differences with the leaders of DMK, and rose to power as Chief Minister of Tamil Nadu mostly with the help of his movie fans and low level cadres. The legacy of politics in Tamil filmdom still continues, though less prominently than in the 1950s to 1970s.

Appendix – 4

Political Use of Media

Mass media have been widely used by Dravidian politicians from the early days of the parties. Initially propaganda was spread through newspapers owned by benefactors or by the organisations themselves and through public gatherings. One early example of media use was the magazine Justice, which carried strong non-Brahmin viewpoints, after which the Indian Justice Party was named. A later example is Kudi Arasu (*The Republic* in English).

DMK had Murasoli (*Drum Beat* in English) as its party organ, and AIADMK published Namathu Dr. MGR (*Our Dr. MGR* in English). Dinakaran, a Tamil Daily owned by Marans, was earlier considered as an unofficial organ of DMK until the family feud within the family of Karunanidhi.

Tamil Cinema and Politics

Tamil cinema first became politicised during the Non-cooperation movement. With the advent of sound in films, large numbers of theatre personnel were attracted, many of whom were already active in politics. Annadurai was a writer, director, and producer of many films that were used as a means of propagation of Dravidian ideologies. Sivaji Ganesan was a member of DK but later moved to DMK as one of its founding members.

Nevertheless, he was expelled from the DMK following his comments on the party being a "glamour party", a reaction which is attributed to his frustration over lack of recognition. M.G. Ramachandran was reputedly the most famous star of any

Dravidian party. Current Chief Minister of Tamil Nadu Karunanidhi has continued be active both in film script writing and politics until recent times. Former Chief Ministers of Tamil Nadu Janaki Ramachandran and J. Jayalalitha were both film stars who paired with MGR in many of his movies. Other stars within the Dravidian parties include S. S. Rajendran and K. R. Ramaswamy.

Role of Television

DMK initially used Sun TV Network for its propaganda until the family feud within Karunanidhi's family, which eventually led to the birth of the alternate Tamil Channel Kalaignar TV. Similarly, AIADMK earlier owned J.J. TV, which was later dissolved. It currently uses Jaya TV for its propaganda.

The Impact

Regional: One of the major impacts of the Dravidian parties is said to be the lack of or limited support to the Hindutva movement, which swept the Hindi heartlands of India, in Tamil Nadu. The announcement in 1990 by the then Prime Minister V.P. Singh that the Mandal Commission's recommendation to extend reservation in employment in the Union government to the Other Backward Classes would be implemented was "in accordance with the resolution to that effect, passed in the State Assembly" is claimed by DMK to be one of its achievements. Listing the benefits accruing to the State from sharing power at the Centre, the DMK stated that "the presence of the DMK Minister (Murasoli Maran) in the National Front Cabinet and the resolution passed in the (Tamil Nadu) Assembly during the DMK regime (1996-2001) resulted in a Tribunal being appointed to adjudicate the Kaveri River Water Dispute in the case filed by the Thanjavur farmers in the Supreme Court".

The success of the efforts of Prime Minister Vajpayee in persuading Karnataka to accept the Tribunal's Interim Award ensuring 205 tmc.ft. of Kaveri river water to Tamil Nadu has been seen as one of the benefits of the DMK's presence in the BJP-led government. According to the DMK, the "creation" of 11 Navaratnas and 97 Mini-Ratnas companies in the public sector, (blue-chip companies which invest 30 per cent of their surplus funds in public sector mutual funds) "with administrative and financial autonomy", during the United Front government at the Centre (1996–98) was because of the party's presence in the Cabinet. Another benefit cited by DMK is the substantial profits the State has received from foreign investments since the start of the liberalisation process. According to a party statement, of the total investment of Rs.13,150,170 millions that has flowed into the country since liberalisation began, Tamil Nadu has received 1,511,870 millions, which is 11.5 per cent of the total investment in the country. It is often stated by the DMK and its sympathisers that DMK chief Karunanidhi played a vital role in the then central government declaring Tamil a classical language.

National: Since 1996, either DMK or AIADMK has been part of the central governments of India. The inclusion of DMK in the United Front government, led by I. K. Gujral, in 1997 came under crisis with the interim report of Jain Commission, which was appointed to oversee the assassination of Rajiv Gandhi, said that the then DMK government was responsible for abetting Rajiv Gandhi's murderers. In 2007 DMK chief Karunanidhi sparked controversy with his remarks on Lord Rama, causing political unrest and resulting in the filing of a First Information Report against him.

International: The Dravidian parties have played a pivotal role in the ongoing Sri Lankan civil war. M.G. Ramachandran, then AIADMK chief, is said to have donated 110 million Indian Rupees to the LTTE. It was also reported by the Jain Commission that the DMK regime was aligned with the LTTE between 1989 and 1991. S. Ramadoss, party chief of PMK, has recently called for the Central Government of India to help work towards an "early political solution in Sri Lanka." In 2007 DMK, AIADMK and MDMK expressed their concerns over the arrest of Tamil Malaysians following a protest.

Tamil Cinema

Tamil cinema, like its counterparts in other languages in India, is known as a melodramatic entertainment form plotted around twists of fate set in exaggerated locales, and filled with songs and dances. Although a few stars from other southern states have tried to use film popularity as a stepping stone in politics, such as N. T. Rama Rao (Andhra Pradesh), Rajkumar (Karnataka) and Prem Nazir (Kerala), it was in Tamil Nadu that it was most prominent, with five of the seven Chief Ministers from Dravidian parties hailing from the Tamil film industry. In a state such as Tamil Nadu, where no single caste is predominant, film stars were considered people with wide acceptability to lead. According to Emeritus Professor K. Sivathamby, the movie halls themselves acted as a symbol of social equality. He states: "The Cinema Hall was the first performance centre in which all Tamils sat under the same roof. The basis of the seating is not on the hierarchic position of the patron but essentially on his purchasing power. If he cannot afford paying the higher rate, he has either to keep away from the performance or be with 'all and sundry'".

Politicising Tamil Cinema

Early Tamil films were mainly based on mythological stories, and movies based on contemporary society started only in 1936. With the end of the era of silent movies in the 1930s many stage actors joined the Tamil cinema, and brought the ideologies of Gandhian philosophies with them. Although the Congress party made use of movie stars such as K. B. Sundarambal to appear at political meetings, some congressmen of that era looked upon movie media with contempt. Tamil Congress leaders like C. Rajagopalachari considered movie media to be a source of moral corruption. K. Kamaraj, then president of the All India Congress, mocked DMK's desire to get into power in this statement: "How can there be government by actors?".

DMK and Cinema

Attempts made by some Congress leaders to use stars of Tamil cinema, however minimal, were limited since this media remained inaccessible to the rural population (who were in the majority). The politicising of movies by the Congress virtually stopped soon after Indian Independence in 1947. With the introduction of electricity to rural areas in the 1950s Dravidian politicians could implement movies as a major political organ.

In post-colonial India, Dravida Munnetra Kazhagam (DMK) was the first — at the time the only party to take advantage of visual movie media. Actors and writers of guerrilla theatre, who were inspired by the ideologies of Periyar, brought the philosophies of Tamil nationalism and anti-Brahminism to celluloid media. The movies not only made direct references to the independent Dravida Nadu that its leaders preached for but also at many times displayed party symbols within the movie.

Murasoli Maran, former central minister from DMK, considered that the DMK movies reflected the faces of both the past (demonstrating the rich language and culture of Tamils) and the future (with social justice). The DMK films espoused Dravidian ideologies through use of lengthy dialogues in its initial movies. Nevertheless, as the party's political aspirations grew, the movies based on Dravidian social reformation themes were replaced with stories that would enhance star popularity.

Censorship in DMK Movies

The initial DMK movies were not victims of censorship since the party was little known to the censors, but as the party gained popularity in mid 1950s censorship became stronger. According to Murasoli Maran one of the techniques followed by the censors was to make sure that the coherence of the movie was lost so that it was a box office failure. At one point DMK, having had been a target of high censorship, had to move back to stage dramas. But the *Dramatic Licensing Act* brought censorship to stage plays as well, and two of Karunanidhi's plays were banned.

To evade censorship DMK script writers chose to use puns and equivocal phrases. The most commonly used pun was *Anna* which is the word for *older brother* in Tamil and also was the popular name for DMK chief C. N. Annadurai. When *Anna* was praised on screen the audience would break into applause.

Script Writers of DMK

C.N. Annadurai: The use of movie media as a major propaganda vehicle of Dravidian ideologies was first introduced by Annadurai, the founder chief of DMK, through his scripts. During his initial days with Dravidar Kazhagam, Annadurai wrote dramas which promoted social reforms and non-Brahmin self-respect ideologies. After the formation of DMK, Annadurai, along with E. V. K. Sampath (Periyar's nephew and one of the founders of DMK) and actor

K. R. Ramaswamy, staged several plays promoting Dravidian ideologies. The DMK party's head office was purchased using the money raised through these plays. Annadurai scripted six screen plays in total. His first movie was *Nallathambi* (Good Brother, 1948), which starred N. S. Krishnan. It promoted cooperative farming and the abolition of the zamindari system of taxation. His movies such as *Velaikaari* (Servant Maid, 1949) and Or *Iravu* carried the hallmarks of propaganda for Dravidian politics. On *Velaikari,* Annadurai said that the movie:

> "made it clear that greed and avarice of the rich did not pay in the long run. Some of the elementary principles of socialism and stressed that we should depend upon our own labour for our progress and well being and not some unknown factor."

Velaikari made direct criticisms of suppressive landlords who were traditionally allied with Jawaharlal Nehru and Gandhi. When DMK won the elections in 1967, Annadurai served as its first Chief Minister until his death in 1969.

Karunanidhi: Karunanidhi, the other major leader from DMK, started his propaganda efforts with *Parasakthi* (1952). *Parasakthi* was a turning point in Tamil cinema, as until then most movies contained up to 55 songs and were mostly based on mythologies. *Parasakthi* was initially banned. When it was finally released in 1952 it emerged as a huge box office hit. Like that of his political mentor Annadurai, Karunanidhi's movies carried elements of Dravidian political ideologies such as anti-Brahminism and anti-Congress Party messages. Two of the movies that contained such messages were *Panam* and *Thangarathnam*. The overall themes of the movies were remarriage of widows, untouchability, self-respect marriages, abolition of zamindari and abolition of religious hypocrisy. Until 1949-50 Tamil film dialogues were in a Brahminical slang of the Tamil language. Annadurai and Karunanidhi introduced Tamil close to formal language and void of Sanskrit influence. According to Professor Robert Hardgrave Jr, the popularity of their movie dialogues made both Annadurai and Karunanidhi "stars in their own right." After the death of Annadurai, Karunanidhi assumed the office of the Chief Minister in Tamil Nadu, and with intermediate periods of in and out of power, he currently serves his 5th term as the chief.

Actors from Dravidian Parties

K.R. Ramaswamy: K.R. Ramaswamy was a popular Tamil actor of both stage and screen in the 1940s and 50s. He was one of the founding leaders of the DMK and it was his earnings that initially financed the party. A talented singer and actor, he was called a *Nadipisai Pulavar* (acting and singing poet) by the popular masses. Improvements in technology in the film industry, including playback singing, along with personal problems ended the career of Ramaswamy. Nevertheless, he was nominated as a member of the Legislative Council (upper house of the State) by Annadurai in recognition of his service to the party.

N.S. Krishnan: N.S. Krishnan, or NSK as he was popularly known, was a Tamil comic actor and, as the times then required, a talented singer. He was never officially a member of any Dravidian party, but served the DMK to a great extent. He was the one of the few non-Brahmins of his era to be popular in a Brahmin-dominated Tamil film industry. His favourite character to play in the movies was a Brahmin buffoon, which he would also enact in DMK meetings. NSK was highly influenced by the ideologies of Periyar and sowed the seeds of anti-Brahmanism in his scripts. NSK served the cause of DMK so much that the last public gathering Annadurai ever attended was to unveil a statue of NSK at a busy intersession in Chennai.

M.R. Radha: M.R. Radha was a stage actor and was popular through his roles as villain on screen. He was an ardent follower of Periyar and was close to most DMK leaders before they split from Dravidiar Kazhagam. Both Annadurai and Karunanidhi were part of M. R. Radha's troupe at different times and had even acted in his plays.

Sivaji Ganesan: Sivaji Ganesan is a veteran actor of Tamil cinema. He started his acting career at the age of six and toured with various drama troupes including that of M. R. Radha. The actor himself was named Shivaji by Periyar E. V. Ramasami after his role portraying the Maratiya King in a play named *Chandra Mohan*. In *Chandra Mohan* the Maratiya King triumphs over Brahmins and the role of the villainous Brahmin was played by Annadurai himself.

Sivaji Ganesan made his movie debut in 1952 with Parasakthi, which opens with a song that glorifies Dravidian culture. Sivaji was a Tamil, whereas at the time he entered the film industry most other major actors were Telgus. He later became one of the founding members of DMK. Although it was DMK movies that brought Sivaji to the limelight he found that the responsibilities that the party threw at him limited his acting career. His association with DK and with DMK gave him an atheistic reputation that acted as a barrier between him and the religious segment of the audience. Realising that DMK was no longer an asset to his career, he attacked it as a *glamour party* and broke party protocol by his pilgrimage to Tirumala Venkateswara Temple.

With the growing popularity of MGR in the party, Sivaji left DMK and aligned with the Tamil Nationalist Party of E. V. K. Sampath. When the Tamil Nationalist Party was dissolved he joined the Congress Party. Although Congress itself lost in the elections in the 1967, Sivaji's fans kept the party alive. In spite of being an active member of the Congress party, he made sure his movies were free of political references. After differences with party leaders he launched his own party, Thamizhaga Munnetra Munnani, in 1989 but with little success, even losing his security deposit in the 1991 assembly election.

S.S. Rajendran: S.S. Rajendran (known popularly as SSR) was initially a theatre artist like Shivaji who starred in many plays for Dravidar Kazhagam. Like Shivaji, he debuted in Parasakthi. Being one of the most popular stars of Tamil cinema in the 1950s and 60s, he raised funds for DMK and acted in movies glorifying Dravidian ideologies. SSR was the first elected member of legislative assembly among actors in India in 1962. Personal problems led to a fall in his film career and in politics. Having spent most of his earnings for the party he found himself in a deep financial crisis. His movie career brought another star of DMK, M. G. Ramachandran, to cross swords with him, and his political ambitions brought Karunanidhi against him. Sensing trouble in all quarters SSR made a highly political movie, Thangarathinam, to coincide with the 1967 election campaign to prove his loyalty to the party. The party won a landslide victory in the 1967 general elections, but soon after the elections the animosity between SSR and Karunanidhi deepened. SSR complained of threats to his life and eventually left DMK to join AIADMK along with his old friend MGR. His aspirations as a political stalwart and as a film superstar were overshadowed by M. G. Ramachandran.

M.G. Ramachandran: M.G. Ramachandran (popularly known as MGR) was the foremost star for DMK propaganda during its peak and was politically the most successful of any film stars in India. MGR had a simple beginning in stage plays at the age of six. MGR was first invited by Annadurai to star in one of his movies in the 1950s. From then on MGR actively participated in the party's meetings. His films such as *Nadodi Mannan* (Vagabond King, 1958), *Enga Vitu Pillai* (Son of our House, 1965), *Nam Nadu* (Our Nation, 1969), *Adimai Penn* (Slave Girl, 1969) and *Engal Thangam* (Our Gold or Our Precious, 1970) displayed a stereotypical image of a philanthropic, mundane hero made out of a vagrant who becomes a King. Unlike other DMK actors, MGR used his screen popularity in social works as well, which included financing the poor, running orphanages and participating in disaster relief. MGR's movies portrayed him as a friend of the poor and downtrodden. MGR himself commented "My roles have been to show how a man should live and believe."

MGR always acted as a hero and made sure that he was always portrayed in a good light on screen. With the departure of Sivaji Ganesan from DMK, MGR's position within the party grew stronger. In contrast to *Parasakthi*, MGR's movies made less reference to social justice but dwelled more on contemporary political scenarios. The movies typically included references to *Dravida* and MGR would be clad in red and black (the DMK flag colours). In sharp contrast with earlier DMK movies where the overall theme was used for propaganda, in MGR's movies the protagonist was shown as a representative of the party ideology, who would fight against evil and support the poor. Thus he played roles that were directly relevant to the filmgoers and displayed himself as a symbol of the fulfilment of their own dreams. MGR, however, made sure that his social image, which he gained by independent charity and social works, did not get merged with that of DMK. With his rising popularity with the common man MGR fell into controversy by referring to K. Kamaraj, the Congress leader, as *My leader*. MGR resigned as a Member of Legislative Council. Soon after, the attendance of his then newly released movie dropped, with DMK supporters boycotting the movie. Just before the 1967 general elections MGR was shot by M. R. Radha in a personal dispute. This incident gained support of sympathising voters for DMK in the days leading up to the elections. Professor Hardgrave claims that at the time of the shooting incident MGR's popularity was slowly declining and the incident helped him regain his stature with the masses as well as the party. Whether DMK gained with MGR's popularity or MGR gained popularity with the rise of DMK remains a question for debate. Although MGR's charisma probably played a significant role in DMK's success, his popularity also cost the party much.

When the party leaders tried to neutralise his powers, MGR launched his own party in 1975, the All India Anna Dravida Munnetra Kazhagam, with support of the lower cadres alone. According to Professor Hardgrave one of the reasons for antipathy between MGR and the DMK leadership was Karunanidhi's attempt to bring his son M. K. Muthu into the party to replace MGR and to convert MGR fan clubs into Muthu fan clubs. The fictionalised account of the troubled relationship between Karunanidhi and MGR was later portrayed in the Tamil film *Iruvar* (The Duo) in 1997. When MGR formed his own party, Karunanidhi underestimated MGR's popularity and commented on AIADMK as *"a successful movie's 100 day run"*. However, with the support from his fans and low cadres alone, MGR won the 1977 state elections with a landslide victory and continued to rule the state until his death.

J. Jayalalitha: Jayalalitha was the last main leading lady to pair with MGR on screen. She was inducted into AIADMK by MGR himself and frequently accompanied him to party rallies until MGR left for the United States for medical treatment in 1984. After his return, MGR was always accompanied by Janaki Ramachandran, his wife of forty years, until his death in 1987. Soon after MGR's death, AIADMK was split between his widow Janaki Ramachandran and Jayalalitha. Although both factions had lost the elections, Jayalalitha's AIADMK won 27 seats when compared to just one won by Janaki's party. Following the election defeat, Janaki retired from active politics and the two party factions rejoined. Although a successful film star of yesteryear, according to Professor Sara Dickey, Jayalalitha's popularity in politics comes from MGR rather than her own success on screen. She served two terms as Chief Minister of Tamil Nadu (1991 – 1996 & 2001 – 2006).

Later Period

In post MGR years, political reference in Tamil cinema had been less sporadic. Rajinikanth, one of the highest paid actors in India, supported the DMK and its ally Tamil Maanila Congress in the 1996 elections. His movie *Muthu* (1995) makes indirect reference to the then AIADMK head and Chief Minister of Tamil Nadu, Jayalalitha. His movies such as *Mannan* and *Padayappa* had characters which were politically identified with Jayalalitha. He later moved his allegiance to the Bharathiya Janata Party in 2004 Parliament Lok Sabha elections. Rajinikanth is no longer active in politics. Another leading actor of Tamil film land Kamal Hassan is a well known follower of Periyar.

Two recent film stars have launched their own parties. Of them Vijaya T. Rajendran was well known supporter of DMK for a long time, although he did not incorporate its ideas into the movies. After a personal feud with the DMK leadership he launched his own party All India Latchiya Dravida Munnetra Kazhagam in 2004. The other Tamil film star being Vijayakanth who had earlier converted his fan clubs into social service organisations, initially as *typical, Dravidian, for-the-Tamils*. His party, Desiya Murpokku Dravida Kazhagam is now placing itself as an alternative to main-stream Dravidian parties. Vijayakanth himself is from a pro-Congress family.

Bibliography

Arnold, Alison: *Pop Music and Audio-Cassette Technology: Southern Area - Film Music,* The Garland Encyclopedia of World Music, Taylor & Francis, 2000.

Arora, N.D. Awasthy, S.S.: *Political Theory and Political Thought,* Har-Anand Publications, New Delhi, 2007.

Beck, Brenda: *The Symbolic Merger of Body, Space and Cosmos in Hindu Tamil Nadu,* Contributions to Indian Sociology, 1976.

Bharata: *The Natyashastra [Dramaturgy],* Manisha Granthalaya, Calcutta, 1967.

Bhaskaran, Theodore, Sundararaj: *Eye of The Serpent: An Introduction to Tamil Cinema,*University of Michigan, Chennai, 1996.

Bjorn Landstrom: *The Quest for India,* Double Day English Edition, Stockholm, 1964.

Bloch, J.: *The Grammatical Structure of Dravidian Languages,* Deccan College Handbook Series, Poona, 1954.

Boulanger, Chantal: *Saris: An Illustrated Guide to the Indian Art of Draping,* Shakti Press International, New York, 1997.

Bukowski, Jeanie J, Swarna Rajagopalan: *Re-distribution of Authority,* Greenwood Publishing Group, 2000.

Caldwell, R.: *A Comparative Grammar of the Dravidian or South-Indian Family of Languages,* Asian Educational Services, New Delhi, 1998.

Chandra, Bipin: *The India after Independence,* Penguin, New Delhi, 1999.

Chinniah, Sathiavathi: *Tamil Movies Abroad: Singapore South Indian Youths and their Response to Tamil Cinema,* Kolam, 2001.

Christopher John Fuller: *The Renewal of the Priesthood: Modernity and Traditionalism in a South Indian Temple,* Princeton University Press, 2003.

Codrington, Humphrey William: *A Short History of Lanka,* Macmillan and Co., London, 1926.

Craddock, Norma: *Anthills, Split Mothers and Sacrifice: Conceptions of Female Power in the Mariyamman Tradition,* University of California, Berkeley, 1994.

Danielou, Alain: *Shilappadikaram (The Ankle Bracelet) by Prince Ilango Adigal,* New Directions, New York, 1965.

Dehejia, Vidya, Richard, H. Davis, R. Nagaswamy, Karen Pechilis Prentiss: *The Sensuous and the Sacred: Chola Bronzes from South India,* 2002.

Dirks, Nicholas, B.: *The Hollow Crown:Ethnohistory of an Indian Kingdom,* University of Michigan Press, USA, 2000.

Dutt, Romesh Chunder: *Open Letters to Lord Curzon on Famines and Land Assessments in India,* Adamant Media Corporation, London, 1995.

Gokulsing, K. Moti Gokulsing, Wimal: *Indian Popular Cinema: A Narrative of Cultural Change,* Trentham Books, 2004.

Gover, Charles: *Folk-songs of Southern India,* The South India Saiva Siddhanta Works Publishing Society, Madras, 1983.

Guy, Randor: *Starlight, Starbright : The Early Tamil Cinema,* Chennai, 1997.

Harris, John: *Successful Populism*, Oxford University Press, 2000.

Hart, George: *Poets of the Tamil Anthologies: Ancient Poems of Love and War*, Princeton University Press, Princeton, 1979.

Hughes, Stephen, P.: *New Perspectives on the Nineteenth and Twentieth Century*, University of Chicago, Chicago, 2005.

James Hough: *The History of Christianity in India*, 1893.

Kallarasa Virachita Janavasya Ed: Manjunathan, G.G.: *Kannada Adhyayana Samsthe*, University of Mysore, Mysore, 1974.

Kasbekar, Asha: *Pop Culture India: Media, Arts and Lifestyle*, ABC-CLIO, 2006.

Keay, John: *India, a History*, Harper Collins Publishers, London, 2000.

Koder, S.: *History of the Jews of Kerala*, The St. Thomas Christian Encyclopaedia of India, Menachery, 1973.

Kohli, Atul: *The Success of India's Democracy*, Cambridge University Press, 2001.

Krishna Iyer, K.V.: *The Cochin Synagogue Quatercentenary Celebrations Commemoration Volume*, Kerala History Association, Cochin, 1971.

Kulke, Hermann, Dietmar Rothermund: *A History of India*, Routledge, UK, 2004.

Leslie Brown: *The Indian Christians of St. Thomas. An Account of the Ancient Syrian Church of Malabar*, Cambridge University Press, Cambridge, 1982.

Lloyd Rudolph, I. and Suzanne Hoeber Rudolph: *The Modernity of Tradition: Political Development in India P78*, University of Chicago Press, 1969.

Lord, James Henry: *The Jews in India and the Far East*, Greenwood Press Reprint, 1977.

McDowell, Chris: *A Tamil Asylum Diaspora: Sri Lankan Migration, Settlement and Politics in Switzerland,* Berghahn Books, New York, 1996.

Menachery, G.: *The Indian Church History Classics,* The Nazranies, Ollur, 1998.

Menachery, G.: *The St. Thomas Christian Encyclopedia of India,* B.N.K. Press, 1973.

Menachery, G.: *The St. Thomas Christian Encyclopedia of India,* B.N.K. Press, 1982.

Miller Innes, J.: *The Spice Trade of The Roman Empire: 29 B.C. to A.D. 641,* Oxford University Press, Special edition for Sandpiper Books, 1998.

Mundalan, Mathias, A.: *History of Christianity in India,* Church History Association of India, Bangalore, 1984.

Nagaraju, S.: *Prehistory of South India: In South Indian Studies,* Geetha Book House, Mysore, 1990.

Nagasamy, R.: *Roman Karur,* Brahadish Publications, Madras, 1995.

Nakassis, Constantine, V. Dean, Melanie, A.: *Desire, Youth and Realism in Tamil Cinema,* Journal of Linguistic Anthropology, 2007.

Nilakanta Sastri, K.A.: *A History of South India,* Oxford University Press, New Delhi, 2000.

Nilakanta Sastri, K.A.: *The Colas,* University of Madras, Madras, 1984.

Nilakanta Sastri, Srinivasachari, K.A.: *Advanced History of India,* Allied Publishers Ltd., New Delhi, 2000.

Phadnis, Urmila, Rajat Ganguly: *Ethnicity and Nation-building in South Asia,* SAGE, 2001.

Podipara, Placid, J.: *The Thomas Christians,* Longman and Tidd, London, 1970.

Poomangalam, C.A.: *The Antiquities of the Knanaya Syrian Christians,* Kottayam, Kerala, 1998.

Prasad, Durga: *History of the Andhras up to 1565 A.D.,* P.G. Publishers, Guntur, 1988.

Rajwat, Mamta: *Encyclopaedia of Dalits in India,* Anmol Publications PVT., LTD., 2004.

Ralhan, O.P.: *Encyclopaedia of Political Parties,* Anmol Publications PVT., LTD., 2002.

Ravindran, Gopalan: *Negotiating identities in the Diasporic Space: Transnational Tamil Cinema and Malaysian Indians,* Korea Broadcasting Institute, Seoul, 2006.

Read, Anthony: *The Proudest Day - India's Long Ride to Independence,* Jonathan Cape, London, 1997.

Sahoo, Sanghamitra; Anamika Singh, G. Himabindu, Jheelam Banerjee, T. Sitalaximi, Sonali Gaikwad, R. Trivedi, Phillip Endicott, Toomas Kivisild, Mait Metspalu, Richard Villems and Kashyap, V.K.: *A Prehistory of Indian Y Chromosomes: Evaluating Demic Diffusion Scenarios,* Proceedings of National Academy of Sciences of United States of America, 2006.

Shohini Chaudhuri: *Contemporary World Cinema: Europe, the Middle East, East Asia and South Asia,* Edinburgh University Press, 2005.

Thomas Puthiakunnel: *Jewish colonies of India paved the way for St. Thomas,* George Menachery, Trichur, 1973.

Trawick, Margaret: *Notes on Love in a Tamil Family,* University of California Press, Berkeley, 1990.

Velayutham, Selvaraj: *Tamil Cinema: The Cultural Politics of India's Other Film Industry,* Routledge, New York, 2008.

Vellian Jacob: *Knanite Community: History and Culture,* Jyothi Book House, Kottayam, 2001.

Velu Pillai, T.K.: *The Travancore State Manual,* Trivandrum, 1940.

Wadley, Susan: *The Powers of Tamil Women,* Syracuse University Press, Syracuse, 1980.

Weil, S.: *Symmetry between Christians and Jews in India: The Cananite Christians and Cochin Jews in Kerala,* Contributions to Indian Sociology, 1982.

Wilkinson, Steven, I.: *Caste mobilization in Pre-independence Madras, Votes and Violence: Electoral Competition and Ethnic Riots in India,* Cambridge University Press, 2006.

Wyatt, AKJ: *New Alignments in South Indian Politics: The 2001 Assembly Elections in Tamil Nadu,* University of California Press, California, 2002.

Zvelebil, Kamil: *Tamil Literature,* Brill, Leiden, 1975.

Index

D

E

F

G

H

I

J

❑❑❑